A **BIRD TALK** Book

PARROT PARENTING

Carol Frischmann

i-5 PRESS

Parrot Parenting

Project Team
Editor: Tom Mazorlig
Copy Editor: Joann Woy
Design: Mary Ann Kahn
Index: Elizabeth Walker

i-5 PUBLISHING, LLC™
Chief Executive Officer: Mark Harris
Chief Financial Officer: Nicole Fabian
Vice President, Chief Content Officer: June Kikuchi
General Manager, i-5 Press: Christopher Reggio
Art Director, i-5 Press: Mary Ann Kahn
Vice President, General Manager Digital: Jennifer Black
Production Director: Laurie Panaggio
Production Manager: Jessica Jaensch
Marketing Director: Lisa MacDonald

Library of Congress Cataloging-in-Publication Data
Frischmann, Carol.
  Parrot parenting : the essential care and training guide to 20+ parrot species / by Carol Frischmann.
     pages cm
  Includes index.
  ISBN 978-1-62008-130-3 (alk. paper)
  1. Parrots. I. Title.
  SF473.P3F754 2014
  636.6'865--dc23
                          2014016309

This book has been published with the intent to provide accurate and authoritative information in regard to the
subject matter within. While every precaution has been taken in the preparation of this book, the author and publisher
expressly disclaim any responsibility for any errors, omissions, or adverse effects arising from the use or application of
the information contained herein. The techniques and suggestions are used at the reader's discretion and are not to be
considered a substitute for veterinary care. If you suspect a medical problem, consult your veterinarian.

i-5 Publishing, LLC™
3 Burroughs, Irvine, CA 92618
www.facebook.com/i5press
www.i5publishing.com

Printed and bound in China
14 15 16 17   1 3 5 7 9 8 6 4 2

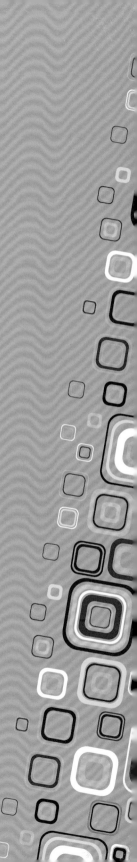

TABLE OF CONTENTS

1

THE
PROS AND CONS
OF LIFE WITH
A PARROT

arrots engage us from the first moment we catch sight of them: Their feathers are gorgeous, they seem to represent an exotic landscape, and they are as interested in us as we are in them. If you have not spent a lot of time with a parrot, you may be surprised at the attention a parrot gives to every detail of a human's movement and tone of voice. And, in response, their attempts to get human attention are fascinating. The sounds they make, the way they move their bodies, the color of their feathers are interesting, but their fascination with us is gratifying—flattering even. Additionally, parrots take us from the mundane, ordinary life of our homes and lead us to imagine life in a foreign and magical place.

Introduction

Living as a companion of parrots for more than twenty-five years—currently with two African grey parrots—and as a writer about parrot behavior, biology, ecology, and husbandry (the keeping of what is essentially a wild animal in a human home), I can tell you that I would not be anxious to acquire a third companion parrot who was neither a cockatiel nor a budgerigar (parakeet).

The principal reasons for this come from the fact that a parrot is a wild animal, evolved to live in places where they fly miles each day, communicate with their flocks with loud calls, and where the detritus from their feeding serves a useful purpose. I and many of my parrot-loving friends have faced difficulties with neighbors over the noise that our parrots make. We tire of cleaning the mess that seems to reappear over the course of an hour. Our partners and friends resent the time, attention, and expense lavished on our birds. We wrestle with our conscience over the difficulty of providing an environment and companionship that is stimulating enough for an animal as intelligent and as persistent as a parrot can be. At times, we have talked with one another about our problems, sought solutions, engaged with consultants, and worked with veterinarians, nutritionists, and experts in animal behavior.

Parrots are only a few generations from their natural ancestors and are essentially still wild animals.

I have thought hard about how to open this book about a species that has brought so much pleasure and richness into my life. Psittacines, as parrots are called in scientific circles, are a very large and diverse group of birds. Mainly, they live in equatorial climates in the wild, and many of their habitats are disappearing at alarming rates. In fact, for some species of parrots, only the skills of aviculturists (bird breeders) have kept them alive.

Thousands of people around the world have dedicated

their lives to studying, raising, and understanding this most fascinating group of birds. Whether a parrot belongs in your home or not is a very personal decision. What I can tell you echoes what everyone else I know who loves and respects parrots will say: think hard about your adaptability, your willingness to commit to a parrot for many years, and your ability to provide what your companion needs, including making trade-offs in order to spend time with your companion parrot.

In addition to being demanding, psittacines are so long-lived that scientists believe they hold a key to unlocking the secrets of staying young. As a result, anyone who has a parrot larger than a parakeet can expect that, unlike most other companion animals, the bird will live for fifteen to eighty years, depending on the species. (Consider this: many of us have difficulty committing to live with another member of our *own* species for that length of time!) Parrots not only speak a "foreign" language, but they also have needs that are completely different from our own. In addition, as companion animals, they are completely dependent on us for their well-being. This is a trust that begins the day you decide to bring a parrot into your home. My goal here is to help you envision, to the extent possible, what your experience of parenting a parrot can be. Depending on your expectations, the choice of species you make, and your flexibility, your experience can be either a lifelong and mostly positive experience or a frustrating and unhappy one for both you and your parrot. Let's look at both the positive and the potentially difficult aspects of this endeavor.

Why Keep a Parrot?

Companionship, admiration, and tradition are among the many reasons people choose to keep parrots. Parrots are good company—they are intelligent, interaction-seeking presences. Parrots sometimes want play but more often they seek a flock relationship: a contact call first thing on waking, a greeting when you return, a desire to be involved in whatever you do. Admiration and fascination for the parrot as a "being" is what initially draws people to these birds, and may be what grips some of us for a lifetime. Finally, some families have a tradition of keeping parrots. Adults remember their family parrots and want to provide that experience for their children.

Companionship

The United States census tells us that more people than ever are living alone. A friendly whistle and a bit of a talk in the morning may be just what you need to shake off some loneliness. Sharing an ordinary breakfast with a parrot offers you moments of genuine affection and reassurance. Your bird may ask to have his beak stroked or to go to your finger so that you can provide him with bites of your own breakfast, which will be infinitely more interesting than whatever you planned to feed him. Before heading out for a very busy day, having a few minutes just to talk things over as you change the paper and exchange yesterday's water for a fresh supply can be gratifying. This may be one of the high points of your day—just the morning routine.

Parrots love their routines, and their needs help give our own lives stability and meaning. By providing for his needs in the way of food, toys, social interaction, and a clean, well-lighted place to live, you enjoy the daily constancy of a relationship. For people who have few demands in their lives, a companion bird provides a focus and a purposeful routine of care, feeding, and interaction. Sometimes, life with your parrot will be an unbelievably rewarding experience.

Link to the Wild

For some of us, parrots provide a link to the wild that is otherwise missing in life. While living and working in cities or suburbs, we long to be elsewhere, living in a remote place filled with trees and the calls of monkeys and birds. In other words, the fact that a parrot is not a domestic animal, molded through thousands of generations of selective breeding to fit in with our lives, is exactly what we're looking for. Before we head out for work, we'd like to be reminded that there is something else in the world, something not quite so civilized as our version of life.

Lifetime Fascination

Some of us cannot stop admiring the beauty, the wonder, and the complexity

Well-socialized parrots are highly interactive and often affectionate companion animals.

of wild birds. We have to have birds in our lives. We cannot imagine life without birds as an integral part of each and every day. We realize that we not only need to have birds in our lives, but we work to preserve birds in their natural habitats so that their species can flourish. These are the people who join various national and international associations to support research into understanding companion and wild birds, and who promote their health and welfare, associating with others who also cannot stay away from these sometimes raucous companions. Even when our parrots are stubborn, we remember that they are doing what they've evolved to do (at least we remember that most of the time!). What makes them difficult is also what makes learning about them so satisfying.

Other Reasons

Parrots have been companions of humans for thousands of years; for many Native Peoples, these birds' feathers provide essential elements for religious ceremonies. For many others, parrots' ability to mimic speech or sounds is an attraction. Whatever the reason you fall in love with these birds, there is likely a species that will suit you and your living situation, if you are willing to provide what that bird needs.

Why Not Keep a Parrot?

There are many reasons not to keep a parrot. The trick is to anticipate them and decide whether you are a parrot person. If you love antiques and oriental carpets and covet the perfect looks from *Architectural Digest*, a parrot is not for you. You will resent the mess, the non-designer cages, and the parrot paraphernalia. If you love the obedience of dogs but want the colors of a parrot, get a poodle and have your groomer sculpt and color his hair. Do not expect a parrot to be obedient. If you want another pet but feel you don't have much time, a parrot is a poor choice.

The Worst Possible Scenario

Whenever I try to explain why one might not want to have a parrot, I suggest the following scenario: Imagine a two-year-old who will never grow up and out of the "No!" phase. Now, give the little tyke a small chainsaw (if you don't believe that is a fair comparison for a beak on a bored parrot, you definitely haven't spent enough time with parrots). Finally, imagine that the chainsaw-wielding two-year-old can fly.

Now, a budgerigar is a bird with a teeny-tiny chainsaw that is targeted toward paper and other easily chewed items like the pages of cookbooks or knitting patterns. A scarlet macaw, on the other hand, can crack a 1 × 1-inch piece of wood with a single closing of his beak. To be a successful parrot companion, you have to be an anticipator, a bad-behavior preventer, and a person who can swoop in and present the feathered two-year-old with something so interesting that he is no longer interested in cracking the leg on your antique chair or chasing after your sister's newly pedicured scarlet toes.

If Decor Is Important

In addition, the larger parrots require large accommodations. If you are a person who values flawless carpets and Japanese wood-carved figures, think again before considering a parrot as a pet. To the parrot, everything in his environment is for chewing, tasting, pulling apart, and examining. Most parrots are jungle natives. Their ecological role is as a spreader of partially digested seeds and a provider of uneaten plant parts and nutrients that serve as fertilizer. This evolved behavior will not change because you have brought a parrot into your home. Although there are cases of people

If you value your furniture and home décor highly, a parrot is probably not a good choice for you.

potty training their parrots, in general, this approach does not work well for a variety of reasons. Inevitably, your most valuable and rare figurines will be the ones that attract your parrot's attention, and you'll need to put them behind glass or in an enclosed display area out of your parrot's way.

Do You Value Obedience?

Unlike domestic animals, parrots have no interest in pleasing you. Training a parrot is a bit like training a cat. You have to find a way to appeal to the parrot's higher want. The trouble is that, without quite a bit of experience, this is much more difficult than training a dog. If you do want to train your parrot, there are simple approaches that work. The issue is that you must follow the experts' directions, because nothing about training your bird is intuitive. This is all practice, repetition, and patience in rewarding very small improvements.

To enjoy having a parrot as a companion, you have to be able to put aside your ideas about what is acceptable behavior and find a way to coexist with an animal who evolved in the treetops, to lives in flocks, and to spend a majority of the day foraging for food. If you cannot provide either these conditions or conditions that mimic the parrots' natural environment in these critical ways, your life together will not be as happy as you both would wish life to be.

Family Cooperation

One of the most practical parrot behaviorists in recent years is Liz Wilson. Her advice about the difficulties of having a parrot as a companion is that not all household members are enthusiastic about living with a bird. Because parrots can be so difficult, for the relationship to be successful, it

Owning a parrot requires a significant time commitment. Most species need more than an hour of interaction each day.

Questions to Ask Before Acquiring a Parrot

How long have I been committed to acquiring a parrot as a pet?

If your answer is less than six months, then think again. Even the smallest parrots are long-lived. Make sure you want to commit to a beautiful (and needy) animal's well-being.

Is my family as enthusiastic as I am about this pet?

Any pet impacts the entire family. Parrots, especially those with loud voices or those who require lots of space, do have a significant impact on everyone in a household. Allergies, as well as attitudes that include being frightened of birds, pressure the bird-lover in the household into relinquishing her pet quickly. Consider waiting until another time in the family's evolution before getting an avian companion.

Do I live in a place that will allow parrots? Will my neighbors be troubled by my new companion?

Everyone dreads living uncomfortably next door to someone who hates pet noise. And an angry neighbor wears on your happiness. Consider whether your apartment, condo, or neighborhood association allows parrots. Also, even when they do, consider those who live near you. If you know in advance that there will be trouble, wait until you (or they) live elsewhere.

Do I understand that parrots are not easy pets and that they are not people-pleasers like dogs?

Many people are under the mistaken impression that parrots don't require much care. Nothing could be further from the truth. Parrots are intelligent animals who need daily attention and companionship, adequate toys, and numerous food choices to keep their minds busy. Without these things, parrots begin to do things to demand your attention. When this happens, most parrots quickly lose their homes.

Am I willing to devote the time and funds required for the proper care of a parrot?

The purchase price of a parrot is simply the beginning. You will need an indoor cage; a way to provide full-spectrum sunlight or an outdoor cage; a continuous supply of destructible toys; fresh (or frozen) fruits and vegetables, in addition to a high-quality pelleted food; and an annual veterinary examination in addition to periodic beak and nail trims. If you don't have forty-five minutes a day to spend with your pet, consider either a very small parrot, such as a budgie (parakeet) or a different type of pet that is more independent than a companion parrot.

is essential for everyone in the home to be enthusiastic about the prospect. Everyone in the family will need to handle the bird, keep the same rules, and cooperate with one another in parrot-related responsibilities. This cooperation begins prior to acquiring a bird. If everyone is not enthusiastic, then acquiring a parrot is a mistake. The placement will not be a success.

Why Parrots Lose Their Homes

Concerned about the number of parrots losing their homes, avian veterinarians Susan Clubb DVM, Dipl ABVP (Avian) and Michelle Goodman studied the reasons that parrots are given up for adoption. Among the unanticipated reasons that parrots are relinquished to adoption agencies or abandoned include "changes in the family structure such as deaths, divorces, financial difficulties and moving into places that do not accommodate pets, etc." However, in addition to those problems that cannot be foreseen, many parrots are given up because their owners' expectations have not been met by the parrot or because new parrot people become either bored with their new pet or upset because the parrot has not behaved well.

Clubb and Goodman found that although "not enough time" was reported most frequently as the reason for relinquishing parrots, further questioning revealed that "dissatisfaction with the relationship," "unfulfilled expectations," or "inability of the owner to communicate to the parrot their wants and needs" played a significant role. Goodman and Clubb believe that although the incompatibility issues that lead to negative behaviors such as aggression, noisiness, and feather

Before getting a parrot, make sure everyone in the household will enjoy living with one.

destruction could be resolved through training and enrichment, in many cases the relationship between bird and owner had already deteriorated past repair.

To Make Good Matches, Education is Key

These researchers concluded that the most important way to keep parrots in their original homes is to educate the prospective parrot owner about "appropriate bird choice and reasonable expectations." Surprisingly, they found that "many [parrot] purchases are impulse buys." Your reading of this book is an excellent first step in learning about what type of parrot might work as a member of your family and what you should expect to do to keep your parrot happy and healthy.

Among many other educational opportunities you can explore include local bird club meetings, online communities, and visiting specialty veterinarians or rescue organizations.

For every family that has a negative experience with parrots, you can find families who treasure their avian companions and who go to great lengths to ensure they are well cared for and have everything a companion bird could want. These parrot lovers gather at local and national meetings, through online communities, and at their local bird specialty stores and behavioral seminars. If you've never visited an avian veterinarian's office, you'd be surprised at the number of people who create friendships there in the lobby waiting for their well-bird checkups or talking about the concerns they have for a bird who needs treatment.

As with any other specialty interest, people who love parrots have an instant affinity for one another. We understand their worries, their difficulties in getting to the best veterinarian for their bird, their need for that expensive puzzle toy that will keep their cockatoo busy while they are on the telephone, the concern they have in the spring when some birds become more difficult because of their reproductive hormones, their worry when a bird begins to barber or pluck his feathers. These are concerns that those who do not have parrots find difficult to understand.

If you decide that a parrot is right for you, I'd urge you to join with some more informed parrot owners who will be glad to share their knowledge and help you begin your long and fascinating journey into the world of the parrot.

With so many species to choose from, each with slightly different anatomies, different dietary needs, behavioral quirks, and challenges, as well as their own endearing qualities, you may be able to find a parrot who fits your lifestyle, your home style, and your personality style. If you cannot, many opportunities exist for you to volunteer to spend your time with parrots while not taking full responsibility for an individual parrot for his lifetime. These opportunities include local rescue groups and humane societies, bird clubs, and events that support behaviorists and researchers as well as companion parrot owners. There may even be opportunities for you to work regularly with a parrot person who lives near you.

2

FINDING THE PARROT OF YOUR DREAMS

Y ou can find a fabulous lifetime avian companion in any number of places. However, some places are more likely than others. Breeders and specialty pet stores are more likely to provide you with a healthy companion who has been socialized in such a way that his diet, manners, and experience of the world is on a track to success as a companion parrot. To continue this successful start, introducing your parrot slowly and carefully to his new environment and the creatures that will be sharing life with him is very important. Remember, you're choosing the companion of a lifetime. Take things slowly; plan. Impulse purchases almost always create an unhappy family and an unhappy parrot.

Sources of Parrots

The many sources of parrots today can confuse even the most experienced bird person. Sources include pet shops, breeders, rescues, and other sources such as friends or newspaper or online ads. According to Amy B. Worell, DVM, Dip. ABVP, in an article in the *Journal of Exotic Pet Medicine*, the sources of birds have changed dramatically since 2009, from aviculturists to major pet store chains. Worell reports that, previously, birds came into the pet trade through breeders and private aviculturists to bird-specific pet stores. Because of the economic recession, many breeders and small bird stores have given up their businesses. Karen Windsor, Executive Director of Foster Parrots, Ltd. presented a paper at the 2012 Association of Avian Veterinarians reflecting the point of view of many rescue organizations: that some breeders, more interested in profits than animal welfare, are responsible for an "overproduction" of parrots. Whether the source is an aviculturist, a pet store, or a rescue organization, most pet parrots are bred in the country in which they are purchased, especially in the United States, where, since 1992, the Wild Bird Conservation Act made importation of wild parrots for the pet trade illegal.

Desirable Characteristics of Companion Parrots

What veterinarians and rescue organizations together have learned is that a physically and emotionally healthy parrot is more likely to stay in his original home longer and to make a successful transition to a second home, if necessary. Factors associated with these physically and emotionally healthy and therefore successful companion parrots include:

- The bird was raised by and with his avian parents, so that he has a sense of identity as a bird.
- The bird learned to fly before his first wing clip, so that his flight skills and physical confidence were fully developed.

In the United States, parrots are no longer imported from the wild; they are hatched out and raised by breeders.

- The bird was fully weaned before he transferred to his new home, so that he was confident about his ability to find food to provide for himself.

In the 1990s many people believed that successful companion birds should be removed from their parents just after hatching and subsequently should be raised by human beings. Although this procedure created parrots who attached to human beings, the unintended consequence was that this method also created parrots who had no sense of identity as parrots. In other words, the parrot imprinted on human beings. When those human-raised parrots reached adolescence, the mates the parrots looked for were human. This created many of the behavior issues that caused parrots to lose their homes after they had made their transitions to sexual maturity.

Many species of parrot are available, and they differ in size, disposition, talking ability, and many other attributes.

In addition to needing their identities as birds, parrots also need confidence in their physical abilities, including the ability to fly. Surprisingly, parrots, especially the heavier-bodied parrots, can take quite a while to learn to fly. If those parrots are not allowed to move through this normal process, which can be difficult to watch because of their clumsiness, the birds also never become fully confident in their balance, climbing, and perching abilities. This lack of physical confidence leads to all sorts of difficulties that a first-time bird owner would never imagine. A frequently seen example of this sort of trouble is that parrots become fearful of leaving spaces they know well.

Finally, the longer lived a creature is, the longer the creature's process of development and maturing from birth (or hatching) to a young, independent bird. A parrot's complicated needs are best filled by his parents until he is of an age to separate. Although the idea of hand-feeding appeals to the nurturers among pet lovers, the complications that can result from improper hand-feeding and rearing are significant.

Selecting Candidate Species and Sources

So, if you want to find a parrot companion who exhibits these three requirements—a parent-raised bird, fully fledged, and weaned—then what is the next step? The most advisable next step is to begin reading about different species of parrots, their suitability as pets, their species characteristics, and their care requirements. In addition, future parrot parents need to meet as many individual members of your "candidate species" as possible, keeping firmly in mind the notion that you are familiarizing yourself and your family with your potential companion species rather than beginning the process of selecting your dream parrot. While gathering information about your candidate species, you will meet representatives from the major sources of parrots: pet shops—specialty and chain—rescues, and breeders.

Whether you find your dream bird in a specialty pet shop, a rescue, or a breeder, the critical point is how much support you can expect if and when you run into questions and problems in caring for your new companion. As you consider the various sources, ask yourself this question: "If I have questions or problems, can I rely on this source to help me through and succeed with my new best friend?" If you're unsure of the answer, move on to another source.

A second aspect of finding your dream bird species is to consider the cost of the species over its lifetime, not the initial cost of purchasing or adopting your bird. Although you might find a perfectly lovely bird of your species that someone is "giving away," the odds are that you will, after several days, discover the reason that the bird is "free." Healthy birds with good manners and habits are usually not given away "for free." This is because rescues, specialty pet stores, or breeders want to be sure that the person acquiring this sort of bird cares enough to recognize his value. Specialty stores and breeders who produce only a few birds each year usually are in business to recover the costs of raising and caring for the birds. (Good-quality food and supplies are the products that allow these stores and breeders to continue to operate, not the sale price of the birds themselves.)

Third, follow your instincts. Plan to visit a variety of sources prior to making a decision about a species. Then visit more sources before making a final decision about acquiring a specific companion. Meet many birds. Talk to these sources about the species, as well as about the individual birds.

Do I Need to Get a Pair?

Many times, people believe that they need to get a pair of parrots because an individual bird will become lonely. The European Union agrees and has recently passed legislation that requires birds, which are flock animals, to be kept in small flocks—in other words, in a natural family grouping.

In general, birds are more comfortable in a small flock. However, the practical realities of keeping a small flock of birds are difficult for most people. This is one reason that the smaller birds, ones that have smaller cage and play area requirements, are easier, especially for first-time bird keepers.

The advantage of a pair or small group of birds is that they keep each other busy. The disadvantage is that unless you handle them a great deal, they often prefer each other's company to yours.

The answer to whether you need to get a pair or three birds depends on your situation. A pair of budgies or cockatiels makes an excellent situation for first-time bird keepers. Similarly, two small conures, such as green-cheeks or maroon-bellied conures, would be a delightful situation.

If you insist on a larger bird as your first, you might have a more difficult time finding two who get along, not to mention the space requirements and the handling challenges this will entail. In addition, in contrast to most dogs and cats, which eventually sort out a hierarchy, birds, especially larger, mature birds, such as male cockatoos, definitely do not get along with others and have been known to harm or kill their cage mates. This is particularly a problem when the birds feel crowded or when multiple adult birds are housed together.

If you decide to get a pair of birds, get help from a behaviorist or avian veterinarian in putting together a pair or small groups of birds who can live happily together.

Every bird is different, and not every bird is a representative of its species' normal behaviors. If you feel that the rescue or specialty store is not clean and the birds do not seem content, move on, even if you are attracted to a single bird. And never acquire a bird because you feel sorry for the conditions in which it is living. Although this may be tempting, birds raised in such environments are usually not healthy, may carry communicable diseases, and will be expensive and heartbreaking to care for.

Acquiring a bird of the species of your dreams requires a bit of looking, return visits, and lots of thought. But if you follow these steps and make an informed decision, you can find the right species. By taking shortcuts, people often find species that make them feel as though they are living a nightmare.

Once you've made the decision to acquire a companion bird, you will need to narrow your choice to a few species. Following this, you'll need

A cockatiel is one of the very best choices for a first-time bird-keeper.

to locate a reliable source for your bird species and get help, including a veterinarian, in selecting a healthy companion of your chosen species. Although making each decision is exciting, move slowly and take the time to think through each step because this is an important decision. In addition, if you have a family, the agreement of everyone in the family is important.

Narrowing the List of Species

The information in Chapter 8: Selected Species should be helpful to you in narrowing your choice to just a few species. Although the process may seem bewildering at first, the key decision points include: (1) lifespan, (2) personality and temperament, (3) noise level, and probably (4) size. If you are a beginning bird-keeper, please consider a bird that is suitable for your knowledge and abilities. If you decide that bird-keeping is for you, you'll have many birds over the course of your lifetime; you can get that raucous pink bird or the very expensive purple bird later, after you've learned to handle an easier species first. For this reason, I recommend budgerigars, green-cheeked conures, cockatiels, and perhaps a pionus or a lovebird for first-time keepers. In addition, although I have no hands-on experience with them, lineolated parakeets are recommended as first-time birds by many experts.

These birds are relatively inexpensive, require small to moderate-sized cages and furnishings, and have dispositions that tend to make them easy to handle during the time you and your family are developing your bird-handling skills.

Bird specialty stores are often good places to find a pet parrot as well as a lot of information about them.

For apartment dwellers, small birds have served as cheerful pets for centuries. Many people I know believe that the best pet for someone who wants a bird is a budgerigar (commonly called a parakeet or a budgie). Beginning with a shorter-lived and less demanding member of the psittacine family gives you much of the pleasure of a larger bird without many of the more difficult problems. For those who question whether smaller birds can be satisfactory as pets who can learn to speak, I direct you to YouTube videos of Bingo, the parakeet with his own channel. As every bird-savvy person will tell you, no one can tell whether an individual bird will learn to talk or not. However, this is one of the benefits of adopting an older bird—you'll likely know if he can speak or not.

Locating a Reliable Source for Your Bird

Finding a good source for a lifelong companion requires searching and patience. Because excellent health, temperament, and socialization are the qualities you want in your companion parrot, the most promising sources are small-scale breeders of birds for the pet trade, specialized exotic bird stores, and parrot rescue networks that have fostering and educational programs. Although you will find birds for sale in newspapers, on Craig's List, and from Internet suppliers, you take a significant risk that your new pet will be unhealthy, unsocialized, or unsuitable as a companion. Furthermore, if you purchase a bird from one of these sources, you have very little recourse if the bird is not as advertised. Think of it this way: would you choose a partner of twenty years based on the recommendation of someone you don't know? That's what you're doing when you purchase a bird from those sources.

An even worse way to acquire a bird is because someone else doesn't want it. If you want to acquire your bird from a rescue, that's a commendable aim. Have the owner relinquish the bird to the rescue organization. Most rescue organizations will do at least some health and behavioral assessment and help you acquire the skills you need to be successful with your new companion. The online advertisers' interest is making money, not in successful lifelong placements.

Breeders

The best bird breeders raise a small number of birds, specialize in a few species, breed for ideal pet characteristics, and sell only fully weaned birds either directly to clients or through small specialty stores. These breeders spend a good deal of time educating potential buyers about the species' needs, as well as about the needs of the individual birds. The best breeders, generally members of associations such as the American Federation of Aviculture, may have received certifications for their breeding operations and aviaries, attesting to the quality of their breeding program and the health conditions of their birds. Breeders become experts in their species, understanding their natural history and the dietary requirements of their particular birds and in providing the amenities that a particular species of parrot needs.

Because their birds were raised with care, these breeders want families to take good care of their new companions. Some breeders will ask you to return your bird at any point in his lifetime if you need to give him up for any reason. Again, this is because of their concern for the welfare of their individual birds.

Visiting a breeder or two who specializes in the sort of bird you are considering is an excellent step to take in the process of finding the right parrot for you. Most breeders are happy to share their knowledge if you contact them and make an appointment to see or speak with them. Many breeders maintain websites with extensive information about their species' natural history, suitability as a companion bird, and requirements for well-being as a lifelong companion.

You will need to do some work to find these breeders, but they can be located with a little research and some telephone calls. A good place to begin is the American Federation of Aviculture (AFA), a local bird club, or national bird group, such as the American Cockatiel Society (ACS). Even if a breeder of your species of interest is not listed for your local area, try corresponding with representative from your region. People from your region are more likely to know others with the same species who live near you. Explain your situation: you want to meet with a local breeder who raises a small number of your chosen species as pets.

Pet Shops

Many pet shops in North America have rethought how they provide their buyers with access to healthy and happy animals. Both local and chain pet stores have partnered with humane societies and animal welfare groups to feature animals that need new homes. For the most part, pet shops feature only small mammals and small birds, including parakeets (called budgerigars outside the United States), finches, and a few of the smaller conures. Despite hard work on the part of these stores to educate their staff and screen birds taken in for sale, the fact remains that the care of the birds is uneven, and some staff members

Visiting a breeder of the species that interests you allows you to meet several different birds and pick the breeder's brain.

are not able to distinguish when a bird is not at his best. Bringing together birds from various suppliers means the opportunity for disease introduction is significant, despite best efforts. However, many stores work hard to create a well-informed staff that can provide high-quality care for their animals and for the companions who purchase them.

The advantages of spending time in pet shops, especially those that specialize in birds, is that you will have the opportunity to see a variety of species, observe the care provided to the birds, and gain some feeling about what will be required to care for your bird.

Exotic Bird Stores

Although many pet stores sell birds, few have staff members who are extremely knowledgeable about birds. However, you can learn a great deal about your

Parrots and Kids

Although many kids get along fine with larger parrots, a safer approach, particularly for a first parrot, is to consider a budgie or cockatiel. These child-size birds are gentler. Their beaks, although still able to provide powerful bites, are nowhere near as powerful as those of a larger parrot. In addition, the cages and accessories are small enough for the child to take an active role in the care, feeding, and training of the pet parrot.

The quick movements and squawks of birds can sometimes frighten children. In addition, the high-pitched voices and quick movements of children sometimes frighten birds, especially those not accustomed to children.

The best approach is to go one small step at a time. Birds are curious and will respond to a child's patient reading, singing, or feeding through the cage bars as a first step. Likewise, children often enjoy the "magical" properties of birds—their soft feathers and their ability to fly.

Children can learn much about responsibility by caring for pets; however, it is an unrealistic expectation that a child can be entirely responsible for a creature as complicated to care for as a bird.

chosen species at one of the few remaining stores that specialize in exotic birds. You can sometimes find these in major metropolitan areas. Locate these stores by using your online search skills and by talking with other parrot people you meet through your research. Even if the store is several hours away, the effort of making a weekend trip and visiting several times over the course of a couple of days will be a worthwhile experience.

Equipped with a knowledgeable staff, exotic bird stores are more likely to have time to work with you and your prospective bird, especially if you call ahead to make an appointment to visit on one of their less busy days and times. Not only will you be able to see a variety of species, but you can spend time observing the staff, the birds, and the various chores associated with keeping a parrot. In fact, you can learn quite a bit about bird handling and caretaking simply by watching.

One caution about an exotic bird store as a source is the possibility that a particular bird might not be as healthy as you would like. Although specialty stores do their best to protect their investment in the birds who pass through their shop, the birds are brought together from many different breeders. Whenever this happens, the potential for disease is higher than it is when you acquire your bird from a small breeder. However, like every reputable breeder, most specialty stores offer a health guarantee. If the store is unwilling to do this, don't take the chance.

Another caution is that once the birds come to the store, staff may have little time to continue each bird's socialization. As a result, each individual may not receive the attention he needs to support his emotional growth. You will be able to observe the staff in the store and the attention that each bird receives. This is a good reason to visit the store several times, even if you have to stay overnight. Nevertheless, most exotic bird stores do their best to create good matches and to provide you with the information and training you need to be successful with your bird.

In addition, many specialty bird stores offer wonderful educational opportunities that you can take advantage of before you choose your species and your individual bird. These stores often arrange for well-known and respected bird behaviorists to visit and hold seminars. Attending one or more of these seminars is another way to learn more about the various species and the demands of caring for fascinating and sometimes difficult psittacines.

Humane Organizations and Parrot Rescue Networks

Shelters or rescue organizations are another place to meet your species. Most humane societies have birds for adoption, as do bird rescue organizations and exotic bird clubs. Keep in mind, however, that a foster and rescue network serves the increasing number birds given up by the people who purchased them. Knowing the reason your potential companion was surrendered is important. Owners who made poor choices about pet selection may be surrendering birds with behavior or diet-related health problems. In addition, the emotional and physical health of these birds is often compromised. Even though a bird may be healthy at the time he's adopted, the stress of being relinquished, kept at a shelter, and then relocated again does not create the best conditions for maintaining a healthy immune system.

Accordingly, as you look at the birds and talk with the organization's staff and volunteers, keep your requirements and questions in mind. The best situation is one where you can visit several sources of the species of most interest to you and take a few days to consider what you've seen. Your relationship with your bird may last twenty or more years, so be selective.

To find a reputable rescue organization, look for a group that has been operating successfully for a number of years, has a board of directors who oversees the operation of the rescue, and is known to local veterinarians and bird clubs as a reputable and careful rescue. A rescue is not a place to acquire "free" birds. In

Unfortunately, many parrots are given up to animal rescues and are waiting for their forever homes.

fact, most reputable rescues have a lengthy adoption process and require you to complete a basic bird care course, and many will visit your home to ensure that you have adequate space and can safely care for a bird. Rescues operate in this way because, when people relinquish their birds, the rescue organization takes on the responsibility to care for the bird in a proper manner. This means finding families who will care for the bird long term.

Seven Safety Tips for Interspecies Relationships

- Clear bird areas of food debris that attracts other pets.
- Clip cats' toenails.
- Confine cats and dogs when your birds are out of the cage.
- Keep aquariums covered.
- Leave a buffer zone between animal species.
- Separate snakes, large lizards, ferrets, and other predatory pets from your bird zone.
- Stop stalking behavior immediately.

In effect, rescue organizations will typically take you through the list of questions at the end of Chapter 1, making sure that you are ready for a bird. In addition, they'll ask you to complete some education to ensure that you know how to care for the bird of your choice. Finally, they'll visit you several times after your adoption to ensure that you are doing well with the bird you've chosen. For the rescue organization, it's about finding the best home for the individual bird. That's their focus.

Other Sources

Other sources of parrots include individuals or companies located through advertisements on local bulletin boards, newspapers, or online sources. Unless the source is well known to you through a web group you've been a member of for some time or through a bird professional, steer clear. The more barriers between you and the individual providing the bird, the greater the chance that something can and will go wrong.

This is not to say that all such sellers are hiding something or are dishonest. This is merely to say that you have many choices in where to acquire your lifelong companion. Why wouldn't you choose a source that is well-known to you and to others in your area (including veterinarians), so that you will have the assistance you need in the years to come?

Exceptions exist. For example, a well-known breeder and expert on eclectus parrots may be downsizing her group of birds because she is aging. She's begun to talk about this on a list-serve that American Federation of Aviculture members participate in. If someone wants a companion eclectus, a bird acquired from this person would be the best imaginable companion. This professional aviculturist has been an acquaintance and friend for more than 20 years, she's been an active member of local bird clubs, a speaker at national meetings on the Eclectus parrot, and is a well-published author on the species. In other words, there's nothing anonymous about this person.

Contrast such a well-known person with one you meet through an online advertisement. The bird has no band, no microchip, no health certificate, and the owner offers you no health guarantee. The bird has never seen a veterinarian because "he's never been sick." Sketchy? Yes, definitely.

A different advertisement tells you about a bird who has come to a local bird club because the owner has recently passed away. The bird has a record at the local avian veterinarian, has a band, was microchipped, and is well-known to the vet and the technicians in her office. This is a different situation. You know something of the bird's history and socialization, and the bird club is handling the placement of the bird. Their interest is in the bird and not the sale.

When it comes to other sources, use your best judgment. You should be able to find how the bird has been connected in the local community through veterinarians, boarding facilities, caretakers, a bird club, or a national organization. With two or three people telling the same story, you have some idea about your bird's history. Without that, the advice of most professionals is to pass on the bird. Let me repeat: never purchase a bird because you feel sorry for its condition. Especially as a beginning bird keeper, you're in for heartbreak—this is a guarantee.

Young Bird or Old Bird?

Birds of all ages are available, from the newly weaned to the senior bird. Since bird life expectancy is 20+ years, age should be a consideration. Mature birds—birds over one year of age—provide the advantage that their personalities are fully formed, their coloration is developed, and their habits are well established. You have a realistic glimpse of your lives together from the beginning. Newly weaned young birds offer a completely different experience. In this case, you have the short-lived pleasure of watching your bird mature and the responsibility for socializing this curious and perhaps clingy creature over the course of your first six months together. Whether you think that a young bird or a senior is right for you, do get to know an adult bird (or maybe several adults) before choosing a youngster.

Reputable sources of parrots will provide a health guarantee for their birds.

Hand-Fed vs. Parent-Raised Birds

The best companion birds have been handled by the breeder very early in their lives. Whether young birds have been raised by their bird parents, by humans, or by a combination, the key is that they have been exposed to and handled by people from the earliest part of their lives. An advantage to birds at least partially raised by bird parents is that they are not imprinted on humans. In other words, parent-raised birds are clear that they are birds of the parent's species. They identify themselves as birds and are clear that their potential mates are birds. Hand-raised birds (meaning removed from the parents' nest and raised only by humans) become imprinted. Generally, these birds are needy and prone to behavior problems. For this reason, many good breeders share rearing with the parents, leaving the chicks in the nest until they are fully feathered and flighted.

Visit Your Potential Bird More Than Once

When you've identified several potential birds, spend time with each in an environment that mimics your home. Bathe the bird or feed him. Observe how the staff handles him.

Discuss the purchasing process. What paperwork does the seller provide? You should expect to receive:

- A bill of sale that provides a description of the bird, the sales price, and the hatch date and band number of the bird
- A care sheet that describes the bird's routine
- A health guarantee for your bird, explaining the right of return. A health guarantee usually provides several days for you to have your bird seen by a veterinarian.

If your prospective seller is unwilling to provide these things, move on, no matter how much you like the bird. An unwillingness to provide them indicates that the seller may not be reliable.

If your prospective seller provides these things, you should return at least one additional time to spend time with the bird you like most. Again, ask to help in the bird's care. Watch the process of caring for your prospective bird and other birds. Talk with the seller about suitable veterinary care in the area, a local bird club, and other resources that may support you in your efforts to become knowledgeable about your companion.

Once you and the seller are agreed, a final step in the process is the health examination. For this, you should use a veterinarian who devotes a large part of her practice to birds. The veterinarian should do a well-bird exam and provide a health screening as a part of this process. As you will learn more in Chapter 7, birds should be screened for the more common diseases that afflict this species. For the screening, expect both blood and feces to be collected from your bird.

Health Check

As you begin your selection process, rely on a bird's general appearance as the best indicator of health. A healthy bird has clear eyes and cere (where skull and beak meet, containing the nostrils), smooth feathers, all his toes, and clear legs and feet. His vent (where he eliminates feces) will be clean. The bird should be active, show curiosity, and perhaps approach you. If you're not sure whether a bird is healthy, or if the cleanliness of the facility is suspect, move on. Remember, a healthy bird is both physically and emotionally healthy.

A healthy bird has clear eyes and smooth feathers.

Molting birds or birds growing new feathers create confusion for a new bird person. The spiky, coated feathers sometimes cause people to assume the bird is ill. Developing feathers poke through the bird's skin from the inside, and new feathers emerge covered with a waxy coating similar to your cuticle. This is normal. Birds replace all their feathers once each year, and, between molts, they replace individual feathers year round.

Another health indicator is the appearance of the bird's enclosure. The room should be well-lit and relatively clean. The cages should not show a buildup of feces or dried food. The birds' food and water should appear to have been changed twice daily. Although birds are messy, the facility should appear clean and the water and food fresh.

No matter whether your bird will be young or old, you want to select a healthy bird. Once you have done the initial screening and eliminated some sources of birds from your list, you can look more closely at a specific bird. You will need to have that specific bird checked by a veterinarian for those things you cannot see. This may be impossible to do before you actually purchase or adopt the bird. If so, make arrangements to have a vet examine the parrot within a few days of acquiring him and have the source agree that nothing is final until you get a clean bill of health from the vet.

Why all the fuss about getting a healthy bird? Your bird is a substantial investment of time and emotional energy. In addition, your financial investment in the purchase of your bird, annual medical care, and proper housing, including toys, is equally substantial. Ensuring that you have a healthy bird from the beginning means that you are unlikely to make these investments and then spend many more dollars providing medical support to a bird who was unhealthy from the beginning.

Choosing the Right Parrot

To find the parrot of your dreams and not the pet of your nightmares, potential parrot parents must be honest with themselves. The first decision is about the parrot species. Only after that decision has been made should the family begin to consider individual parrots as potential pets. Liz Wilson, a well-respected parrot behaviorist who was known to say the things that everyone needed to hear—but not everyone wanted to hear—published widely on this subject. In choosing the best parrot species for a family, Ms. Wilson suggested the following questions be part of an honest family conversation about acquiring a parrot before the decision is made:

If you live in an apartment, you will have to select a quieter species, such as a masked lovebird.

Question 1: Does everyone in the household agree that a parrot would be a happy addition?

If the answer to this question is yes, then the next step is to decide on the species.

Question 2: Are there chronic health issues in the household that might affect the decision about a pet parrot?

One of the most frequently seen health issues, especially with children and older adults, is allergies or respiratory problems. If any family members suffer from these sorts of health problems, have them handle multiple species of birds. By handling various species and being exposed to the feather dander, they can determine whether there is a species of bird that does not aggravate their health condition. For fragile individuals, potential parrot parents should consult with a physician because, despite air filters, birds produce a certain amount of "feather dust," and frail individuals may become increasingly sensitive over time. For these families, an alternative to purchasing a bird of your dreams is to share responsibility with a friend for a bird or to work with a bird rescue organization. There's no reason to purchase a pet you know will aggravate the health of a family member.

Question 3: Are you limited financially?

If your family is limited financially, this will restrict your choice of species to a smaller, more common parrot. Not only will the price be smaller, but also the size and price of cages and toys will be smaller. For a larger species of parrot, the initial purchase price can be more than a thousand dollars; the toys and furnishings, including cages, can be more than twice the purchase price; and the ongoing costs of toys, veterinary care, and a proper diet can cost as much each year as in the first year.

Most people find as much joy in a small parrot, including budgerigars (parakeets), as in a bigger bird, and there is the relief that they are not financially extending themselves more than is comfortable. Not only are these small parrots cheerful, busy, and interesting to watch, but also they are amusing in their antics. Many budgies can learn to talk and make excellent companions. In addition, budgies have a life span of no longer than ten years or so. If you feel insecure financially and insist that you must have a parrot in your life, consider a budgie.

Your new parrot will be nervous in his unfamiliar surroundings for several days or even weeks.

Question 4: Are you already too busy and feeling stressed about getting everything done?

Parrots need lots of daily interaction to remain psychologically healthy. If you must have a bird to be happy, Ms. Wilson always suggested considering a songbird, such as a finch, rather than a parrot. Finches, like other songbirds, do not require the same commitment of face-to-face interaction that all parrots do.

Question 5: Do you live in a noise-sensitive situation?

If you live in an apartment or in a neighborhood where the houses are close together, you need

Should I Get a Male or Female?

Although there are many legends about one sex of bird or the other talking or behaving better than another, the choice of one individual parrot or another is more about the personality of the individual bird rather than about the individual's sex. Many companions are never sure of the sex of their birds. Although some species have differing feather patterns for males and females, many species have feather patterns that are exactly the same no matter which sex the bird. The only way to be sure is with DNA testing. (Okay, if your bird lays an egg, you do have a female.) From the shape of the head to the mystical (and fake) method of sex detection using a pendant, the only sure ways to determine sex are the (unlikely) production of an egg, DNA testing, or an internal examination by your veterinarian.

Rely on your instincts about an individual bird, rather than on legends about the capabilities of one sex versus another. (By the way, the only way to be sure that you are getting a parrot who will talk is to purchase a parrot who is already talking.)

to limit your species to those parrots who are considered "quieter." Being a "quieter" species, of course, is a relative thing because there is no such thing as a truly *quiet* parrot. However, some species, including budgerigars, cockatiels, and members of the *Pionus* group are somewhat quieter than most other parrots. Ms. Wilson famously said "trying to keep a parrot quiet so it does not aggravate others invariably leads to excessive screaming."

Question 6: Does everyone in your family feel comfortable with your choice of bird?

If family members are frightened of the enormous beak of a macaw or cockatoo, then you must look at smaller birds that aren't so intimidating. No matter how much you want a particular species of parrot, the feelings and opinions of others in the environment *must* be considered. Otherwise, you're saying that your desires are more important than those of other household members; this is unfair to everyone, including the bird.

Bringing Your Bird Home

Bringing your parrot home will undoubtedly be an exciting time. Although you are looking forward to this occasion and are excited about your new family addition, your bird may need more time than you do to become enthusiastic about his new surroundings. Depending on your bird's temperament, the best thing for you to do when you bring your bird home is to make this a non-event. Simply follow the routine you've thought about and planned for, and keep excitement and handling to a minimum to give your bird time to adjust.

Several things may be helpful in the process of adjustment. First, keep to the same feeding routine for the first few days or weeks. Everything will be unfamiliar to your new best friend; do him the favor of keeping a few vital things the same. Be sure to provide a favorite toy, exactly the same one he's already used to. If you can also keep to his familiar schedule of "lights out" and "time to get up," this will help your bird make a large number of adjustments more easily. As with any situation that involves relocation, the stress is enormous.

Prior to bringing your bird home, you will have decided on his housing and purchased all the necessary supplies. Those many decisions and the options available are presented in Chapter 3. His cage will be on site and in place. In addition, you'll have a suitable carrier to bring your bird home in. The carrier should be one he's familiar with. You may want to take the carrier to your breeder so that she can familiarize your bird with this over a series of days in an environment that is familiar and not stressful.

Your breeder will supply you with some food, and you should get the name of the supplier and a local outlet, if available. You should also receive a list of the fruits and vegetables that your bird has been eating, along with any special treats he is fond of. You might also look at the appearance of the food the breeder offers because, again, familiarity creates a better experience for your bird.

At the time of purchase or adoption, you should receive a health guarantee, along with the name of the veterinarian your breeder uses. Also, you should ask for a copy of the bird's health records to date. Most breeders also keep records of hatch date and weights at various stages in your bird's development. Finally, she should also supply you with several toys that your bird particularly likes. Hold at least one of these back, so that you can use this toy to offer to your new bird to help him in his adjustment to the new play gym, cages, and all his other new things. You can also do this with a particularly favored food treat.

Some birds adapt quickly and act as if nothing has changed. Other, more sensitive birds will need more time to adjust. Don't rush the process. Let the bird go at his or her own pace. As with any creature, things take as long as they take.

Introducing Your Parrot to Family and Other Pets

Bringing your parrot home is a time of great excitement and enthusiasm for you. For your parrot, the experience may be quite different. Although your entire family will be anxious to pick up the bird, feed the bird, talk to the bird, and dance with the bird, the fact is that your bird will not be anxious to meet your four children, the cat, and the dog, all in a matter of hours.

Consider the fact that your parrot's emotional development is similar to that of a two-year-old child. Now imagine if you brought a two-year-old, new to you and your family, home. How would you go about introducing the people and animals in your household to this new child? Although parrots and children are not the same, the idea will help you understand the experience from the parrot's point of view.

Introduce Over a Period of Days

A reasonable idea would be to bring the parrot home during a time when your children and other pets are elsewhere. Give your parrot a few days to acclimate to his new surroundings. Then, one by one, introduce the children and the other pets, giving your parrot plenty of space and time to adjust.

Plan introductions to coincide with your parrot's active times of day, when he has had enough rest and has eaten. Your parrot will need plenty of sleep during his period of adjustment. And proper meals are important, so that he has the energy to cope with the change of just about everything in his life. Again, think about that two-year-old. Without enough sleep and a decent meal, anything, even something that should be pleasurable, will be a trial.

Prepare the Family Members

Prepare your children to talk quietly and to keep their approach slow and soft, especially if your parrot was not raised around children. Their high voices and sudden movements take some getting used to. Slow, short, and quiet first meetings leave your parrot curious and wanting more.

Make the first introduction through the cage bars, and allow family members to offer a piece of fruit (or other treat your parrot particularly likes) or to sit next to the cage and talk quietly with the bird for a few minutes. If your bird retreats to the back of his cage, allow this, and don't encourage him into a situation in which he feels unsafe. Instead, have the visitor back up and give a bit more space. When your parrot feels safe, he will approach because his curiosity—eventually—wins.

Birds are quick to pick up on a person's energy. Never try to force a bird to come out of his cage or go to a person he doesn't want to. This is not a good beginning to their relationship and an expectation that your bird should simply obey you is not productive.

Although these first few days are excellent for establishing your parrot's manners and behavior, what is not appropriate or useful is for you to expect that "manners" will overcome fear. This doesn't work for children, and it doesn't work for parrots either. More about this will become clear in the chapter on training.

Of course, this is the time that the family will establish ground rules for handling the bird, for making sure the doors and windows are closed and opened according to a set of rules, and who has responsibility for feeding and making sure the bird has clean water at set times of the day.

How to Catch a Parrot in the House

The strategic elements of catching a parrot indoors are: (1) calm, (2) darkness, and (3) a gradual reduction of the area in which the parrot can fly or roam. The tools you need are either a net or a sheet or pillowcase, depending on the size of the bird. This scenario assumes the parrot can fly and is not yet socialized.

If you have a family of five, designate two as the bird catchers. More participants do not equal more success. Next, if you know which room the parrot is in, close the doors between that room and the rest of the house. If you don't know, close off every room, and search one room at a time. Make sure doors and windows to the outside are closed, and lock the outside doors so that no one can accidentally let the bird outside, which will make your job much harder.

Next, confine any other pets. Keep the interior lights off and close the drapes. This will prevent your bird from flying toward the light and injuring himself on the window. Birds are calmer in small, dark places.

Once you have discovered which room your bird is in, gradually close off hiding places, such as under beds or behind desks or dressers using blankets or sheets. Guide (don't frighten) your bird into a smaller and smaller spot. If your bird will go willingly into a cage, bring his travel cage and his favorite treat. If your bird will not go willingly into a cage, sit with his favorite treat and see if you can entice him to come out. If your bird is not tame, position the sheet, pillowcase, or net over him and gently immobilize your bird's head so that you will not be bitten. Do this by placing your thumb and forefinger around the back of the bird's skull and gently but firmly holding his lower jaw near where it joins the skull. Carry your bird gently and calmly to his cage. Make sure he has fresh water and some high carbohydrate food, such as fruit or seeds. Cover the cage to allow both of you to recover from a very stressful experience.

Neutral Space

Often, introductions go well in a neutral space, particularly if your bird is older and has a history of being a bit protective of his cage. You can provide a neutral space outside the cage on a stand, such as a play gym. If your bird is without the protection of his cage, allow even more space between the family members to be introduced and the bird. Each bird, each situation is different. Try to consider things from the bird's perspective. "Everything is new, and I'm not sure about any of this." That's probably what your bird will be experiencing for the first few weeks in your home.

A great thing for a family to do together, with your parrot perched on his play gym, is to watch some videos—either purchased or from the library—about your species of parrot and some basic handling and training techniques.

Parrots and Other Pets

Mixing birds with other animal companions is tricky. We know this, but we are encouraged to dream about perfect interspecies relationships because we've all seen the YouTube videos with the parrots playing with dogs, cats, skunks, horses, and pot-bellied pigs. As your mother would say, "Just because all the kids are doing it doesn't mean it's a good idea." Although some birds do enjoy playing with other species, the videos never show the heartbreaking stories that happen more often than you would imagine. When a cat's claw nicks your parrot's air sack, your parrot has a "collapsed lung" and will require extensive veterinary care of a surgical nature. If your dog punctures your parrot's skin accidentally, a week-long course of antibiotics is needed for your bird. Of course, if your dog closes his jaws just a little too hard, your avian friend can sustain even more serious, perhaps life-threatening, injuries. For every fictional bird hero, there's a real-life story of heartbreak.

Your bird and your other pets will not necessarily get along. Introduce them carefully—if at all.

Every individual—bird, dog, cat, or ferret—is different, but we can generalize about things that transcend individual animals' personalities.

What's Natural?

Birds are prey animals. Whether your pet dog or cat or ferret will act on the thought that your parrot smells like food, your parrot will probably see your mammal companions as the carnivores and predators they are. Your parrot depends on you to keep his territory and body safe from the creatures that, if he were in the wild, would eat him—a tricky business if you have other pets at home. Factors that affect the success of a parrot mixing with other species include the age at introduction, the species, and companion-enforced limits and supervision.

Cats and Dogs

Well-known parrot behaviorist Mattie Sue Athan has both cats and birds. Athan has explained that parrots, because they are social by nature, can have meaningful relationships with other pets. A typical playful relationship between parrots and dogs and cats is a game that parrots start. In this game, the bird calls the pet, sometimes by name, then hangs upside down or flaps to taunt the pet. When the pet comes very near, the parrot screams and lunges at the pet. This game is relatively safe when the parrot plays from inside the cage.

It is always best to keep cats and birds separated; any meeting between the two is a potential disaster.

By the way, many parrot-people have stories of their dogs becoming indifferent to being called. By accident, usually, they discover that the parrot has been calling their dog, often by name, and then shouting, "Bad dog," when the dog appears. The parrot finds this game incredibly amusing. Again, think of the joy of controlling such a fabulous toy—which is what the dog becomes from the parrot's perspective.

With cats and dogs, larger parrots have the advantage because of their hard beaks, intimidating size, and domineering personalities. Small birds that flutter, like parakeets and cockatiels, however, become irresistible to both cats and dogs. Both dogs and cats will bump cages in order to evoke this response from the birds. This creates an impossible situation for the bird, which is constantly being frightened. The only solution is to ensure that the dog or cat cannot reach the area around the cage. This is more easily done with dogs than with cats.

Because of the range of dog breeds, it's hard to generalize, but behaviorists Sally Blanchard and Athan mention two cautions. Larger parrots, such as cockatoos, macaws, and Amazons, may develop a screaming habit if they are housed with barking or noisy dogs. These habits, once established, are very difficult to eliminate. Their other caution is that once a dog (or cat) has traumatized a bird, the parrot may be unable to tolerate that species, even one of a different breed.

The goal is to keep your parrot as flexible and as well-adjusted as possible because, in the long life you have together, you have no idea what will happen next. Preventing trauma that could create lifelong terror is relatively simple, although it takes knowledge and planning. Dealing with the long-term results of a terror of dogs or cats could be difficult for a family, as well as a constant source of horror for your parrot.

Other Companion Pets

Reptiles represent minimal danger to birds, except that large snakes at liberty have been known to eat pet birds. Pond and aquarium fish and aquatic turtles are not a threat to birds, but their aquatic habitats are drowning hazards. Ferrets have been known to kill even large parrots, so small parrots like budgies and cockatiels are a bad choice for mustelid lovers.

Success Factors

Experts do not agree on a preferred species mix or whether animals must be caged or allowed to roam free. They do agree that training, thoughtful introductions, and limit setting are factors that promote mixed-species relationship successes.

Each species has a different way of indicating comfort and discomfort. Each species has a different tolerance for the other. Pet owners, in order to avoid heartbreak, must learn the body language of each of their pets; additionally, the pets must understand the body language of the others. What does "You're too close to me" look like in the language of each animal? Training of some sort, whether from a professional, a good how-to book, or a friend who has had success, will reduce chances of interspecies injuries or death.

Training, thoughtful introductions, and setting boundaries are factors that promote mixed-species relationship success.

Well-planned introductions help establish the tone of pets' relationships. Introducing young animals is best. Next best is a slow, supervised introduction, one-to-one at a time. Athans claims that cats raised with companion birds become trustworthy with that particular kind of bird. As a precaution, she suggests claw clipping in advance of meeting and underlines that any break in a bird's skin by a cat requires antibiotics to prevent that bird's death from a bacterial infection. Athans suggests that introducing a dog into a home with parrot should be done with the guidance of a dog behavior professional.

Sally Blanchard, in her *Companion Parrot Handbook,* emphasizes limit setting. "People who have happy, well-behaved dogs usually have well-behaved parrots." Good behavior comes from the companion's background of rule setting and correction when rules are broken.

Both Athans and Blanchard agree that close supervision of interspecies friendships is essential. Just like small children, pets cannot be depended on to behave in the manner they know you expect. Unfortunately, the price for the parrot can be very high. My suggestion is not to allow interspecies interaction.

The best approach is to keep a neutral zone between your parrot and dog or other pet. This is a space where neither the second pet nor the parrot is allowed. A space about three feet wide is enough to keep the parrot from pitching out food to the other pet. In addition, the space gives the owner enough room to come and go without having the dog slip through to the cage or the other way around. There is nothing a mischievous parrot enjoys more than taunting another pet by calling it or tempting it with food. Of course, the parrot, like a small child, will have no idea of the potential consequences of a too-close encounter. As a pet parent, one of your jobs is to protect all of your pets.

Meeting the Parrot Before He Comes Home

An alternative to having the entire family meet the parrot after he has come home is to have the family, one or two at a time, meet the parrot in his former home. This has the advantage of letting the parrot feel as secure as possible and having the newcomers learn some handling basics from the breeder or shop owners. Similarly, if your bird is coming from a rescue, this is an opportunity for the entire family to take the course that is required by most rescues as a prerequisite for adopting a bird. In addition, this allows the family to become familiar with the bird, and vice versa, prior to the decision to finalize the adoption.

Handling Basics

Handling basics can be learned by watching and through practice. You must be committed to keeping your bird's comfort in mind and as the priority. With this commitment, anyone can learn to competently handle a well-mannered parrot. A key to good handling is to learn the body language of the parrot. In the same way that people judge whether or not to approach a dog or cat based on their body language, parrots "tell" you whether they wish to be approached or not. The difference is that a parrot's feather and body movements may not be as familiar to you as the posture of anxious dogs or arched-backed cats. Nevertheless, once you've learned what to look for, parrots give signals that are every bit as clear.

In addition, never force a family member to handle a bird in a situation that feels uncomfortable for that person. The anxiety of a bird handler can cause negative behaviors, including threats and biting by your normally well-mannered parrot. Parrots can feel stress in their handler. A confident handler calms a sensitive bird. A stressed handler stresses a normally confident bird.

The most important skill to learn is having your bird step onto your hand so that you can move him to a perch and then off your hand and onto a perch. Similarly, you need to be able to return your bird to his cage when it's time for him to go in.

If you did your homework during your visits to the breeder, you and members of your family have observed the process of asking your bird to step onto and off your hand. Again, this is another point on which you and your family should agree. The "commands" or "requests" that you make of your bird should always use the same recognizable word, so that your bird understands what you are asking of him. In addition, you want to create a situation in which your bird sees an advantage in complying with your requests. For example, as you are becoming familiar with one another, try rewarding your bird with one of his favorite treats for returning to his cage willingly. In fact, for the first few times you invite your bird off your hand and onto a perch in his new cage, offer the new treat as a lure to make stepping onto that perch a very attractive and potentially rewarding decision.

If you have a family member who is nervous about handling the bird, try placing your parrot on a stand where the person can read, talk to, or sing or dance with the parrot, away from the cage. This neutral area keeps both the parrot and the nervous person on the same footing: neutral ground. This is not the parrot's cage, so he doesn't have to defend it or oppose going back when he's having a good time out of the cage. And the person doesn't have to enforce anything. She is simply there to interact with the parrot in a neutral spot, to establish whatever connection is possible between the two.

Parrots, like all learners, must have the power to operate positively on their environment to live behaviorally healthy lives. We facilitate this power when we interact with them in such a way that they choose to do what is required of them. This makes for lasting companionship in our homes.

For more information on handling and socialization, see Chapter 5: Behavior, Training, and Life with a Parrot.

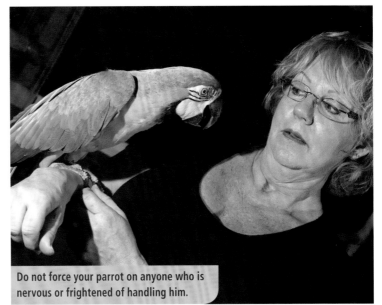

Do not force your parrot on anyone who is nervous or frightened of handling him.

A Summary of Parrot Qualities

The Quieter Species

The species listed here tend to be quieter and less prone to screaming than most others. However, every parrot is noisy sometimes, and each bird is an individual.

- budgerigars (parakeets)
- cockatiels
- eclectus
- pionus parrot
- Quaker parakeets

The Best Talkers

The ability and desire of a bird to talk is not only related to his species, but also to that individual bird's personality. The only way to be sure you acquire a bird who talks is to find an older bird who already talks. Still, you won't know the extent of the vocabulary the bird can acquire nor the conditions under which your bird will use it. Bird species that can produce individuals who learn to talk very well include African greys, Amazons, and budgerigars.

Parrots Who Are Best for First-time Owners

The American Veterinary Medical Association suggests that both budgerigars (parakeets) and cockatiels make excellent first-time birds. Both these species come in a variety of colors, can sometimes talk, and have a life expectancy of between five and twenty years (as opposed to the longer life spans of larger birds). In addition, these species tend to be relatively easy for beginners to manage. Because these are smaller birds, their cages and furnishings also tend to be less expensive.

If you believe you will not be happy with either of these types of bird, but you are still convinced a bird is for you, try a Quaker parakeet, one of the small African parrots (including Senegals, Meyer's, and Jardine's), a pionus parrot, or possibly a green-cheeked or maroon-bellied conure, members of the quieter side of the conure family, the *Pyrrhura*.

If the parrot of your dreams is not one of these, I'd recommend fostering a bird for a few months prior to purchasing or adopting another species. Some people are extraordinary animal handlers from the beginning, but most people find that parrots are a larger commitment than they first imagined and that their exotic animal handling skills develop more slowly than they wish.

- Best bets: budgerigar or cockatiel
- Alternatives: Quaker parakeet; Senegal, Meyer's, or Jardine's parrot; pionus parrot; lineolated parakeet; lovebird; or a green-cheeked or maroon-bellied conure

Parrots Who Are Best for Experienced Owners

- Amazons
- cockatoos (all except cockatiel)
- lories and lorikeets
- macaws

Parrots Who Are Good at Learning Tricks

- caiques
- cockatoos
- conures
- macaws
- Quaker parakeets

3

HOUSING
AND
SUPPLIES

In determining how to advise potential parrot parents on the very best bird-keeping strategies, equipment, and methods, giving some thought to animal behaviorists is time well spent. One of the very best and most well-known behaviorist is Dr. Temple Grandin. Dr. Grandin's book, *Animals Make Us Human*, is based on her study and work with animals kept by humans for many different purposes—livestock, zoos animals, and companion animals. Grandin uses the British Government's Brambell Committee's list of physical and mental freedoms that kept animals should have:

- Freedom from hunger and thirst
- Freedom from discomfort
- Freedom from pain, injury, or disease
- Freedom to express normal behavior
- Freedom from fear and distress

When you bring your parrot home and provide him with housing and supplies, you will be well on your way to being an excellent caretaker if you place these freedoms at the top of your list of concerns. These freedoms belong at this point in this book because the decisions about housing, diet, health, and training, in this chapter and in the chapters to follow, define the sorts of freedoms that your parrot will have. Every loving parrot parent will want his or her companion to have these freedoms. As you make the decisions that bear on your parrot's freedoms, you will be in a position to say, "Yes, this extra cage space is necessary," and "Yes, our parrot really does need these thinker toys."

Buy the largest cage you can afford, but also make sure the bar spacing is appropriate for your parrot.

At the beginning, the number of purchases and decisions you need to make can seem overwhelming. However, if you take the pieces in order and make notes as you talk with people, you'll find the points for and against each decision become clear. For example, whether or not you've identified a source for your parrot, notice and make notes about the housing and supplies that the various breeders, pet shops, and bird companions use. Ask not only about how the bird likes the setup, but also about the practical aspects of his daily care. Cage features can make the difference between a quick, convenient daily care routine and one that feels like drudgery.

Of course, each parrot species has different needs and preferences; additionally, you may also make decisions based on the needs of your individual companion parrot. Take the case of a parrot who does not like going back into his cage: this bird will benefit from a short perch placed on the inside of his cage's swinging door. Once you set him on the "outside" of the cage, you swing the door, with your perched parrot, inside. If you have purchased a cage with "guillotine doors," this strategy is not available to you. So what is a guillotine door and why aren't these ideal? Read on. But, before you do, remember, the key points with cages are: (1) buy the largest cage you can afford and (2) buy a safe cage.

Dome-top cages offer your bird more head room than flat-top cages, but horizontal space is more important for parrots.

Cages

In selecting a cage, place your bird's comfort and the cage's ease of cleaning above aesthetics. Except when you take your bird out during cage cleaning or for playtime, the inside of that cage is the boundary of your bird's universe. Thinking of your bird's enclosure in that way underscores his need for the largest cage you can afford. Because your bird spends most of each day inside his cage and because you clean the cage (at least briefly) each day, the right choice will repay you and your bird every day for as long as you both shall live together. Freedom from discomfort for a bird definitely means somewhere to stretch her wings, climb for exercise, and also have a hidden roost for sleep.

If you live in a location with a bird specialty store, breeders, or rescue organizations, you're lucky. Look at the various types of cages offered there. Examine cages during your visits. Notice the sizes and shapes, the bar spacing, and cage materials. Study placement of cage doors and food dish holders.

Ask caretakers about the different cage styles. Which are easiest to clean? Which do their birds prefer? What would they change about the cages they have? Although their priorities may not be yours, you will learn a lot from professionals who spend their days working with and around cages. Their information will save you uncertainty and the cost of having to sell a poorly suited cage and purchase one more suitable.

If you don't have the luxury of seeing cages in person, order several catalogs, purchase some pet bird hobby magazines, and look online. Take time to consider the various options. You might even solicit suggestions from well-established online forums that specialize in the sort of bird you're planning to acquire. If you look at enough styles and ask enough questions, you'll find what's right for you and your bird.

Not only do you have choices as to size, bar spacing, door placement, style of top, materials, and construction, but also many cages have extra features, such as wheels, built-in stands, feeders, seed guards, and grates, and trays, and latches. What seems like a small feature can make or break your long-term happiness with this, your largest investment after your bird. Let's first examine the styles.

Styles

Metal wire and plastic cages are usually the least expensive option. Although these cages may work well for smaller, shorter-lived birds, they may not be your best choice for a parrot who will be in your life for many years. These wire-topped cages typically detach from their plastic bottoms. Not only can a larger-beaked parrot gnaw through the plastic, but also the plastic becomes fatigued during removal, cleaning, and replacement.

Dome-top cages do provide extra "head room," but unless you have a large bird in a small cage, this can be a false advantage. Birds typically move from side to side more than they do up and down. Although dome tops do offer more interior space, you might do better with a wider cage with a shelf underneath to store extra perches and toys. Flattops with optional play tops offer a place for your bird to perch and play while you clean the cage. In the best of all possible worlds, a cage will have a removable play top to put elsewhere. Both dome and flattop cages tend to be made of powder-coated metal or stainless steel. (More about those cage materials shortly.)

Indoor and outdoor flight cages, sometimes called *aviaries*, should be examined with an eye toward the species you will select. Although these cages are often called *flights*, imagine whether your chosen parrot species could make four or five wing beats across the cage. Again, flights tend to be taller than they are wide, which seems to make little sense because (except for hummingbirds) birds fly side to side, rather than up and down. Indoor and outdoor flights are made either of woven mesh, which works only for very small-beaked birds, such as budgies, or from a wire mesh of various thicknesses or gauges that tells you the resilience of the wire. Some wire meshes are made of galvanized wire; others are powder-coated. The gauge of the wire that makes up the mesh, the size of the openings in the mesh, and the construction quality will give you an idea as to whether you can consider this flight cage or aviary for your bird.

Powder-coated steel cages are one of the best options because they are both safe and durable.

In considering the style of caging, remember that safety and size are the two most important considerations. Your parrot will spend a majority of his life in this enclosure. Be sure that you are providing enough room for him to live an interesting life among toys and foraging areas while you are at work or busy with other things. A bored parrot is a naughty parrot, and nothing is more boring than an enclosure that is too small.

Materials and Construction

Materials and construction are two attributes that contribute to the safety of an enclosure. Whether you can afford only a coated metal cage or the luxury of stainless steel, the design of your bird's

The Dangers of Antique and Used Cages

Antique and used cages pose so many different hazards that using them is out of the question. Not only are these cages built of dangerous materials with dangerous designs, but there can also be dangerous "left-behinds." If Aunt Gladys is dying for you to use her cage, turn the cage into a planter and place it in a "spot of honor" on the front porch for everyone to see.

Dangerous metals, fungal and other disease remainders, inappropriate design, and dangerous decorations are the four most obvious hazards. In times past, not much was known about cage birds, and certainly it never occurred to people that metals could be dangerous. After all, look at the fact that lead-based paints were used in homes until the 1970s, where children could chew the moldings.

Not only are old cages likely painted with dangerous paints, but the metals themselves will poison a bird over time. Grandma might not have noticed; when we knew less about birds, they died from many unexplained causes. Metal toxicity or poisoning was simply one of the reasons.

Spores and other traces of disease can persist in cages for many years. The fact that time has passed is no insurance that a disease-carrying materials is not lurking in the cage. The rougher the metalwork and the more crevices the metal has, the more likely that a problem is lurking there.

Another issue is that the cage designs were created to appeal to people and not to birds. The cages were small and had not enough space for the bird to maneuver, exercise, and play. In addition, the modern conveniences of slide-out trays and the clean designs that makes for easier cleaning for us and climbing for the bird were rarely present.

Decorative scrollwork and converging cage bars pose a threat to bird's free climbing. When cage bars converge, birds become confused, and it's easy for them to catch a foot, a wing, or their heads between the bars. Once the bird panics, injury will occur. The question is whether it is an injury from which your best friend can recover.

Honor your Aunt or your love for antiques in a different way. Your bird needs a new, modern cage. If you feel so strongly about your antique that you cannot say no, then perhaps you should consider saying no to the bird. This is his home, after all, and a bird is not a decoration.

cage is critical. Fancy scrollwork and bars that come together at anything but right angles are unsafe. Birds who extend their feet or wings through the bars and move toward the end where the bars narrow panic when they realize they cannot pull their foot or wing back through. This creates injuries, sometimes injuries that cannot be repaired. Although fancy scrollwork looks decorative, this sort of embellishment is dangerous for you bird.

An acrylic or Plexiglas cage will aesthetically blend with your furniture, but you will eventually regret buying this type of cage. Not only is keeping a proper amount of air flowing through these cages difficult, but the barrier between you and your bird is similar to the effect of keeping a child in a plastic box. The opportunity for interaction and your bird's ability to literally reach out for you are extinguished. If the advantages of keeping the dander and all the bird-related refuse inside are that appealing to you, reconsider whether you want to manage life with a pet who evolved to spread seeds and fertilize jungles. Although Plexiglas or acrylic is not suitable material for a cage, some birds seem comfortable in carriers made of these clear materials as night cages. More on this in the section on carriers (see page 67).

Similarly, wooden cages or cages with wooden parts are not appropriate for parrots. Not only are they difficult to clean and sanitize, but also your parrot will chew the cage material, making cleaning even more difficult. Besides, wooden cages will not keep your parrots inside: one day you will come home to your parrot's idea of living room redecoration.

Although wood and Plexiglas are not good cage materials, there are excellent materials available for cage construction. In a review of cage materials originally presented to the International Aviculturists' Society, Fern Van Sant, D.V.M. reviewed the types of materials commonly used in cage construction. Because most of us are not familiar with how metals are treated, Van Sant explains the ideas of mixing metals and coatings to produce different finished products.

Quick Safety Check Before Buying a Cage

The cage should not have:
- converging bars or scroll work
- guillotine doors

The cage does have:
- powder-coated metal or stainless steel as its material
- the designation "manufactured in the United States" to ensure safe materials standards
- door and food cup latches unreachable by a parrot's beak and feet
- wheels so that it is easily movable (optional, but useful)

Steel wire must be finished with a coating material to prevent rusting and weakening of the wire. The preferred method is to add chromium and nickel, which creates stainless steel. Although they are the most expensive option, stainless steel cages have become popular as safe and beautiful enclosures designed to last for 50 years. Van Sant says, "Stainless steel cages are most commonly used to house larger psittacine species [and] are particularly well suited for large macaws and cockatoos... capable of dismantling inferior materials."

If stainless steel is not within your budget, the next best alternative is powder-coated steel. This durable finish protects the steel, and it is created using an electrostatic application of a specialized paint. Most cages you can purchase for medium and large birds are finished in this way. Properly manufactured, powder-coated cages provide functional, safe enclosures that can be refinished when necessary.

Some less-expensive cages, Van Sant cautions, are made of powder-coated galvanized wire—not the same as powder-coated steel. Van Sant's concern is that birds who chew the coating can quickly ingest toxic levels of metals. She explains that in less costly cages designed for smaller psittacines, steel wire is covered with an inexpensive metal, usually zinc, to prevent deterioration. Most electroplated finishes, including shiny silver or gold, contain some zinc. Electrostatically applied plating is unlikely to be consumed by a bird as long as the finish is smooth. Once the cage shows signs of wear, it must be replaced. Grates, in particular, should be watched.

Other inexpensive cages feature steel or galvanized wire (steel coated with molten zinc) coated with plastic or vinyl. Because lead is a common ingredient of plastic and vinyl, pieces of coating ingested by birds can expose them to toxic metals. When a vinyl or plastic coating is used over galvanized wire, there is the added risk of zinc ingestion if the wire is chewed on and eaten. Again, this leads to effects of metal poisoning, which are life-threatening.

What does this mean for you? If you can afford stainless steel, that's the way to go. Most people can't do this and still have money left over for the toys and behavioral support they need to live a happy life parenting a parrot. As a result, compromise is needed. Powder-coated steel is a great material, and this is what most people turn to for the primary cage.

Cage Shape

Choose a square or rectangular cage instead of a round one. Birds climb and rest more easily in a cage with straight sides. In addition, most manufacturers design accessories such as food dishes, perches, and toys to fit straight-sided cages.

Although pet suppliers make most cages taller than they are wide, most birds use the width and depth of the cage rather than its height. A bird's habit is to use the highest available perch. A rectangular cage—longer side to side than it is tall—provides more usable space, from your bird's perspective. And that's the perspective that counts; after all, who is inside the enclosure?

Cage Bar Spacing and Arrangement

Cage bars with too narrow a spacing do not give the bird's feathers and feet enough room to freely move between the bars when climbing. This creates the possibility of feet becoming caught and can also cause excessive feather wear. Bar spacing is a balancing exercise. Like Goldilocks and the bears, the spacing needs to be "not too small," so that it doesn't constrict climbing, "not too big" so that your bird's head can slip through, but instead be "just right."

Cage bar arrangement also affects how easily your bird can use the space inside his cage. The ideal is a cage with horizontal bars on the sides, and vertical bars on the front and back. In addition to creating a better climbing surface, horizontal bars create less wear and tear on your bird's feathers. Different species and sizes of birds do best with different bar spacing. Chapter 8, Selected Species, will give you the details on recommended bar spacing, and this information is also in a chart on page 49.

Horizontal bars allow your parrot more climbing surfaces than vertical bars do.

The best type of cage door swings down like a drawbridge.

The Danger of Decorations and Bar Spacing that Narrows

New parrot parents also should be aware of the problem presented by bar spacing that narrows toward the top of a cage or spacing that is inconsistent due to cage decoration. A bird can pass his head or leg through the bars at the broadest span and climb until the narrow placement does not allow him to withdraw his head or foot. Injury results when your panicked bird cannot free herself.

Door Position and Latch Style

The most important cage feature a large, free-swinging, hinged door in the cage front. Large means an opening at least two times the width of your bird and at least one-and-a-half times his height. Be sure the main cage door swings out and not into the cage. You will not only need plenty of space to move your bird in and out of his cage without tempting him to grab onto the doorway with his bill, but also to change the paper, sweep with a brush and dustpan, or add a large shallow pan for bathing. One additional note on cage door positioning: when doors open at the middle of the cage, you can reach all parts of the cage for cleaning.

Doors should be hinged and not "guillotine" style. Although guillotine-style doors are frequent features of less expensive cages, the fact is that your bird can easily open these doors and escape, or worse, be injured by the door. This style door, sometimes used to provide access to food dishes or for returning your bird to his cage, is not the best option. See if you can do better.

Door latches are an issue, especially if you have a bird who likes to play with metal objects or is a cockatoo (a.k.a. "expert escape artist and cage disassembler"). For food service doors, the latch should be outside and behind the bowl, and the handle for the latch should not be accessible to an inquisitive beak or foot. Otherwise, birdie will grab on, pull up, shove the bowl out, and voila! It's party time in the living room. Also, if you are planning an outdoor enclosure or one with an outside door, make sure the lock is sturdy enough to dissuade people who might take your bird. With outside locks, think security from people. With indoor locks, think security from beaks and feet.

Extras

Because you ideally purchase a cage only once, if you can afford it, purchase the one you feel really suits your needs. Extras include wheels, seed guards, cage bottom grids, and built-in feeders.

Wheels

Wheels are an almost essential feature unless your bird's cage is very small. If your bird's cage is small, consider purchasing a wheeled stand with a cabinet below to hold supplies. Wheels make moving the cage for daily vacuuming and for emergencies much easier. Cage and stand cleaning requires wiping the surfaces, perches, and vacuuming underneath. If you're cleaning the cage daily—and you should—you'll appreciate this feature. With wheels, moving the cage out for cleaning is a snap. Some experienced keepers place a clear plastic shower curtain or clear contact paper on the wall behind the cage to keep bits of food from sticking to and ruining finished surfaces.

Seed Guards or Skirts

Some cages come with their own seed guards. Although many people like them, others find the guard is just another surface to clean. An alternative to seed guards and skirts is simply to use a good shop vacuum cleaner to remove the hulls, feathers, dust, errant droppings, and food from the floor instead of having to deal with space-consuming or awkward skirts. Guards do help to catch cage-side liquid poop. Again, you may prefer to clean a tile floor rather than the cage guard, which you will lean over (and possibly smash your shins into) frequently.

Cage Grates and Slide-out Trays

Most cages come with grates in the bottom and, beneath the grate, a slide-out tray to make removing soiled newspaper simple. Although grates prevent your bird from escaping while you change the paper and from walking through fouled food or droppings below the grate, those items do fall onto and sometimes through the grate, creating yet another surface to clean. If you purchase a cage with a removable grate, you have the option of deciding whether to use it or not.

If you find the perfect cage, except that the grate is not removable, consider putting newspaper on top of the grate instead of below, in the pullout tray. Droppings fall onto the paper, leaving the grate clean.

Built-in Feeders

Choose a cage design that allows you to provide clean food and water without opening the main cage door. You'll appreciate this when your regular bird-sitter is out of town and your friend—who may know nothing about birds or even be afraid of them—volunteers to feed as long as she doesn't have to open the cage door. Built-in feeders should be completely removable for a thorough cleaning. If you have the option, purchase two sets, so that you can keep one set in the dishwasher and the other set in use.

Cage Location

Once you have selected your bird's cage type, materials, and construction and its various extras, the next question is the best placement of the cage. Cage placement is one key to preventing many behavior problems. Wilson, Linden, and Lightfoot, in a chapter on companion bird behavior in *Clinical Avian Medicine*, suggest companions consider height, stimulation, sense of safety, and comfort.

Placing the bird cage in a corner helps your bird feel secure.

Most birds feel relaxed when allowed to perch between chest and shoulder height of their companion human. Lower positions can reinforce the tendency of a bird to be shy; higher than this can reinforce the tendency of some birds to be domineering and aggressive.

Your parrot's personality will help you decide the balance he needs between safety and stimulation. Select a location that allows him to see what's going on in your home, but allows him to rest when your parrot needs quiet. A wall makes one side of the cage safe for your parrot's retreat and provides a sense of security. The three remaining sides allow him to see approaching family members. Additionally, a position that allows a view out of a window provides interest and stimulation when the family is away. The ideal cage position is one that provides both a wall and a window, where your parrot can choose to watch the goings-on and yet feel secure that one side of his cage is always protected. By the way, in addition to the protection of a wall, parrots appreciate being able to hide behind a cage toy or inside a bird hut for privacy.

Safety regarding cage positioning is tricky because interior conditions (think temperature and sunlight) change during the day, especially if the cage is positioned near a window. Before you decide your parrot's cage position (especially if you are not home during the day), purchase or borrow a thermometer that registers highest and lowest daily temperatures. Place the thermometer in the proposed cage position. If the location varies in temperature more than you would feel comfortable, then you need to make modifications to stabilize the temperature or find a different location.

Remember that the "weather" inside your home not only alters during the day as the sunlight strikes different faces of your exterior, but also changes with the seasons; for example, the wind and damp find the loose caulking around the windows in your home each fall. If you decide your bird's cage position in the summer, reevaluate and redo the thermometer check during the fall and winter. Anyone who has been forced to sit in a draft, even for a few minutes, knows that a day in that position could cause a parrot to become quite ill.

Because positioning is a tricky art, here is a gentle reminder that you must never place a cage beside a door, an unscreened window, or under an air vent. The door and window not only create issues of air movement that can affect temperature in a radical way during the day, but also these openings provide escape possibilities. In addition, the vent, while maintaining an even temperature in the room as a whole, is very uncomfortable to sit under. Just think about the last time you were seated under a vent in a restaurant. Brrr.

Perches

Your parrot stands on his feet day and night. As a result, foot condition is important to his comfort and health. To ensure healthy feet, provide a variety of perches and keep them clean. Regular inspection of your parrot's feet will tell you whether the perches you're selecting work for him.

Perch Basics

Clean, disinfected perches are essential to your bird's health. Perches are not only a place of rest and comfort, but they provide foot exercise. Perches that differ in diameter and materials exercise the feet, vary the pressure across the different parts of the foot, and keep the skin of the feet and nails evenly worn. Because wild birds stand on surfaces of every conceivable size, material, and texture, they rarely suffer from foot sores. In contrast, many parrots with ill-informed or overly busy parents do.

To prevent this problem, the more choices you give your parrot for perching surfaces, the better. Provide perches of not just the ideal diameter for your parrot's species, but also a size larger and smaller. This variety allows him to choose what is comfortable at any one time. At one extreme, the perch diameter should allow your parrot's foot to wrap nearly around the perch. At the other extreme, the perch diameter should barely allow your parrot's foot to grip the perch. In addition, using perches that include all the diameters in between, such as a natural branch with graduated widths, allows your bird to choose the foot position that is most comfortable for him.

Appropriate Cage Sizes for Various Species

Species	Minimum Cage Size	Bar Spacing
Budgerigars, caiques, cockatiels, conures, lineolated parakeets, lovebirds, parrotlets, pionus, poicephalus, ringnecks	24 × 24 × 36 inches 60 × 60 × 91 cm	½ to ¾ inches 1.3 to 1.9 cm
African greys, Amazons, eclectus, small macaws	24 × 36 × 48 inches 60 × 91 × 122 cm	¾ to 1 inches 1.9 to 2.5 cm
Large cockatoos and macaws	36 × 48 × 60 inches 91 × 122 × 152 cm	1 to 1 ½ inches 2.5 to 3.8 cm

The most appropriate cage size is the largest that you can afford. The cage sizes shown here should be considered minimums and are adequate only if your parrot will have the opportunity to exercise outside his cage daily on a play stand or other alternative space, such as in an outdoor aviary.

Many parrots seem to like rope perches.

Determining Perch Size

How do you determine what size perch is correct for your bird? Perches, like shoes, need to be appropriate to foot size. A standard perch size is listed in Chapter 8 for each of the species profiled there. Make your main perches the listed size, which should leave a gap of about one-quarter inch between front and back nails. This gap allows your parrot's nails to rub against the perch, allowing them to wear normally and helping keep them short. More in-depth information and advice about perch size and materials is available from the association that represents your species type. Many times, members of these groups have kept a certain species for decades and have much useful information to share.

Types of Perches

One of the many advantages of a large cage are the many sizes and number of perching surfaces you can provide; variety in what is under his feet is one spice in your parrot's life.

Perches are manufactured of acrylic, natural wood, rope, and flexible braided cotton; in addition, cement or abrasive perches are advertised as maintaining your birds' nails. Each perch material has advantages and disadvantages. The best strategy usually is to provide a variety of surfaces and allow your bird to choose his favorite. (Note: Parrots typically move toward the highest perch in the enclosure. Be sure to provide several perches at a uniform height so that your parrot's decision can be based on the material and not on his natural desire to spend time higher in the cage.) Natural branches are the best choice because they provide the necessary traction, irregular surfaces for foot and toe exercise, and a soft material for chewing. By the way, some manufacturers still sell plastic or wooden perches of uniform diameter. These are not good choices for your bird. The plastic surface is slick, and the uniform diameter does not provide the variety of perching sizes your bird needs.

Natural Wood Perches

Natural wood perches are ideal because the perch diameter varies along its length. In addition, natural wood allows chewing. The disadvantage is that wood perches need frequent cleaning and disinfecting because feces and food become caked in the crevices. One common natural wood, manzanita, chosen for its resistance to destruction by chewing, can be very slick and not provide a secure footing. However, parrots with sharp nails may perch on manzanita very comfortably. If, after you invest in a manzanita perch, your parrot dislikes the texture of the wood (you can tell by observing whether he avoids using the perch), try winding vet wrap (a self-sticking, stretchy bandage material) around the perch and see if that makes a difference. If you and your bird are satisfied with this solution, then simply change the wrap frequently.

Rope Perches

At least one flexible braided perch or one made of natural rope is nice for variety. Although these perches are difficult to clean, the work is worth it because most parrots seem to love these perches. Remove feces with a brush. Use a mild detergent to wash the perch and be sure to dry thoroughly after disinfecting. Alternatively, these perches can be cleaned and sanitized in a washing machine or dishwasher, using hot water. Remember to trim any loose threads before returning the rope perch to the cage.

Cement Perches

Cement perches (also called concrete or abrasive perches) are advertised as good for wearing down your bird's nails so they do not need to be trimmed. One interesting use of abrasive perches is suggested in Harrison and Lightfoot's *Clinical Avian Medicine*: hang the perch vertically so that your bird can use the abrasive surface as a beak cleaner. Birds need a place to clean their beaks (called feaking). Not only is this helpful to the bird for his cleaning and beak maintenance, but it also provides an easy focal point for cage cleaning. Most professionals don't use cement perches because they can easily abrade the skin of a parrot's foot, creating the possibility of an infection that is difficult to cure. (Similarly, although your bird may need minerals, his occasional nibbling of the perch will not provide them. When your bird needs grooming or a mineral boost, see your veterinarian for a toenail trim and a checkup.)

Perch Maintenance

Keep more perches than you need so that you can install clean perches as you remove and clean soiled ones. As you remove the perches, clean and sanitize them and store them near your bird's cage so that they are ready to use. All perches should be washed carefully and disinfected at least each week. (If you notice that the perches are quite dirty, this is a sign that you are not removing them often enough.) The fewer perches you have, the more important cleaning and disinfecting is.

Many people use a stiff brush to remove most of the food and feces on the perch, then soak and scrub again to remove the remaining sticky material. This is also a good time to check for wear and replace perches if necessary.

Appropriate Perch Diameters for Various Species

Freedom from discomfort from a bird's-eye perspective has a lot to do with comfortable places to stand. For your parrot, this means a perch of the right width, and then some of other widths and surface types. Alternative widths are necessary because birds need exercise for their feet. In addition, having several places to perch means that your bird will not be forced to keep his feet in an uncomfortable position, even if they are tired or sore. Consider your discomfort if you were always standing in high heels too small for you or always walking in boots too wide for you. The analogy is not exact, but it suggests your bird's physical feeling.

Medium-sized perches ¾–1 ¼ inches (1.9–3.2 cm) in diameter should be the primary perch sizes for these species:
- Jardine's
- most smaller conures
- pionus
- ringnecks
- small macaws, including severe and noble
- smaller cockatoos, such as bare-eyed and Goffin's cockatoos
- Timneh African greys

Large perches 1–1 ½ inches (2.5–3.8 cm) in diameter should be the primary perch sizes for these species:
- Alexandrines
- Amazons
- Congo African greys
- eclectus
- larger conures

Extra-large perches 1 ½–3 inches (3.8–7.6 cm) in diameter should be the primary perch sizes for these species:
- large macaws, such as scarlet and green-winged
- large cockatoos, such as the Moluccan

Making Your Own Perches

If you have the time and talent, make your own perches. The DIY revolution is alive and well in producing parrot paraphernalia. And, this is a terrific way to get members of your family involved who are more tool-oriented than parrot-oriented.

Because every companion and parrot's idea of a great perch is different, search the Internet for designs and videos. In addition, consult your online species discussion group and your local bird club members. However, there are a few tips that are important to note that might not be covered in the videos and plans:
- Select nontoxic perch materials. (Avoid metals, most plastics, and treated woods.)
- If you're using found perch materials, such as wood, rock, or recycled PVC pipe, sanitize them. An inexpensive disinfecting solution is presented on page 79.
- Use stainless steel metal parts, if needed.
- The glues and caulking you use must be ones that you wouldn't be afraid to eat (in small quantities) yourself. In other words, check the labels. Parrot beaks, toes, and tongues are remarkably persistent in picking out anything that you might think is hidden.
- Allow your bird to become acquainted with new objects before you put them inside his cage. Shy birds especially take time to trust that something new isn't a predator in disguise.
- Never use a design that you suspect is unsafe. If you have a question, don't use it.
- Make sure you're not putting a new perch in and leaving town. You may find unanticipated problems with a perch design that is new to your bird.

Safe Woods for Perches

Let's start with what's unsafe. Unsafe woods include any pressure-treated wood and anything with paint, preservative, shellac, or a coating of some kind. The reason that these woods last so long is because an additive that is poisonous to wood-eating insects has been incorporated into or painted onto the wood.

While researching "safe woods," many sources make the point that "safe" is a relative concept. What is safe for a parrot to chew depends on how much he chews and how much he swallows.

Because no one is testing woods for toxicity in parrots, lists are created from reports of accidental poisonings that are believed to result from ingesting wood. Remember that any wood can be toxic if the grower used systemic poisons for pest prevention. Many lists from reasonable sources use terms such as "believed to be safe" and "believed to be toxic," and "toxic." However, keep in mind that it is the amount of the wood ingested and any treatment that the wood may have undergone that can allow a parrot to live very well with a "toxic" wood and become ill from a "wood believed to be safe."

Believed to be safe:

- acacia
- almond
- apple
- ash
- aspen
- beech
- birch
- citrus
- cottonwood
- crab apple
- dogwood
- elm
- fig
- fir
- grape vines
- hickory
- ironwood
- manzanita
- maple
- mesquite
- mimosa
- mulberry
- pear
- pecan
- pine
- poplar
- rose
- sassafras
- spruce
- sweet gum
- sycamore
- vine maple
- walnut
- willow

Once you rinse the perch, use a dilute bleach solution—one part bleach to ten parts water—to disinfect. Just wipe this on with a sponge kept just for that purpose. After fifteen minutes, rinse and dry the perch and return it to the cage. An alternative method for cleaning and sterilizing is to use the extra hot cycle in your dishwasher. Many parrot parents remove the worst of the debris with a stiff brush then wash the perches along with their bird's food and water bowls, using the high temperature rinse and heat dry that many dishwashers feature. Most dishwasher manufacturers' settings are high enough to kill bacteria and many viruses.

Perches that include rope, fabric, or other stringy material need to be inspected and trimmed once each week. Your bird's toenails can become dangerously entangled in stray threads or strings. Remember, you need to dry these thoroughly before returning them to the cage, and this process can take several days.

Perch Placement

When you place perches, consider two principles. First, birds will usually perch on the highest surface offered. Consider offering varied perch widths at the same height in the cage so that the width and composition of the perch becomes the deciding factor for your bird, rather than the perch height. Second, locate perches away from water and food bowls. Finally, a favorite trick for gaining cooperation from birds reluctant to leave or enter the cage is to place a short perch on the swinging door. This odd trick overcomes the reluctance of birds to enter and exit the cage.

If you notice that a perch is not being used, consider why. Similarly, if only one perch is being used, consider this also. By watching where your parrot perches, and for how long or often, you'll learn quite a bit about the cage environment, your parrot's reaction to what's around him, and possibly the composition and placement of your perches.

Cage Substrate

Although many different cage substrates are manufactured, the simplest and best bedding—and the one recommended by veterinarians—is newspaper. Readily available, newspaper absorbs enough of the droppings to be effective, but leaves the impression of the droppings intact. A clear view of your parrot's droppings is important because the quality of your bird's droppings is an effective monitor of his health. (More about this in Chapter 7.)

One trick that makes changing the newspaper quickly is to layer the sheets, arranging them so that the entire top layer pulls off and can be folded and recycled, all in one quick motion. This allows you to do a fast cleanup to remove the remains of food or heavy droppings without the time required for a full cleaning.

Because your bird may chew the newspaper, use the newsprint sections rather than the slick advertisement sections. Newsprint ink is not harmful in the quantities to which your bird is exposed.

Poor beddings include kitty litter, corncobs, crushed walnut shells, grit, sand, wood shavings, and artificial grass. Not only do these materials provide poor visuals of your bird's droppings, but also they are harmful if your bird eats them. Most likely, your parrot will sample them because parrots are naturally curious creatures. Instead of purchasing substrates that your veterinarian will tell you can be harmful, spend your money on toys to destroy. Use newspaper for bedding: you, your parrot, and your veterinarian will be glad you did.

Cage Covers

Parrots require twelve hours of dark, quiet time each night for rest and sleep. Whether you help your parrot achieve that dark, restful time by using a sleeping cage that you move to a dark room or you create a "good night" routine in his main cage, your bird will be grateful for a cage cover. A cage cover mimics the dark cover into which birds naturally retreat at night for roosting. A cage cover is particularly necessary in households in which the lights and activity continue well past dusk. Like children, parrots will stay up as late as you will allow, and everyone will be the worse for this the following day. Enforce bedtime, and if

Newspaper is the cheapest and likely the safest substrate for a parrot cage.

your bird's cage is in a central area, do consider removing your parrot to a quiet place and cover his night cage, which can also be his travel cage.

You can purchase covers that fit your bird's cage up to and including custom-made monogrammed blackout curtains, create fancy covers yourself, or use old towels or sheets. When choosing a cover, consider its washability, ventilation, and effective darkness. Wash the covers frequently because they can accumulate powdered down as well as dirt and food residue from the cage bars. Regarding ventilation and cage temperature, be sure that you leave enough of an opening so that air can pass in and out of the night cage without difficulty. You don't want the temperature to rise appreciably during the night. Finally, the covers should create true darkness to be effective as a night-time haven for your bird.

Birds who do not get enough rest at night become, as children do, upset and show signs of stress. A nighttime routine in which you have a ritual treat and cage covering can be a wonderful bonding routine between you and your bird; in addition, you will be rewarded with a well-rested parrot who will be glad to see you in the morning.

Food and Water Bowls and Bottles

Your parrot's habits will guide you regarding the types of food and water bowls or bottles that work best. There are a few guidelines, but tailor your plans to your experience—and perhaps that of the breeder or adoption agency from which your parrot comes. Not only are species preferences somewhat different, but parrots are as much individuals as people are.

Stainless steel food and water bowls are easy to disinfect and will last many years.

Food and water bowls should be easy to sanitize and inexpensive enough so that you can have at least two sets to speed your feeding routines. If you are using a water bowl, you'll change the water at least twice each day, once in the morning and once at night, because your parrot must have access to clean water at all times. (Don't assume he makes pellet and poop soup because he wants to drink the water that way.) In addition, you will need at least two and preferably four food bowls: one for wet food and one for dry. As with water, your bird should always have clean, fresh food available. Purchasing enough bowls to wash them with your regular dishwashing routine is important.

If you wash your dishes by hand, disinfect with a dilute bleach solution (1 part bleach, 10 parts water). Alternatively, clean your bird's dishes in a dishwasher with a high-temperature setting that kills bacteria and virus. This will help you keep your bird's water and food fresh.

Materials and Styles

Ceramic, glass, and stainless steel containers are easy to clean and disinfect, and cage furnishings made from these materials last for many years. Plastic is less resilient and less easy to disinfect. If your bird's cage is on the small size, purchase small bowls that lock into a holder that attaches to the cage wire and take up little cage "real estate." In larger cages, ceramic crocks, heavy enough so that they cannot be overturned and with low sides are best for food bowls. A large version of the same bowl is best for bathing.

"No mess" feeders and water bowls come in both Plexiglas and ceramic. Although this concept works well for some birds, consider your bird's natural history. Ground feeders, like budgies and cockatiels, may not dig through layers of seed hulls to reach bits at the bottom of a bowl. A more satisfactory experience for these types of birds is a saucer, with one layer of food on the bottom.

In addition, your bowls must be safe for your bird to use when you're not available. Plastic bowls or decorative bowls made of lightweight painted ceramic may be easily chipped or broken by your parrot's beak pressure, leaving the swallowing of small parts a concern. For most birds, heavy commercial ceramic dishes, sized to fit the cage's built-in bowl holders, are an excellent option. Alternatively, stainless steel bowls are excellent, if they are secured in a holder. Light-weight materials tend to be pried out of their holders and tossed by many parrots as a source of entertainment.

Even if you have built-in bowl holders in your bird's cage, you may prefer to use another type of bowl. For parrots who are food flingers, there are bowls and feeders that form a hood to keep food inside the bowl. Other parrots make a study of overturning water and food dishes. For these birds, try locking bowls that frustrate all but the most determined birds. Typically, a plastic composition bowl, a special birdproof mechanism attaches the bowl to a perch.

Water serves two purposes for your bird: drinking and bathing. Many companions supply a heavy, shallow dish of water on the cage floor for bathing. A separate, secured water bottle dispenses clean drinking water. Glass bottles, with a substantial rubber stopper and a stainless steel spout that affixes to the outside of the cage are easy to clean and disinfect. A water bottle also solves the dilemma of both the parrot who overturns his water bowl and the parrot who fouls his bowl no matter where you place the bowl or the perches, making the water undrinkable. However, do be aware that some parrots make a game of emptying those water bottles or somehow detaching them from the outside of the cage. Before you rely on a water bottle for your parrot, be sure you have observed that he is not guilty of enjoying this particular game. Also, make certain your parrot understands how to drink from the bottle.

There are many types of food and water containers and contraptions; explore the options, keeping the habits and personality of your bird in mind.

Play stands make it easier for your parrot to spend more time out of his cage and interacting with his human flock mates.

Play Stands

Every bird needs a change of scenery, and play stands are the perfect way to give your parrot an out-of-cage experience as well as an outing full of flapping, climbing, swinging, tearing, shredding, and tossing his toys for you to retrieve. Yes, the play stand also makes interaction with your bird easy and natural. (By the way, the play stand has a different purpose than a T-stand. A T-stand is for training, and a play stand is for...well...playing.) By this point in your reading you may be thinking, "Is there no end to what a parrot needs?" The answer is that you're defining the limits of his world. Unlike a child who goes to the playground or to school, your parrot will live in the world of his cage and his play stand. Yes, you'll take him other places inside and outside his home, but, for the most part, cage and play stand are his universe.

Why a Play Stand?

The play stand is where your parrot is allowed to be active without close supervision, similar to the function of a fenced back yard for a child. Use his play stand from the beginning, and your

T-stands are useful for training your bird.

parrot will become accustomed to hanging out with you nearby. Be sure to return the bird to his play stand if he leaves it without your permission. As a result, you'll develop a bird who is reliably nearby, but without hanging on you every minute he is outside his cage. This is extremely convenient when you have household chores, for example. Parrots love to watch others work, and they benefit from the attention you can give them by telling your bird all about the work that you are doing. In addition, the play stand helps keep your bird flexible about his environment, but still feeling safe and secure in a familiar place. Some bird people have play stands in several rooms of their home, giving their bird a point of reference for his safe area in that room, and giving the bird person one main area to clean up after the bird has left the room.

Materials and Features

Play stands come in a variety of sizes, shapes, materials, and prices. You can purchase a play stand, or you can make your own. Or, you could do both. Play stands sometimes come as a cage-top accessory—some removable and some not. Removable play stands give you the option of setting up an area in a different room. Given that you may move during your parrot's lifetime, consider not just your current room arrangement, but possible future needs as well. Play stands as separate rolling units are composed of a variety of materials including PVC pipe, powder-coated metal, or wood. The usually less-expensive PVC pipe is easy to clean but tends to have slick surfaces and a single perch diameter. Powder-coated metal has the easy-to-clean advantage, and these stands usually feature several fixed perches, toy hangers, and cup holders for food. Wood play stands, often made of a very tough wood such as manzanita, come in a variety of sizes and configurations; with irregular surfaces, they are more difficult to clean but they offer a feel and texture different from that of the cage.

Consider the size and physical and personality needs of your bird (acrobatic, small and quick, large and cautious, etc.) as well as your perspective on cleaning, durability, and convenience before buying a play stand. Consider whether you need a flat surface or bowls for feeding at the station and/or a flat surface for games with your parrot(s). When thinking of extras, such as wheels, if you're a single parrot parent, you'll need those. Otherwise, moving a large play stand becomes quite a burden. Also, for stands with round bases, consider whether you can fit the base through an interior door without disassembling it.

If the expense of purchasing a play stand is too great, and if you're good with tools, you can make your own using one of the many do-it-yourself gym patterns in *Parrot-Toys and Play Areas* by Lauren Shannon Nunn.

Toys

After healthy food and a safe cage, toys are the next most critical feature for your parrot's well-being. Why? Let's look to natural history for the answer. The largest component of a wild parrot's day is spent foraging for food. Because the companion parrot is the same creature as his wild cousins, the time and energy that would have been required for this wild foraging must be replaced with an equally absorbing mind and body activity. After all, many parrots have the intelligence and emotional development of a two-year-old human child. If you consider the importance of playtime for the development of a child's physical and emotional health, you'll understand the parrot's situation: play stimulates development, thinking, and coordination. In addition, play provides a productive energy outlet. This makes sense: all animals, including parrots and people, need to work out both body and mind to stay healthy.

In their natural environment, parrots spend most of their waking hours looking for food—both a thinking and physically exhausting job. In the artificial environment that we provide, foraging for food is relatively easy and not physically very taxing. As a result, your parrot needs a variety of toy types, accessible in various locations in his main cage as well as his play stand, to replace these natural activities. With assorted toys and varied perch locations, you can help your bird to experience a range

Most play stands have spots where you can attach food bowls and toys.

of behaviors reminiscent of those that he would experience in the wild. The toys should stimulate flapping, climbing, chewing, tossing, holding, preening, singing, and talking. In addition to colorful hanging toys, parrots (except for budgies and a few other small parrots) also need foot toys for chewing and manipulating. And, all parrots need various puzzle toys, selected for the strengths of your particular species, for problem solving. As you consider toys for these various purposes, your first concern about each should be, "Is this toy safe for my bird?"

Toy Safety

Think safety first and variety second. One factor in safety has to do with the size of your bird. Toys that are perfectly safe for a budgie may be dangerous for a macaw. This is because of the enormous difference in the size and power of their beaks; in the same way that one toy can be appropriate for a child of one size and developmental stage, the same toy in different hands (or beaks) can be dangerous.

Toy safety means choosing good-quality toys with parts that are built for the power of your bird's beak. The most dangerous aspect of toys is that your bird might break off and swallow small parts or become entangled in the toy and unable to free himself. To help you select toys that are appropriate for the beak strength of your bird, suppliers sometimes tag their toys as appropriate for a range of birds (small, medium, large) to help new companions begin to select toys that will be safe for particular species. Stores or online suppliers that specialize in birds can offer personalized advice. In addition, a good breeder or specialty store can help you learn about bird toys.

In addition, take care to select toys that are made of safe materials and that are well constructed. The materials should be nontoxic, as should any paints or coloring used in the toy. Small pieces, such as tiny bells or glittery attachments, can easily be removed by your parrot's beak. Stay away from cheap plastic toys manufactured overseas. There are virtually no safety regulations that apply to the use of paint and other possibly toxic materials. If you wouldn't let your child chew on it, definitely don't consider giving it to your parrot.

In addition to the construction of the toy itself, consider the way in which the toy is suspended in the cage. The best approach is a style of hanger called a safety link. These are stainless steel o-shaped hangers with an attached screw closure. Metal loops and snap hooks, such as those used on key chains or on the ends of leashes, bring with them the danger of your parrot's beak or tongue becoming caught in the closure. If you must use another material, short, thick rawhide strips or short

Only buy toys that are designed for your bird's size and species.

chains with large links help you avoid trapping beaks and toes.

Once you've selected safe toys and hung them in a safe manner, relax. Toys should be used, abused, destroyed, and replaced.

Toy Variety

Select a variety of toys to keep your bird busy, challenged, and excited about life when you are not available for play. Because the variety of toys available is staggering, here are a few tips for selecting toys that will work best for your bird:

Rotate your parrot's toys regularly so he frequently has something "new" to play with.

- Of course, the best teacher is your bird himself. Notice which toys he spends the most time with and which toys he never touches. (Keep in mind that just because he ignores the toy now, he might choose the toy as a favorite next week. That's *so* parrot.)
- Also, ask your breeder and other companions of similar-species parrots which toys their parrots like and which they ignore.
- Parrot toy suppliers often suggest particular toys for species. Online catalogs sometimes suggest the appropriate toys for different types of parrots. Online forums dedicated to a variety of parrots or stores that specialize in birds can make excellent recommendations about toys that will appeal to your new best friend.
- Most parrot people suggest that you purchase at least two of each of the following types of toy for your bird: (a) thinking or puzzle toys, (b) action toys, (c) comfort toys, and (d) toys to destroy.

A trick that parrot toy people suggest is that you use only one-half of the toys each week. When you do a thorough cage clean at the end of the week, install a new set of toys. That way, your bird has new toys each week; in addition, you have a chance to wash and disinfect the "old" toys for the following week.

So, how do you know which types of toys are which?

Thinking or Puzzle Toys

Stores or catalogs call toys that stimulate your bird's mind "puzzle" or "thinking" toys. Designed to keep your bird's mind mentally fit, the excitement of these toys is in figuring out how to get to the "thing" that interests them. Many birds love untying knots and twisting toy parts. A small cardboard box of foot toys, playthings your bird can pick up and manipulate with one foot, will keep your bird's feet, beak, and tongue busy for hours. Most birds like to rearrange shiny things, such as beads and

Ideas for Making Your Own Toys

With a few basics, such as metal skewers, some inexpensive consumables, and a few simple techniques, you can make plenty of inexpensive toys. Add a trip to the local dollar store and an order of bulk toy parts from a good supplier, and you can go wild (and so will your parrot). Finally, if you are a DIY wizard, plenty of patterns and sample photographs of home-crafted toys exist on the Internet. However, use your judgment about the construction. If you feel that your creation is overwhelmingly large, or perhaps has too many dangling parts, it probably does.

Some Useful Toy Basics

The following items can be used either as hangers for consumables or to contain or wrap around consumables.

- cage-like structures, such as those for washing baby bottle parts in the dishwasher
- paper cups
- paper plates
- rawhide strips
- skewers
- slender natural-fiber rope

Some Inexpensive Consumables

The following items can be hung from skewers or rope, put inside cage-like structures, or folded inside paper plates or cups.

- adding machine tape
- cardboard and newspaper from recycling bin
- dried fruit, nuts, pasta
- magazine subscription cards
- manila envelopes and folders
- recovered toy parts from mostly destroyed toys
- safe plants from backyard (see www.aspca.org/apcc/nontoxplants.pdf)

Some Techniques

These are techniques used to combine items in the first two lists, or to practice on the inexpensive consumables using the cage bars as holders. Think of ways to attach, braid, conceal, stack, stuff, or weave the toys to cage bars, perches, play stands, and the like.

Examples

U-shaped roll made from newspaper. Thread two ends of a rolled newspaper section into the cage, through the space on either side of a cage bar. Finding the right thickness for different size birds requires practice.

So long as your bird has enough food in his cage to feel secure, foraging for hidden snacks is fun. Newspaper, lunch bags, and paper cups are fun to open. Show your bird what you are doing as you roll treats into the paper or tuck them into the bags. Once your bird gets the idea, then stuff the concealed goodies into a box or bowl for more advanced fun. Most larger birds love wrestling a crushed paper cup out of a newspaper-packed box and extracting a prize such as a piece of dried fruit or a nut.

For birds who climb, there's nothing as exciting as ripping and flinging leaves, fruit, or vegetables. Hang thoroughly washed and plentiful herbs like mint and parsley or vegetables like squash through the cage top. If you have friends who are gardeners, ask for their excess foliage. They'll be glad to put it to good use.

Use skewers or leather strips to secure materials to the cage top and sides. Extra fun for tiny birds like parakeets and finches include stringing cereal O's onto cotton string. This is an excellent way to involve small children. Have them take cotton string and tie knots 1 inch apart, with the cereal O's between knots.

Some birds like to bat balls around their cages during the day. Small birds can use whiffle or ping-pong balls or marbles to roll around a jar lid. Select a ball your bird can't swallow or break and swallow!

Interactive Toys

- Make a good gentle tickle toy by folding and knotting a paper towel.
- Mail time is exciting. Hand your bird envelopes as you open the mail. Encourage your bird to chew and then hurl each into the recycling bin. Tah dah! Applause please!
- Paper and whiffle balls are fun to toss and catch. Birds easily train their humans by tossing balls or batting them with their beaks. Once the companion catches the ball, they're hooked.
- Make a pull toy made of braided strips of old tee shirts. Braid in interesting objects such as large beads, rings, or leftover pieces from old toys. Tiny birds enjoy miniature versions of this toy hung in the cage from a stainless steel hanger. The width of the strips controls the thickness of the toy.

Remember to give your parrot time to calm down before you try to pick her up after interactive play. When your bird plays and becomes excited, he may forget that your finger is not the toy.

mirrors. Similar mental stimulation comes from "busy boards" or "abacus style" toys. Which part of the toy is most exciting? When your bird can't decide, he tries them all again. In addition, some thinking or puzzle toys include nuts or other treats inside. Cardboard boxes, plastic foraging wheels, or drawers that your bird can open—these toys come in many different configurations.

Action Toys

Think of an action flick—noise, destruction, and physical stunts of derring-do—that's how action toys engage your parrot. The noise the toys make—bells, buzzers, and recorded sounds—stimulates play that parrots need. For sheer physicality, nothing beats a parrot flapping to power a whirling ride on a length of rope, a coiled "boing," or a sphere made of rope. Swings, ladders, and knotted ropes also stimulate physical activity: swinging to the beat of music, ladders set up to reach otherwise inaccessible favorite toys, and knotted ropes to encourage a different form of climbing—climbing with a wing-powered assist. Select action toys properly sized for your bird. Bigger is not better; even with properly sized toys, shy birds may need gentle encouragement to use more active toys. When you are selecting your bird's cage, remember that you'll need a cage large enough to accommodate one of these large toys and to accommodate your parrots' wings flapping during his full action play. Please select a cage large enough for one of these action toys. And you'll need a second action toy for your bird's play stand.

Lovebirds and other smaller species seem to really enjoy swings.

Toys to Destroy

A parrot's gotta gnaw. Gnawing is the way that parrots maintain their beak length and shape; in other words, gnawing is in their nature. Rather than having your favorite companion look longingly at your dining room chairs or your partner's duck decoy collection, provide toys that are made to destroy. Some toys to destroy are little more than blocks of wood, so interpret "toy" in the broadest possible sense.

You can purchase toys to destroy, or you can harvest them from your yard or other projects. You can also purchase destroyable toy parts and make your own. What are these items to gnaw? They include sticks of various lengths and thicknesses, corrugated cardboard, newspaper, pine cones,

Toy Safety Tips

Because we're familiar with small children swallowing things they shouldn't, a parrot parent might assume this to be the most common hazard for birds. Certainly, biting off small bits of things and mouthing them is what parrots do. Some parrots swallow these toy parts as well, and sometimes these parts don't pass on their own and have to be removed.

However, a larger danger for parrots is traumatic injury. The injury comes either from getting a toe caught in the chain or fibers onto which the toy parts are strung or from having the beak stuck on a hanger. The initial "getting stuck" is not the worst part of the problem. When your bird can't free himself, he panics and begins to thrash, trying to free himself. At that point, whatever part is stuck, as well as his wings, is in serious jeopardy. Feathers break as wings hit cage bars or other objects in the cage. A toe can be pulled, broken, or bitten off to get free, or the bird can expire from the stress of being stuck and unable to free himself.

A third hazard, mouthing toxic substances such as galvanized wire, lead, or toys with harmful paints, is serious, but preventable. Simply refuse to purchase cheap imported toys, and spend more to know the parts are safe.

To ensure that your bird doesn't become injured from playing with his toys, try the following:

1. Take a look around his cage each morning. Are the toy hangers closed?
2. As you consider toys for purchase, look to see if the hangers are stainless steel with screw-close safety bolts. If not, replace them.
3. Never use key rings, snap hooks, or carabineers as toy hangers or in other capacities in your bird's cage. Although they look safe and convenient, they are not. They are an invitation to your bird's getting injured.
4. At least weekly, take toys with fibers out of the cage. Scissor off the loose fibers before returning them. When these toys, perches, or furnishings are worn, replace them. This is much less expensive than a veterinary bill for broken leg or wing—or worse.

Select and arrange toys with your companion's size and habits in mind. Some toys are dangerous for any bird. Ask yourself:

- Would I be worried if a baby licked or chewed this?
- Could my bird get a toe, beak, head, or wing caught in this toy?
- Could my bird swallow all or part of this?
- Could a pesticide, glue, or other toxic substance cover this?

If the answer to any of these questions is yes, then throw out the material or toy.

and unfinished wood of various sorts. Having these sorts of materials available for your bird to chew satisfies a basic need. Keep a good supply handy because most parrots gnaw daily.

Safe targets you have at home include old telephone books and cardboard boxes. Untreated, unsprayed tree branches with bark and leaves attached are excellent diversions, but be sure your source plants have not been treated for pests with systemic poisons. Those treatments make them unsuitable because the poison will also be toxic for your bird. In addition, make sure that the plant you intend to use as your wood or branch source is included on the American Society for the Prevention of Cruelty of Animals' (ASPCA) nontoxic plants list.

If you're concerned about the cleanliness or suitability of plant material, don't use it. However, branches can be treated in a solution of 1 part bleach to 25 parts water for 15 minutes, rinsed with plenty of fresh water, and left to dry. This technique eliminates any harmful bacteria or viruses. Another technique for eliminating bacteria and other pests from wood is to oven bake your found materials at 200°F for 20 minutes.

Toys don't always have to be manufactured. Make toys yourself from simple household articles. Chayote, sisal, palm fronds, and softwood blocks are common materials for toys to destroy. You can buy toys assembled from these materials, or you buy the materials and make toys yourself. Bulk bags of these materials are available from online sources, as well as from some local bird specialty stores.

Parrots love to chew, so a piece of wood your bird can shred makes a fine toy for him.

Comfort Toys

After a busy day, with foraging, action toys, toys to destroy, and thinker toys, a parrot needs to slow down. Your parrot may enjoy preening cotton rope or retreating to a sleep hut for privacy. Some parrots enjoy cloth toys that they preen without destroying. In other words, they seem to view the toy as a "preening buddy."

Changing Toys for Changing Moods

Your bird's needs can be satisfied if you pay attention to the toys he's playing with now and provide more of those. Like any individual creature, a bird's needs and interests change with mood, age, health, and seasons. During molting season, more chewing and comfort toys may be needed. During the season when hormones are running high, toys that make noise when they are attacked may be favorites.

Other Types of Entertainment

While you're out during the day, your parrot is at home. You want him busy and using use all five senses, so that he has an interesting day. When you thoughtfully consider your parrot's needs, you are rewarded by a well-behaved bird who is glad to see you at the end of the day, as opposed to a desperately bored parrot ready to explode with energy or depressed from his lack of stimulation.

Think about your bird's five senses: what he sees, smells, touches, tastes, and hears.

1. Give your bird something interesting to watch: a television, a bird-sitter video, an outdoor bird feeder, an aquarium.

2. Your mp3 player or a radio station gives a whole day of listening pleasure. Birds love to chatter and whistle at media of all sorts.

3. Most birds don't have a great sense of smell, but you might leave a little citrus and mint for your bird to chew. You'll appreciate the fresh fragrance when you return.

4. Make sure your companion's food is varied and that there's work involved in getting to "the good stuff." Try using treat dispensers, hanging delicious leaves from the cage top, and skewering fruit so that your parrot must climb and stretch to reach them.

5. Use toys and perches of different textures.

Carriers

What at first looks to be a carrier or travel crate can serve other important functions. Before you choose your carrier, consider the various uses this handy necessity can serve: emergency evacuation carrier, travel or car carrier crate, nightly use as sleeping roost, transport to the veterinarian, and an outside cage for mild days.

Designs for carriers can be as simple as a Plexiglas box, as common as a small dog kennel, or as elaborate as a carefully created small transport cage made of aluminum with built-in food and water holders and a cage-top perch. Before you go shopping, place a checkmark next to the uses that you can foresee to help you select the features important in this purchase.

You will need a carrier or travel cage for trips to the vet and other outings.

Top Hazards for Parrots in the Home

The most common types of injury for parrots in the home include trauma, drowning, poisoning, and escape. In addition, the most dangerous times for parrots include the holidays and other events when visitors come to the home. When you first bring your parrot home, rethink your house rules to minimize the danger to your bird.

To protect your parrot from traumatic injury (an injury that breaks or crushes a bone or organ), keep your parrot away from the following top trauma causes:

• ingestion of pins, needles, or string from craft projects
• knickknacks on shelves
• other pets
• rocker or lounge chairs with moving parts

Drowning is not an obvious hazard; however, when birds fall into water, their feathers rapidly become laden and heavy with water. The more the bird struggles to free himself, the more tired he becomes until he drowns. The top sources of water for drowning include:

• deep pans or bowls of water for other pets
• drinking glasses—small birds like budgies and parrotlets can drown in these
• laundry or dish sinks full of soapy water
• open fish tanks
• open toilet lids
• pots of water on the stove

Accidental poisoning has many causes that often are not obvious. Not only are the substances that poison other pets a problem, but also birds are especially susceptible to fumes and gases. (Remember the story about coal miners using canaries as the first indicators of poisonous gasses?) *Fumes from self-cleaning ovens, candles, incense, propane, or Teflon pans can be fatal to your parrot.* In addition to those hazards, the following are the top pet toxins:

• chocolate
• insecticides
• paint, glue, or solvents from craft projects
• plants and associated lawn and garden products
• prescription and over-the-counter medications for humans and pets
• rat and ant poisons

Escape is every parrot parent's nightmare. Once parrots escape, a gust of wind can carry them to a location they're not familiar with. In addition, once parrots are frightened, they often go silent, not making any response to their companion's call. To minimize the possibility of escape, it's best to have at least two doors between your parrot and the outside world. However, this is not always possible.

Your best friends in keeping your parrot indoors are well-fitting storm windows and doors, as well as window and door screens. If your parrot is outside his cage, no one should be holding the door open to bring in groceries.

Although the family is aware of the parrot and his whereabouts, the most dangerous times for birds are during holidays, when everyone is distracted and routines are interrupted, and when visitors come to call. Although visitors are often anxious to spend time with your parrot, limited visitation in a controlled and extra-safe environment is the best policy. Many long-time parrot people relocate the cage to a bedroom where the bird can be comfortable, away from the stress and dangers of holiday rituals and visitors. In addition to visitors, decorations and paraphernalia can also be both intriguing to and dangerous for your bird. What self-respecting parrot could stay away from brilliant red poinsettias (poisonous to birds), glass ornaments on a tree (crunch, followed by ingestion of glass fragments), Easter grass or tinsel (require surgical removal)? When it comes to holiday guests and decorations, err on the side of caution. Keep your birds out of the fracas, and you'll both be glad you did.

When you acquire a parrot, you'll need to rethink "house rules," so that an ordinary chore such as taking out the garbage or bringing in the groceries does not become a heartbreaking experience.

For emergency evacuations, prepare for two to three days of displacement. Similarly, if you plan to car camp with your companion, you want an enclosure that would work for two to three days there also. For visits to the veterinarian, nightly sleeping, or an afternoon outside, you could do with something less well-equipped.

The critical aspects of the carrier are similar to those of the larger cage: safety (the material, bar spacing, and the latches), well as ease of carrying for you, the companion. For example, a 3 × 3 × 2-foot cage makes a great carrier for a medium-sized bird to travel in, but it takes two people to lift it and not all cars can accommodate it. So, think as small as would be comfortable for your bird to spend the day with you, given that he will have lots of opportunity to flap and play at the end of your travel.

Sleeping cages simply allow your companion to roost at night as he would in the wild. What he needs is a perch, proper ventilation, and a decent closure. Most birds enjoy the routine of a "good night" and a transfer to a safe, dark place. Then, in the morning, a transfer to the larger, day cage mimics the natural "fly out" that parrots do each morning to begin their foraging.

If you decide to use a small dog crate, be sure to make holes that allow you to secure perches. In addition, check the bar spacing and door closure to be sure your bird cannot be caught in the mechanism. If your parrot is not a real chewer, this solution can work as transport and overnight for many years. However, it's important that, if your parrot is not sleeping in the transport cage, you spend time working with your bird so he knows how to enter and exit the carrier, perhaps for special treats, so that getting into and out of it is an easy, natural activity for him. If you ever have an emergency, that is not the time you want to be fighting with your parrot, looking for a towel, and creating more stress for both of you. Be ready, not just with your carrier, but with your comfort in using the carrier also.

Other Helpful Equipment

Once you've completed your acquisition of the essentials, there are a few other nonessentials that might be very important to you and your bird. Full-spectrum lights, air filters, and humidifiers, as well as harnesses, hanging beds, and misters, might be essential for your bird in your environment. Keep in mind that individuals have different needs. Lights and air filters are essential for my birds. When we moved, a humidifier became an essential. So, in different circumstances, the same birds might need different forms of environmental support.

Lights

Why lights are not considered essentials by everyone is unclear. Veterinarians recommend full-spectrum lighting or daily outings not only to keep your parrot's plumage gorgeous, but also to allow her body chemistry to function correctly.

Some calcium metabolism studies referenced by Stanford in *Clinical Avian Medicine* (Chapter 5, pages 147–150) suggest that inadequate amounts of ultraviolet (UV) light cause a deficiency of vitamin D. UV light allows the body to make vitamin D. In turn, vitamin D allows birds (and other organisms, including humans) to absorb calcium from food. If the level of vitamin D is insufficient, the parrot will not take in enough calcium. Birds need calcium for the health of bones, beaks, nervous systems, and much more.

What many companions do not realize is that windows block most UV light. Even when your parrot spends all day next to the window, she is not getting adequate amounts of UV light. In addition, simply adding more vitamin D to the diet does not solve the problem. The mechanisms of light absorption and the activation of various metabolic pathways in your parrot's body are poorly understood, although they can affect your parrot in significant ways, causing bone deformation and liver and thyroid problems.

For these reasons, full-spectrum lighting is a relatively easy and inexpensive way to create a healthy and safe environment for birds who are not located where they may often be taken outdoors. In fact, full-spectrum lighting is essential for the health of people who live in climates where sunlight is scarce.

There are a few buzz words to know so that when you purchase a lighting system you get what you need. Incandescent lights, the light bulbs with filaments that glow, do not meet the standard needed for birds. Bulbs that will meet your bird's needs have full spectrum with a color rendition index (CRI) of greater than 90 and a color temperature (CT) of more than 5,000. We don't have to understand the details of CRIs and CTs. All we need to do is to read the package's fine print for this information. These special lights also have electronic ballasts to eliminate a flicker that your parrot will notice but our differently functioning human eyes don't. Several manufacturers make lights that meet this standard. Your local or internet bird supplier or lighting store can advise you on availability and pricing.

When you are planning your system, be sure to install these lights overhead for best effect. Your bird sees into the blue and violet range, which people don't, so the environment looks brighter to your parrot than to you. Also, match natural daylight hours with indoor lighting. Use a timer to turn on your light one hour after sunrise and off an hour before dusk. Every two to four weeks, adjust the timer to the shortening or lengthening daylight hours. The minimum light use recommended is an hour each day. However, parrots who live on a sunlight schedule tend to have better feather condition and better circadian rhythms.

An online search will help you find specialty lighting that will meet the needs of your birds. Alternatively, consult a specialty bird stores. Although aviaries often offer built-in lights as features, few cage manufacturers offer this option. In fact, the best day-to-day cages don't. Another source of UV light systems is a store that specializes in reptiles, as—not surprisingly—reptiles require similar UV light as birds.

Harnesses

If you acquire a parrot accustomed to a harness, you are a lucky person. Although many parrots can be trained to tolerate a harness for the purpose of going outside, this training is less complicated if a breeder begins with a young bird. Harnesses that are easy to slip over your parrot's head and wings are best. The diaper-style harness is designed for you and is not particularly safe or healthy for your parrot. (Clean feathers are essential for parrots. Worse, only a parakeet or a cockatiel *might* be secured by a Velcro mechanism. For most of us, "might" is not enough.) Online retailers can suggest the sizes of sturdier and more secure harnesses that will most likely fit your bird. Catalog listings and packaging typically includes the species the harnesses are designed to fit. In addition, ask your local bird specialty retailer for suggestions.

Hanging Beds

Some parrots love hanging beds and some look at them and seem to wonder, "What were you thinking, human?" Before you go to the expense of deciding that a hanging bed or sleeping hut is what you need, see how your bird likes an approximation of the style you're considering. For example, find a way to drape a towel over two perches placed right up against the roof of the cage and let the ends hang down to the perch your bird sleeps on. See whether your bird will use this improvised sleeping hut as a privacy screen. Some birds head right for the perch and peek out; other birds head in the opposite direction. Similarly,

It takes some patience and training to get a parrot comfortable with a harness, but it's worth the effort.

the bird hut is a bit like a dark chamber to which your bird can retreat. You can create a faux hut for a trial run with a cardboard box through which a perch runs. Support the box against a cage side. The bird enters from the open side and steps onto the perch. He's covered on three sides. If this sort of arrangement works for your bird, take the next step and try a hanging bed or a hut.

Caution: if you have a bird who is coming into breeding season, a dark place can literally increase the breeding hormones. Usually, the behavior a companion bird displays during this time (most often early spring) is unwanted. During that season, most veterinarians and behaviorists recommend you remove anything that simulates a dark cavern, which is a stand-in for the hollow tree trunks in which parrots typically nest.

Humidifiers

If a person could possibly be more comfortable in your home with a humidifier, consider having one near your parrot's day cage. A great deal about a parrot's health is related to his skin and feathers. The natural habitat for most parrots is near the equator and mostly in moist areas along rivers. (There are exceptions.) In a human home, with heating and air conditioning systems taking much of the natural moisture from the air, skin can become dry and flaky. For parrots, this is more than a painful experience—as it is for people—because he cannot simply grab a bottle of lotion and relieve his discomfort. (Never, ever put lotion or oil on your parrot's skin.) What he needs is an increase in humidity. A humidifier will not only relieve your parrot's discomfort but improve your own respiratory system's natural moisture, helping it work better.

Air Filters

Parrots produce a fine dust called "powder down," which they use to clean and lubricate their feathers. In particular, African greys and cockatoos can create quite a bit of dust from this powder down. To help keep the air in your home cleaner and reduce the job of wiping down surfaces, an air filter is a tremendous help. Some household heating and cooling systems have air filters built in. With parrots, you'll find you need to change your filter more often. However, you might also consider installing a separate filtration unit near your parrot's cage.

Several considerations are important in selecting an appropriate filter. First, consider the noise. For a filter to be effective, it has to be working much of the day. The noise from machines such as air filters and humidifiers can add up to a lot of background racket. Second, think about the cost of replacement filters. Some air cleaners are electrostatic: they attract floating particles. As a result, there are no filters to change. Instead, as often as necessary, simply pull out the metal blades and wipe them. A second type of air filter physically pulls the air through a fine mesh that traps particles. These filters, like those in your home air filtering system, must be changed periodically—and the cost can add up. The most effective mesh filters are high-efficiency particulate air (HEPA) filters.

An air purifier will be helpful in controlling the dust your bird creates.

If you dust and vacuum each day, perhaps you don't need an air filter. If you have one small maroon-bellied conure, you don't need an air filter. If you have an African grey, a bare-eyed cockatoo, and an Amazon, consider getting a filter.

Misters

Many books talk about installing misters for birds, but without an outdoor aviary, a mister system is an unnecessary complication. For daily misting, use a bottle that emits a fine mist when you squeeze the handle. Some of us use misters to add moisture to the air just before changing the newspaper. Not only does your bird get his feathers damp, but also the dust particles from the newspaper, moistened and heavy, do not enter the air.

Make sure you label the plastic bottle, "Bird Water Only." Never, ever use the bottle for anything else. Tip: Make sure the plastic bottle looks nothing like the plastic bottles you use for your cleaning products. One squirt of something that's not water can be very serious for your bird.

Setting Up the Cage

Cage setups have a few universal principles and many personal and creative attributes. The most important idea about cage setups is that your bird feels comfortable, has plenty of room to move around without hitting his wings on something, and has easy access to food and water that stays clean during the day. Cage placement and set up is an important part of a bird's freedom from discomfort. Many parrot parents enjoy discovering new ideas for cage setups to solve husbandry problems and to create a more enjoyable environment for their companion.

Birds feel at home when they have something to hide behind that conceals them

Although your parrot needs toys, perches, and bowls, he also needs space to move around and spread his wings.

from anything that might appear frightening. Instead of seeing mostly ahead of them, as cats and dogs do, parrots have about 270 degrees of vision. As prey in the wild, they're adapted to see motion from almost any direction. As a result, parrots are constantly monitoring what's around them. In the same way that people like to burrow into a safe nook when they're nervous or tired, companion parrots feel relief when have a hiding place. This could be a bird hut, a large hanging toy to sit behind, or strips of newspaper hanging down into the cage that obscure him from view.

Next, secure perches are important to a parrot's comfort. Especially with a young or heavy-bodied bird who is not particularly acrobatic, you might want to position most of the perches low in the cage, so that moving from floor to perch and down again is relatively easy. For young birds just beginning to perch, a towel in the bottom of the cage is a good idea. You want to be sure that the bird can't hurt herself in her new home.

All parrots appreciate a variety of widths and materials of perches. Choice should be the primary goal, so that not only does your companion have a variety of foot positions to choose from, but also your companion is able to decide which perch suits her at that moment. For companion parrots, the ability to exercise choice is important.

Safe and Unsafe Cleaners

If you've taken a look at your cleaning products' labels recently and seen, "poison," "caution," and "dangerous," you might want to reevaluate their use. Parrots, like small children, investigate everything by putting it into their mouths. If you've investigated the meanings of label warnings, you'll know that "poison" means that, in amounts up to 1 teaspoon, a fluid can be fatal to a human being. If you imagine the relative weights of a human being—about 150 pounds—and the weight of a bird—less than 1 pound—you'll realize that a lick of such a fluid could be fatal to a bird.

What to do? Rethink your cleaning ingredients and methods. Here are some tips:

- Dust: With a damp or a static-charged cloth, remove dust that's made of synthetic chemicals, insect parts, dust mites, the feather leavings of your bird, and other allergens.
- Vacuum and sweep: Remove the major detritus in your home after dusting. You might investigate a new vacuum with a HEPA filter. However, don't use any powdered carpet fresheners.
- Scrub: Using white vinegar and water or lemon juice in equal parts disinfects and deodorizes. Baking soda removes stains. Castile soap cuts grease.

In recent years, because their customers have asked, many companies have created cleaners without the most toxic chemicals. The least harmful ingredients are basic and natural, rather than petrochemical. If the manufacturer does not disclose the ingredients on the label, there is a reason. That reason often includes that the ingredients are toxic.

The question of safety revolves around how much of a substance is required to do the job. If you can do the job with common, inexpensive substances such as baking soda and vinegar, why purchase expensive products?

Bleach is a very toxic ingredient that is recommended as a disinfectant for periodic deep cleaning of cages and parrot furniture. The reason that bleach is needed is because of certain categories of serious viruses that are not eliminated without the strongest disinfectant. For more information about the recipe for this disinfectant, see the sidebar on page 79.

(The information for this section comes from Chapter 6, pp. 146–151, of *Pets and the Planet: A Practical Guide to Sustainable Pet Care* by Carol Frischmann.)

Although a variety of toys is important, also important is that your bird not have too many obstacles to avoid while flapping his wings. Typical set-ups include a perch that runs from one side of the cage to the other as the starting point. To either side towards the corners, are spots for toys or a platform-type perch or swing.

Positioning food and water bowls is an art. Be careful not to place the bowls under perches. Rather, place them to the side, so that they can be reached easily but cannot be defecated in from any perch. Keeping these bowls or water bottles properly positioned will save you time as well as the cost of replacing fouled food. In addition, this helps your bird remain healthy.

The best ideas about cage setups come from seeing what other people do successfully. Consult with your breeder or specialty bird store and with the members of your parrot association; observe as many different cage setups as possible. From these, you'll get ideas that will keep your bird feeling great about his new home.

Cage Cleaning and Maintenance

Cage cleaning and maintenance drives home the concept that parrots are wild animals. Parrots who have an abundance of food types, foraging systems, and toys to destroy create quite a mess. In addition to the down feathers stuck in the leftover banana on the cage bars your bird used for cleaning her beak, the bottom of the cage will probably look frighteningly dirty. Keeping a parrot's cage clean is a balancing act: the tension is between preventing messes that are difficult to cope with and cleaning frequency and depth. As you and your parrot adjust to life together, you will find a routine that works most of the time. Know that you won't be able to stick to your best parrot-keeper self every single day. Nevertheless, do something that's quick to maintain your parrot's "area of influence" whenever you have just a minute or two or while you talk on the telephone. Put on a Bluetooth headset and grab a broom or a rag. If you do basic maintenance each day, you'll find your "deep cleanings" take less time.

The Basic Equipment

Soap and water are key to cage maintenance. You don't need to buy anything expensive or sophisticated. Use a damp rag with soap and water and wipe the cage bars after removing the cage-bottom paper and vacuuming or sweeping around and under the cage. (This is the reason that a wheeled cage or cage stand is critical.) Many companions seem to enjoy watching your cleaning activities. Keep a stack of washcloth-sized rags and a metal bowl with soapy solution always on hand; dip and wring out your rag, and you can make short work of most of the food and poop that clings to your bird's cage bars and bottom.

For deeper cleanings, use an old toothbrush and a paint scraper or one of those plastic gizmos that remove caulking. The key to excellent maintenance is, rather than being a perfectionist, being consistent. If you live in an area that allows you to take the cage outside, your work may go faster. Spray the entire cage with water, use the soapy rag, then wipe

It's best to avoid positioning perches directly over food and water bowls.

Cleaning Chore Checklist

Daily
- Change the cage-bottom paper.
- Replace food and water with clean food and water in clean dishes.
- Spot vacuum to pick up worst of feathers and dust.

Weekly
- Remove and replace all perches and toys from cage and play gym.
- Thoroughly vacuum cage and play gym.
- Use a damp cloth with soap and scrub the cage bars and tray inside and out; also scrub play gym surfaces.
- Move your bird's cage and play gym and vacuum around and underneath.
- Place clean washable rugs (if used) under cage and play gym, or steam clean linoleum or tile under play gym and cage.
- Replace toys and perches.
- Machine wash cleaning rags, cage cover, rugs, etc.
- Replace for next use.

Monthly
- Use the weekly protocol, making sure to use the small, stiff brush on all surfaces to remove the cage grime for a thorough cleaning.
- Wipe the walls (or the contact paper) surrounding the cage.
- Disinfect the cage, play gym, and all toys, perches, cage covers, rugs, etc.

it dry. Keep a hamper for the used rags and wash them in the heavy-duty cycle with bleach. *Voila*! You're ready for the next deep cleaning.

Trade Secret Short Cuts

For those with carpets in areas your bird frequents, consider using a washable rug underneath the cage. Choose one that extends as far beyond the cage as your bird's usual "flinging" distance. You can easily vacuum the washable rug or take it outside and shake it before putting it into the washing machine with the rags from the week. Use a closed hamper for your rags, and don't attempt to wash the rags each day. Let this be a weekly job. As with all other parrot supplies, have two under-cage rugs so that one can be in use while the other is being washed.

Cover the nearest walls with transparent contact paper. Although the contact paper isn't completely invisible, it is more resistant to repeated scrubbing to remove bits of apple and grape than your paint—unless you've used special wall paint that is meant to be wiped. By the way, if you're sure that your bird's cage location is correct, applying a scrub-resistant paint to nearby walls is a very good idea.

Depending on cage arrangement and your bird, you may be able to use a "top layer removal" method for keeping the cage bottom clean. Some birds are neat keepers: they don't shred the cage paper. For these birds, place several layers of newspaper on the cage bottom so that you can simply remove the top layer as it becomes soiled. This quick removal technique keeps everything cleaner, especially if you are feeding foods that stick to your bird, the perches, and elsewhere. Pulling out the top layer of paper twice a day keeps your bird's cage much cleaner overall.

Quick Wipe Process

Anytime you have a couple of free minutes and a soapy rag in your hand, give the cage a quick wipe, especially around the bottom where everything accumulates. You'd be surprised how much cleaning time this saves in the long run. Antibacterial quick wipes that work for kitchen counters also work for cages, but read the labels carefully. If the contents aren't something you'd be comfortable putting in your mouth, don't use it on your bird's cage. If you have to wipe off the residue, then quick wipes aren't quicker than soap and water.

Deep Cleaning Process

As with any household, periodic deep cleaning and disinfection is needed in your parrot's cage. Think of it as the equivalent of cleaning the baseboards and the blinds and wiping out the closets in your own home. When you begin, be sure you have enough time to finish the entire job. As you gain

Reducing the Cleaning Burden

Here are a few tips that can help you minimize the drudgery of cleaning your parrot's cage and surroundings:

- As you see how your bird prefers to perch, make sure that his water and food are not located underneath favorite perches. Savvy perch and bowl placement will help you reduce the amount of poop that goes into the bowls.
- In addition, if you've never considered a water bottle, consider a glass bottle that attaches outside your bird's cage. If you buy a good-quality bottle and keep it out of the direct sunlight, this reduces cleanup by guaranteeing that your bird has clean drinking water for the day. If you have a bird who is a "dunker," you know the mess that the soup makes when his bowl overturns or splashes onto the cage floor.
- Next, remove the paper after your bird has his first large poop in the morning. Some birds wait until after eating breakfast to eliminate the waste from overnight. If you change the paper afterward, this ensures your bird will not walk through and spread this mess to every cage surface during the day.
- In addition, when you remove the paper, if you vacuum the loose seed, wet food, and feathers from the cage bars, you'll find your weekly "detox" goes much faster because less material has adhered to the sides of the cage.
- Try waiting to remove the paper until the daily misting of your feathered friend has been done. After misting, wipe the cage bars (no scrubbing needed) and then do the vacuuming. You'll find that your weekly cleaning has just been halved.
- Each bird's habits are different. If you observe, think, and plan, cleaning can be a much smaller chore.

experience, you'll find your own shortcuts and ways to speed the process. However, in the beginning, there's nothing so discouraging as thinking you can finish in an hour and finding that the process really takes three hours. The smaller the cage, the shorter the process. There's quite a time difference between cleaning a cage for two budgies versus cleaning a cage for a couple of African greys.

First, vacuum up all the loose dirt. Remove the bottom tray and vacuum both the tray and the cage again. Next, pull everything else out of the cage: perches, toys, and bowls. Put those to soak or into the dishwasher, depending on your method of choice. Be sure to include the washers, the nuts and bolts, and the toy hangers as well.

Next, if you're cleaning the cage outside, use the hose and spray the surfaces thoroughly. If you're cleaning the cage inside, put down painter's plastic from the hardware store in an area much larger than you think you'll need. (You can wash it with your cleaning rags, small rug, and cage cover and reuse.) Wipe a generous amount of soapy water onto the cage bars, top and bottom and allow the solution to rehydrate the dried-on material.

Allow the dried-on food and feces to soften. Then use a rag, a plastic scraper, and a small brush such as an old toothbrush to remove any adhered material bit by bit. Listen to great tunes or an old movie. This makes the work go faster. If your bird can be perched nearby, perhaps in his travel carrier, he will enjoy watching the process and discussing the movie with you. (Okay. He'll really be listening ... but these times together can be helpful to your relationship.)

If you spot-clean your bird's cage daily, your weekly cleaning chores will be less laborious.

Inexpensive Disinfecting Solution

Many people do not realize that disinfectants do not work until organic materials have been removed from the surface with soap and water. The "organic materials" include feces, food remnants, other pets' saliva, and similar substances.

Use disinfectant once you've cleaned and dried the cage, play gym, or other surface, including your counters, sponges, and any cleaning rags and your washing machine. You can buy commercial disinfectants formulated for cage cleaning.

For general disinfection, use 1 tablespoon (15 mL) of bleach to 1 quart (946 mL) of water. This solution is the choice of most wildlife hospitals, which are without the greater resources of veterinary hospitals that usually purchase premixed disinfectant.

If you have a specific contaminant, for example one sick bird at the veterinarian's and your remaining birds at home not yet showing signs of illness, use a much stronger solution of 2 tablespoons (30 mL) of bleach in 1 cup (237 mL) of water. *After fifteen minutes, rinse thoroughly and wipe dry.* It's best to rinse until the items no longer have any trace of bleach scent. Two precautions must be mentioned. First, bleach is a skin irritant, so use gloves. Second, the solution loses its effectiveness over time. Accordingly, mix a new batch each day.

Remember: Once you've wiped on the bleach and waited the requisite 15 minutes, you must rinse to remove the bleach solution.

(The information for this sidebar comes from Chapter 6, p. 151 of *Pets and the Planet: A Practical Guide to Sustainable Pet Care*, Frischmann, Wiley Publishing, 2009.]

Once you've finished the cleaning, wipe on a dilute bleach solution. Allow the solution to dry for fifteen minutes. Then wipe the cage dry. You're ready to move the cage back inside or remove the plastic drop cover that you've used to protect your carpet.

Toy Cleaning

Between the application of the soapy water and the time for the initial scrubbing, wash soiled toys in a mild soap and water solution, using a small bristle brush. Use the same disinfecting bleach solution on the toys.

Reassembly

Reassembly goes quickly if you've got a standard cage set up with a supply of perches, toys, and dishes from your second sets that are immediately ready to go. Again, your parrot will be fascinated to watch you reassemble his cage. A good conversation with your bird about his toy selection and perch placement is good for your progress and mental attitude while taking care of this necessary but messy and sometimes annoying cleaning process.

Safe and Unsafe Houseplants

The ASPCA Poison Control Center (ASPCA-PCC) maintains three separate lists of plants known to be safe and known to be toxic to cats, dogs, and horses. Birds are not included in this list because few veterinarians treat birds and report poisonings and because there is little research done into toxicity of plants to exotic birds.

Although the ASPCA's plant lists are based on other species, assume that if a plant is toxic to other pets, the plant will be toxic to your bird. However, the converse is not always true.

Just because a plant is safe for one species does not mean a plant is safe for another. Groups of bird fanciers keep track of reports of poisonings and continue to update lists. Nevertheless, these more informal lists are not the result of tracking research papers or incident reports from poison control centers.

Common house plants and cut flowers known to be toxic to parrots include:

- amaryllis (*Amaryllis* spp.)
- autumn crocus (*Cholchium* spp.)
- avocado (*Persea americana*)
- azalea (*Rhododendron* spp.)
- castor bean (*Ricinus* spp.)
- chrysanthemum (*Chrysanthemum* spp.)
- crocus (*Crocus* spp.)
- cycad, ago, and zamai palms (*Cycad* spp.)
- cyclamen (*Cyclamen* spp.)
- English ivy (*Hedera* spp.)
- kalanchoe (*Kalanchoe* spp.)
- lilies (*Lilium* spp.)
- marijuana (*Cannabis* spp.)
- mother-in-law plant (*Monstera* spp.)
- peace lilies (*Spathiphyllum* spp.)
- philodendron (*Philodendron* spp.)
- pothos (*Fpipremnum* spp.)
- tulips and narcissus (*Tulipa* spp., *Narcissus* spp.)
- umbrella plant (*Scheffleria* spp.)
- yews (*Taxus* spp.)

Even if the houseplants themselves are safe, and a few are listed below, think about fertilizer pellets, systemic fertilizers, and "top dressings." Any of these could contain poisons.

The safest thing is to forget about houseplants. After all, don't you have enough to care for with your bird? If you are a person who just has to have plants, be sure that you (or your supplier) do not use systemic fertilizers (ones that you cannot see) or fertilizer pellets in the soil, which are prime targets for inquisitive bird to eat. In addition, consider the safety of ingesting whatever is on top of the houseplant's soil. Small glittery bits will also go right into your bird's mouth. If you must have houseplants, the following are believed to be safe:

- African violets (*Saintpaulia ionantha*)
- Christmas cactus (*Schlumbergera* spp.)
- coleus (*Solenostemon scutellarioides*)
- ferns (*Pteridophyta* Spp.)
- roses (*Rosa* spp.)
- spider plants (*Chlorophytum comosum*)

Check for updates at the ASPCA Poison Control Center at www.napcc.aspca.org. (The information in this section comes from the ASPCA Poison Control Center and from Chapter 31, "Implications of Toxic Substances in Clinical Disorders," pp. 711-721, Harrison and Lightfoot, *Clinical Avian Medicine*.)

Disaster Preparedness

The American Red Cross has created a list of plans to make and things to do to prepare for an evacuation. Since emergencies are, by definition, times when you don't have time to "throw a few things together," plan for your new companion before he comes home.

Advanced Planning: Where to Stay?

You're going to take your bird with you. Because many shelters do not allow pets, you're going to need to know which hotels will accept you and your parrot during an emergency. The Red Cross suggests that you ask whether the no-pet policies could be waived in an emergency.

In addition, make a list of friends, relatives, or veterinarians who can care for your bird in an emergency. Prepare a list with phone numbers. If you have other pets, you may not be able to house your pets together, so be prepared for that.

Other Advanced Planning

Practice evacuation with your parrot so that he is not upset by entering the carrier and being placed in the car. Make a copy of your parrot's health records and keep a copy of those with your evacuation supplies.

Make sure your parrot is microchipped by your veterinarian and carry the number with his medical records. Many pets are lost during emergency situations. A microchip gives you the best chance of recovering your best friend.

Create an emergency supplies kit for your parrot. Be sure to use a container that is sturdy and easily carried. Include:
- at least three days of food, bottled drinking water, and bowls
- carrier with favorite toys and cage cover
- current photos of you with your parrot in case your best friend is lost
- first aid kit (see Chapter 7 for details)
- harness (if bird normally tolerates one)
- lists detailing the feeding schedule, any medical conditions, behavior problems, and the name and number of your veterinarian
- medications and copies of medical records, stored in a waterproof container

As the disaster approaches, confirm emergency shelter arrangements for you and your parrot. You should inspect the contents of the emergency kit regularly, checking to make sure that the foods and medications have not expired and that the other components are still up to date and in working order.

Expect that no one, parrot or human, will be at their best during an evacuation. Be aware that the stress during the evacuation may keep everyone on their best behavior or the stress may bring out the worst in everyone. Often parrots can become aggressive or fearful, so protect them from as much of the stress as possible. For yourself, know that your parrot may become very territorial about her carrier and unwilling to come out or go in willingly. Try not to take this personally. This is a natural reaction of parrots to fearful situations.

For more information about disaster planning, consult www.RedCross.org or www.Ready.gov.

4

DIET
AND
NUTRITION

n the same way that a new parent can become overwhelmed with advice about how to feed a child, parrot parents can become exhausted by surveying the many choices available for feeding their parrots. Long gone are the days of grandmother's parrot, who ate seed and chewed on a cuttlebone and a mineral block. We now know that this is the equivalent of feeding a child a diet consisting only of potato chips. Today's range of choices includes feeding a bewildering variety of commercial pelleted diets, many different types of cooked diets, and complicated sprouted seed diets. As with people, diets are formulated to match various philosophies of feeding.

What's important for novice parrot parents to keep in mind is that diets not only serve parrots' nutritional needs, but also support the behavioral needs of this companion who is, with few exceptions, only two or three generations from his wild counterparts. Finding and selecting items to eat and experiencing the texture and color of food take up most of a wild bird's day. For companion birds, food provides a way to experience choice and variety in life. Assuring that both your parrot's nutritional needs and your bird's food-related behavior needs are met is critical to a long and happy life together.

Today, with more than ten million companion birds in the United States, avian diets and health have assumed a greater economic importance than in past years. As a result, researchers now investigate the specific needs of different companion bird species, rather than limiting avian nutrition research to chickens and ducks. University researchers and pet supply manufacturers have combed the literature and sponsored research to determine what dietary components keep different companion bird species healthy. As a result, our understanding of ideal diets for each bird species is improving. This new research also tells us that the all-seed diets of the past limited companion birds to about one-fifth of their natural life span.

In nature, parrots eat a little bit of one thing, drop it to the forest floor, and move on to something else.

As with people, a diet of preferred foods is not the basis for a healthy body. In the same way that you would not allow your two-year-old to eat only the foods he requests, part of your job as a parrot parent is to help your bird make healthy choices. After all, your parrot's well-being, happiness, and long life depend on good nutrition. The quality of his feathers, temperament, and zest for life come from being properly nourished. In fact, veterinarians say that poor nutrition causes most companion bird health problems. The healthy parrot's human parents provide abundant food, balanced nutrition, and foraging experiences that meet his behavioral needs.

Dangerous Foods

Do not feed your parrot these foods; they are harmful or toxic to birds:

- alcohol
- avocado
- caffeine
- chocolate
- cured meats
- dairy products (small quantities okay)
- roasted and salted nuts
- sugared products

If your parrot eats these foods, immediately check with your veterinarian or Animal Poison Control Center at www.napcc.aspca.org/pet-care/animal-poison-control.

Abundant Food

In the same way that a person's diet defines his or her health and emotional well-being, so does your parrot's diet define his. Nothing makes a creature as confident as abundant food that meets not only his nutritional needs but also his psychological needs. Just as people consume food to build their bodies and fuel the activities that give our lives meaning, so does your parrot's diet do both for him. Not only is the body built through nutrition, but the activities of daily life are powered by nutrition, with the assistance of proper vitamins, minerals, and lots of fresh water.

Balanced Nutrition

Balanced nutrition comes from a mix of proteins, carbohydrates, and fats, along with vitamins, minerals, and water. Each of these components has an important role to play in your bird's health, as well as providing energy for his life activities. A well-balanced meal twice each day, early in the morning and late in the afternoon, will keep your bird healthy and happy, secure in the fact that he will always have enough food.

Proteins

Proteins not only build body tissues such as muscle, but they are also required to keep the immune system and the metabolic pathways working properly. Proteins from parrots' diets are broken into smaller pieces—amino acids—which in turn are used as the building blocks for the proteins that your parrot needs to produce strong muscles and other tissues. In addition to beans and nuts, proteins are also gathered by wild parrots who eat insects and pollen.

Carbohydrates

Carbohydrates give your parrot's body energy. Some carbohydrates, like those in some fruits, are absorbed directly into the bloodstream for quick energy. More complex carbohydrates are digested slowly; therefore, they produce a longer lasting effect.

Fats

Not only are fats necessary as energy sources for the body, but fats also aid the body in metabolizing (using) various vitamins including A, D, E, and K. Brain tissue is created from these fats, and fats also play an essential role in delivering nutrients throughout the body.

Minerals

Minerals build and maintain bone, nerve, and muscle function, as well as help maintain the body's fluid balance. Minerals, which originate in the earth, are concentrated in plants that are consumed by your parrot. Some minerals, such as calcium and phosphorous, build bones. Other minerals, such as iron and sodium, aid in the manufacture of blood cells and other tissues. Some other minerals that your bird needs include copper, magnesium, and potassium.

Vitamins

Vitamins are a critical part of a parrot's diet. Vitamins, needed by living things for good health, must be taken in as food because the body cannot manufacture them from other nutritional elements. Because they play an important part in almost every bodily process, vitamin deficiencies cause serious health problems, including vision problems, bone fractures, and inability to fight off infections. Vitamins regulate many body processes; your parrot needs thirteen essential vitamins that are included in a varied and sufficient diet.

Your parrot should never have to worry about where his next meal is coming from; keep food available at all times.

Putting the Components Together

Parrots require a mixture of proteins, carbohydrates, fats, vitamins, and minerals. Presenting those essential nutrients in a way your bird enjoys assures that you've done your best for his health. In other words, you must provide healthy food that your bird is eager to eat.

Most experts agree that the essential nutrition for a companion bird comes from clean, fresh

Sprouting Seeds

Some companions regularly feed sprouts to their birds. Sprouts are shoots of germinated seeds. Not only is the nutrition of the seed increased in this process, but also the process adds variety to your bird's diet. Sprouted seeds are excellent sources of protein, vitamins, and minerals. The most common types of seeds used for sprouting are alfalfa, mung bean, soybean, radish, and rye seeds.

To grow edible sprouts be sure you *buy only those seeds labeled for sprouting.* Seeds for sprouting are generally available from health food stores and the produce section of many grocery stores. This is important because garden seeds are often treated with fungicides, which can be harmful if eaten.

Technique

1. Use a clean, wide-mouth glass canning jar, a screw-top ring, and cheesecloth or fine wire mesh (preferably stainless steel or aluminum) cut to the size of the screw-top ring.
2. Add seeds. Cover with cheesecloth or mesh and secure with screw top or rubber band.
3. Rinse the seeds and drain.
4. Soak the seeds for 12–24 hours in water twice the volume of seeds.
5. Drain, and then rinse the seeds.
6. Keep the jar in a dark place at room temperature (68° to 72°F/20° to 22°C).
7. Rinse the seeds two to four times a day until the sprouts are the desired length, usually 2 to 5 days. Drain all excess water to prevent fermentation.
8. To remove the husks, place the sprouts in a pan of water, stir, and remove the seed coats as they rise.
9. Refrigerate sprouts in a sealed bag or jar for up to 2 weeks. Discard if they get moldy or start to smell bad.

Seed Type	Sprout to	Time	Starting	Result
Adzuki	½-1 inch	4-5 days	1/4 cup	1 cup
Alfalfa	Seed length	1-2 days	1 cup	2 ½ cups
Barley	Seed length	3-5 days	½ cup	1 cup
Bean	½-1 ½ in	3-5 days	¼ cup	1 ¼ cups
Cabbage	½-1 inch	3-5 days	¼ cup	1 ¼ cups
Chia	⅛-½ inch	1-2 days	¼ cup	1 cup
Chickpea	¾-1 inch	5-8 days	1 cup	3 ½ cups
Millet	Seed length	3-5 days	1 cup	2 ½ cups
Mung bean	½-3 inches	3-8 days	1 cup	4 cups
Pea	¼-½ inch	3-4 days	1 cup	2 cups
Radish	½-1 inch	2-4 days	1 Tbsp	¾ cup
Soybean	¾-1 inch	4-5 days	1 cup	3 ½ cup
Sunflower	Budded only	5-8 days	1 cup	2 cups
Triticale	Seed length	1-3 days	1 cup	3 cups
Wheat	Seed length	4-5 days	1 cup	4 cups

[This information comes from University of Wisconsin Extension, http://learningstore.uwex.edu/assets/pdfs/A3385.PDF]

water; a basic diet of high-quality pellets; and daily addition of fresh fruits, vegetables, proteins, and small amounts of seed.

Foraging Satisfies Behavioral Needs

Well-reared parrots have a love and acceptance of many different foods. In fact, this is one important reason to acquire a parrot from an excellent breeder. If the parents are nutritionally fit, they teach the chick to eat a variety of foods. If the parrot is not well-reared, then he may not know that many of the items you present are actually delicious and nutritious foods. As with people, offspring learn to eat the foods that their parents eat.

In foraging groups, wild birds select seasonally among flowers and tree buds, insects, fruits, and seeds. After parrots eat what's ripe, they move on to the next tree where produce is fresh. Parrots forage in flocks. Young birds learn what is good to eat at different times of the year from the flock. As a companion, you can use this inborn search for guidance to your advantage. When your bird is reluctant to try something you feel she would enjoy, eat some in front of your parrot, and make a fuss about how delicious the morsel is.

Festive Amazon enjoying a nut. Nuts provide fats, protein, some minerals, and a good beak workout.

Forshaw's *Parrots of the World* and Arndt's *Atlas of Parrots* provide excellent information on wild diets. Keep in mind that the specific plants available in your parrot's homeland may be different from a similarly named plant in your home country. However, you'll be amazed at the variety and kinds of foods your parrot eats in the wild.

You will not be able to duplicate your parrot's natural wild diet. It would be impossible to obtain the plants and grow them successfully. Even more important, wild flocks may be eating whole categories of food that researchers are unaware of. Still, what comes through in reading these accounts is how varied the parrots' diets are and how much time and care they devote to acquiring and eating healthy wild foods.

Wild parrots spend most of their day hunting for and consuming food as they find it. In fact, a majority of their energy goes into this vital activity. Most birds fly miles from their night roosts to gather food from trees, grasses, and plants that provide grains, flowers, and fruit. Most parrots in the wild eat a varied diet. The few that don't, such as lories, are specialized to eat a particular diet. Those parrots are in the minority.

What is fundamentally different about wild birds and their companion parrot counterparts are their energy requirements. Birds who are flying miles each day need quite a bit more food—more calories—than do birds who are sedentary or lack enough activity.

Ingredients of a Healthy Parrot Diet

You can group all the varied ingredients of a healthy parrot diet into a few broad categories: seeds, pellets, nuts, and fruits and vegetables. Let's look at each category in more detail.

Seeds and Their (Limited) Place in the Diet

Some avian veterinarians believe that we've gone from one extreme (the all-seed diet) to another extreme (the no-seed diet). Seed has a place in your parrot's diet: behaviorists suggest that you withhold either seed or nuts and provide those as training treats. There's nothing wrong with this. During training (see Chapter 5), you'll definitely need an incentive to reinforce your parrot's compliance with the desired behavior.

Seed, as with any other dietary component, should be the freshest you can find and appropriate to your parrot's size. The best way to do this is to purchase from a quality supplier. However, most seed, even when carefully grown and processed, contains insect eggs. To ensure that insects do not hatch and consume your seeds, freeze the seeds for at least twenty-four hours following purchase. To keep seed fresh, you may freeze it for up to six months, withdrawing small amounts as you need them for your parrot.

Parrots enjoy taking the hull off the seed and nibbling the exquisite flesh underneath, which contains as much as 50 percent fat. Aside from the amounts of fat seeds contain, they lack nutrients necessary for a healthy life: two critical amino acids, ten important vitamins, and many minerals and trace minerals. Fed exclusively on seeds, a bird's health suffers, and he becomes unwilling to eat anything else. Feed only a small amount of seed as part of a healthy varied diet. This same advice, by the way, applies to an exclusive diet of anything else. Variety is part of a healthy diet.

Making your parrot forage for some of his food helps keep him mentally and physically fit.

Pellets

High-quality pellets ensure a proper base of nutrition, eliminating much of the uncertainty pet companions have in

Edible Flowers to Feed Parrots

If you are an organic gardener or can cut flowers from a friend's garden, those listed in this table, adapted especially for parrots from the North Carolina State University Cooperative Extension list, should be delicious eating and another variation to add to your bird's diet. By the way, a warning that can't be repeated too often is that eating flowers sprayed with pesticides or given a drink of an elixir to make them last longer could be fatal. Stay away from anything grown for floral display.

Common name	Scientific name	Flavor	Color	Comments
anise hyssop	*Agastache foeniculum*	anise	lilac	self-seeding perennial
arugula	*Eruca vesicaria sativa*	spicy	white	annual; once flowers form the leaves become bitter
basil	*Ocimum basilicum*	herbal	white, lavender	annual
bee balm	*Monarda didyma*	minty, sweet, hot	wide range	perennial
chervil	*Anthriscus cerefolium*	herbal	white	annual
chicory	*Cichorium intybus*	herbal	blue	perennial
chrysanthemum	*Chrysanthemum* spp.	strong	perennial	use the florets; strong flavor
dandelion	*Taraxacum officinale*	sweet, honey-like	yellow	perennial; use young flowers, mature flowers become bitter; flowers close after picking
dianthus	*Dianthus* spp.	sweet clove flavor	wide range	perennial; remove the narrow base of the petals (bitter)
dill	*Anethum graveolens*	herbal	yellowish-green	annual

Common name	Scientific name	Flavor	Color	Comments
elderberry	*Sambucus canadensis*	sweet	white	perennial; do not wash flowers since it removes much of the flavor
English daisy	*Bellis perennis*	mildly bitter	pink	perennial
fennel	*Foeniculum vulgare*	mildly anise	yellow-green	normally grown as an annual
hibiscus	*Hibiscus* spp.	Sour	wide range	perennial; common houseplant
lilac	*Syringa vulgaris*	varies	lavender	wide variation in flavor from no flavor to green and herbaceous to lilac
lovage	*Levisticum officinale*	celery	white	perennial
marigold	*Tagetes patula*	bitter	yellow, orange	annual; Lemon Gem and Tangerine Gem have the best flavor
mint	*Mentha* spp.	minty	purple, white	perennial; each type of mint has its own unique flavor
nasturtium	*Tropaeolum majus*	spicy, peppery	wide range	Annual
pansy	*Viola xwittrockiana*	vegetal	wide range	annual; has a slightly sweet green or grassy flavor; petals have a mild flavor; whole flower has a wintergreen flavor
pineapple sage	*Salvia elegans*	sweet, fruity	red	perennial; flavor has a hint of mint and spice
rose	*Rosa* spp.	perfumed	wide range	perennial; remove the white, bitter base of the petal
rosemary	*Rosmarinus officinalis*	herbal	blue	perennial
Scented geraniums	*Pelargonium* spp.	varies	wide range	perennial; the flavor is usually similar to the scent of the leaves
squash	*Curcubita pepo*	vegetal	yellow	Annual
thyme	*Thymus* spp.	herbal	white	perennial herb
violet	*Viola odorata*	sweet, perfumed	purple, white	perennial; use candied or fresh

ensuring a proper diet. The best suppliers blend diets based on research into species-specific nutrition needs. As dog and cat dietary needs differ, so conure dietary needs differ from those of cockatoos or parakeets. Additionally, diets are formulated for life stage, as well as for beak size. For value's sake and to provide the best nutrition, buy the best quality diet available, one that's packaged and distributed with freshness a priority.

Complete

The advantage of using these pelleted diets as a base for your parrot is the knowledge that your bird has available all the nutrients he needs. The pellet form also answers the problem of your bird picking through his food, selecting only those bits he wants. With pellets, you know your bird is eating the nutrients he needs, not just the items he likes. Formulated pellets include a mix of proteins, carbohydrates, and fats. The balance among these classes of nutrients gives your bird the proper nutrition.

Species-Specific Diets

Pelleted foods contain the required nutrients for a particular species of bird, including vitamins and minerals. Selecting pellets of correct size for your bird's beak is important. Macaws, for example, eat much larger pellets than do parrots. Purchase an appropriately sized pellet. Generally, good quality pellets are marked for the appropriate species.

Life Stage-Specific

Some diets have also been developed to match a bird's life stage. You may be familiar with the formulated diets for young parrots from which they graduate when they wean to pelleted diets. Young birds who are still growing, as well as birds who are transitioning to pellets for the first time, usually prefer a diet higher in protein and fats. Some species can or should then transition to a lower protein and fat diet. Likewise, birds who are consistently overweight should be seen by a veterinarian, and together you should determine whether to decrease the amount of diet given or the makeup of the diet.

If your parrot will not eat pellets, mixing them with foods he likes can convince him to accept them.

Helping Your Parrot Recognize a Manufactured Diet as Food

If you need to convert your bird to a healthier diet including pellets, your bird needs to recognize pellets as food. Just because those expensive square things contains excellent nutrients doesn't mean your bird will understand they are food, especially if they don't look like any food he's had before. A proven strategy, in a gradual plan, is to mix the pellets with a high-preference semisolid food such as strained carrots or fruit. As your bird eats the carrots and fruit, he'll begin to taste the pellets and, if they're high quality and contain nuts, seeds, and the nutrients he needs, he'll become a convert. Do monitor your bird's weight to ensure that you do not progress too rapidly. Of course, the other strategy that always works is to have your bird watch a parrot who already knows how delicious some of these pellets are. Then, the two-year-old mentality kicks in: Your parrot will immediately think, "If he is eating it, I want it."

Selecting the Right Manufactured Diet

Once you have decided to feed a manufactured diet to your parrot, the work of selecting one begins. Manufacturers formulate pellets in a wide range of qualities, from those you find in a bulk bin at a discount pet store to premium diets available only from an avian veterinarian or specialty store. The best manufacturers use organic ingredients that are free of pesticides and additives. In addition, these high-quality products balance nutrients, vitamins, and minerals.

Companions can choose among pellets, crumbles, balls, and square-shaped cakes. Some companions blend different formulations to add variety to their parrot's pellet cup.

Good sources of information include your breeder and your veterinarian. In fact, an excellent plan is to discuss diet with your veterinarian during your initial health exam and prior to making your purchase final. Take a sample of the diet your parrot is eating and ask for your vet's comments and suggestions. Several avian diets are available only from veterinarians or from the manufacturer directly to ensure freshness. Do consider these top-quality suppliers.

Although a veterinarian-supplied diet may seem to serve the veterinarian best, remember that the number one cause of illness in parrots is an inadequate diet. Avian veterinarians are so busy that they could survive just fine without offering manufactured diets. The truth is that most veterinarians are concerned about their patient's health.

Many other choices are available. If you are considering a diet other than one offered by your veterinarian, examine the labels carefully. Discuss the choice, based on the contents, with your veterinarian. Then, choose what you think will work best.

Food Waste

Parrots do not eat all their food. In fact, if your parrot is not dropping food, you're probably not feeding him enough. What looks like wasted food to you is part of a parrot's natural behavior. Parrots tend to pick up a piece of food, take a bite, and drop the rest. In their native habitat, dropped food acts as a fertilizer. In your bird's cage at home, dropped food looks like a terrible mess, but this is not a sign you're feeding too much. Consider that the amount of food you provide is not large, and your bird is getting the value of knowing that he has abundant food. That confidence gives you an emotionally healthy parrot instead of a neurotic one.

If you cannot stand waste, use the newspaper and the parrot meal castoffs as elements in your compost. Compost benefits from dropped food, your bird's droppings, and the dry newspaper. Each provides something the compost needs to form a nourishing mix for your garden plants

Making Food Fun

Wild birds spend a major portion of each day foraging; that is, they locate food and extract the tasty bits from a larger fruit or plant. Make your companion birds' lives more interesting by providing food in a way that requires work, as it would in the wild. Foraging exercises birdie brains and brawn.

Make food more interesting! Hang it up, wrap it up, and mix it up. Two cautions. First, provide sufficient food in plain sight for your bird to remain healthy. Second, use organic produce when possible and wash thoroughly to remove fertilizer and pesticide residues when you can't.

Hang It Up

Weave anything flexible into cage bars or dangle it from the top into the cage. Greens such as parsley, dandelion, cilantro, cabbage, carrot tops, and kale are more interesting when offered in locations above birdie eye level.

Skewer fruit and vegetable chunks. Hang the skewer in a different position each day. Try vegetables and fruits that hold their shape when cut into chunks. Ask your pet store for bird-safe skewers.

Use rawhide ties or cotton string to arrange firm vegetables and fruits that hold their shape cut lengthwise. Try carrots, celery, turnip, yam, apple, and green pepper tied on cage bars at the ends of perches or on the sides of a swing. Move them around. Think color.

Wrap it Up

Don't work too hard for your birds. Leave the natural wrappers on corn (husk and cob), nuts (the shells), grapes (the skin), and beans and peas (pods). If your bird doesn't understand there's a goodie inside, demonstrate to him. Make it fun.

For birds who like to chew, wrap anything safe in plain paper, newspaper, or light cardboard. Make sure the bird knows that you're putting treats inside. Leave the box or paper open the first time.

Treat cages or containers of metal, natural fiber, or plastic are available in every size and shape. Put his favorite treats inside and stand back to watch the fun.

Mix it up

Mix foods your bird loves in with chunks of things he doesn't like as much. He will forage through the bowl of seed and pellets, beans, rice, and red pepper to select the foods he prefers first. The choice is good brain work.

Change the locations of food and water in the cage while keeping them accessible. Make sure your bird uses the entire cage space to get a new outlook.

Change the form of the food. If you serve yams sliced, serve them mashed the next time. Check out serving ideas below.

Food	Serving Idea	Variations
banana, plantain	open one end and hang from skewer or rawhide	peel and roll sections in seed to tempt suspicious birds
corn	for big billed bird, leave husk on; for smaller birds, cut into rounds and hang from skewer.	
egg	hard-boil, chop egg and shell, and serve in bowl	scramble egg with hot peppers
grape, berry	skewer	alternate with pepper chunks
kale, spinach	weave in bars	chop and mix in with seed and chow daily diet
melon, apple, citrus	slice in half and hang from skewer	chop and mix with cooked rice and chopped greens
nut	leave in shell	place inside treat containers for extra foraging challenge
uncooked pasta and cereal O's	string on skewer, rawhide, or cotton string, knots between pieces	use different colors and shapes of pasta and whole-grain cereals
yam, squash, carrot, turnip	cube and add to treat cage	mash and serve with seed mixed in

Diet Form

The form of pellet diets varies; companions can choose among pellets of various sizes. Selecting pellets of correct size for your bird's beak is important, and the size can affect your bird's willingness to accept the pellets. Generally, good-quality pellets are marked for small, medium, and large species of parrots. Some manufacturers color and scent their pellets to make nuggets more appealing to human shoppers. However, coloring and scent are not necessary. Furthermore, the long-term effects of food dyes and other chemicals are of concern to many veterinarians. Pellets colored with natural dyes, such as beet juice, are preferable. You can provide your parrot with more colorful foods by including fresh fruits and vegetables in his diet.

Cost

A good-quality pellet is expensive, but is a quality diet much more expensive than cheaper varieties if you consider the density of nutrition? You feed pellets in small amounts because the nutrition is very dense. To reduce costs, some keepers make bulk purchases and freeze pellets in small bags that, when removed from the freezer, stay fresh for a week or so. Also, consider the cost of poor-quality nutrition on your avian friend's health.

The manufacturer usually provides recommended amounts to feed based on your parrot's weight. For any of us, seeing that precious organic pellet lying uneaten on the bottom of the cage is upsetting. While we know that parrots are notorious for dropping uneaten food to the bottom of their cage (or the jungle soil), that we paid so dearly for this wasted pellet is almost untenable.

To combat their sense of resentment, many parrot companions try to increase the value and decrease the waste of that "nutrient gold," by offering pellets in a foraging system. When your parrot works hard to extract a pellet from his foraging system, he's less likely to drop it. In addition, these systems keep the not-yet-selected pellets from becoming soiled in droppings.

Nuts

Feeding nuts can be an excellent addition to your parrot's diet. Nuts provide built-in foraging amusement with their outer shells. Parrots will appreciate your sizing the nuts to the size of their distinctive hooked bills. For example, African greys can usually crack almond shells, but their beaks are not large enough to crack Brazil nuts and walnuts. Macaws, on the other hand, need the challenge of Brazil nuts and walnuts, because almonds may be too easy for them. As with seed, there is quite a bit of energy packed into a small space with nuts. Be sparing in providing these supercharged treats to your companion.

Fresh Fruits and Vegetables

Fresh fruits and vegetables provide a satisfying visual experience as well as foraging fun. While he is receiving excellent nutritional value, your parrot also receives the mental exercise of choosing which items to eat, as well as the physical experience of maneuvering, crunching, and discarding textures and tastes that don't suit him. Presenting fresh foods in a variety of attractive ways allow parrots to strip the stalks like forest foliage, work through a stack of less desirable skewered vegetables to get to his favorite, and get plenty of exercise manipulating the various foods.

Why Feed Fruits and Vegetables?

Reproducing the behavior that birds would follow in the wild is key to keeping a behaviorally healthy bird, and providing vitamins, minerals, and carbohydrates is the nutritional role of fruits and vegetables in a parrot's diet. Unlike domestic household pets, parrots—closer to their wild origins—instinctively spend a good deal of time foraging for food. Selecting ripe foods and eating takes up most of their early morning and late afternoon time. Vegetables and fruits can form up to about 50 percent of a parrot's diet; variety in both the content and the presentation of this portion of the diet are very beneficial.

Vegetables are a source of carbohydrates, vitamins, and minerals. Varying in their nutritional content, darker vegetables with lower water content tend to provide more value. Parrots will enjoy both uncooked and cooked vegetables. Additionally, variability in presentation is also helpful. For example, corn could be presented on the cob one week; two weeks later, corn kernels can be part of a vegetable mix.

Fresh fruits and vegetables can form about half of your parrot's diet.

Vegetables that create an excellent basis for diet include the following:

artichoke	green and red peppers
asparagus	jicama
beans (garbanzo, kidney, peas, limas, black-eyed peas)	kale
	mustard greens
beet and beet greens	peas
bok choy	potato
broccoli	pumpkin
Brussels sprouts	radishes
cabbage	spinach
carrot and carrot tops	sprouts (all kinds)
cauliflower	squash
collards	Swiss chard
corn	turnip and turnip greens
cucumber	yam and sweet potato
dandelion greens	zucchini

Fruits provide quick energy and are a natural part of all parrot diets. Up to about 10 percent of your parrot's diet should be fruit. When feeding fruit, be aware that the sugar content does attract ants and bacteria. Fruit, along with cooked vegetables, is the source of quite a bit of the "sticky mess" in your bird's cage. Wipe up with soap and water after feeding fruit, and you'll be glad you did when cage cleaning time comes.

Fruits that are attractive to your birds, especially when fresh and in season, include the following:

apple	mango
apricot	melons (cantaloupe, honeydew, cassava, watermelon)
banana	
berries	papaya
citrus (lemon, orange, grapefruit, lime, tangerine)	peach
	pear
fig	persimmon
grape	pineapple
	pomegranate

Preparation

Fruits and vegetables, for parrots as for people, should be as clean and colorful as possible. Rather than regarding your bird as a consumer of your rejected produce, remember that your bird eats very little. It is not expensive to feed him well. Birds react to the soggy, the overripe, and the overcooked in the same way you do; the taste and texture just isn't right, and they just don't like it. Unless you are using organic produce, do scrub fruits and vegetables to remove pesticides and appearance-enhancing waxes.

Birds like variety, not only in what foods they eat, but also in their presentation. What works best is to vary the presentation of different suggested foods. One week, chop chard into small pieces. The next week, offer chard whole from a skewer or threaded between the cage

This Major Mitchell's cockatoo is about to enjoy a healthy meal of cooked grains, fruits, and green vegetables.

bars. Changing the form of the food, chopped to skewered, skewered to chopped, rolled in pellets, cut in different shapes, entices your bird to expand her appreciation of different foods.

People Foods

Your parrot wants to eat what you eat. Share a salad for dinner. If you eat broccoli, he will eat broccoli. If you eat a garbanzo bean, he will imitate you. Even small amounts of eggs, meat, fish, poultry, and yogurt can work for your bird. In other words, most human foods prepared from fresh ingredients and low in salt can be shared with your parrot. If you feed dairy products, do not feed more than a half-teaspoon (2.5 mL) in one meal because birds do not have the enzyme lactase that allows them to digest dairy products. For birds smaller than an Amazon parrot, reduce the amount proportionately. In other words, for a parakeet, one mouthful is enough dairy.

By the way, most of us feel compelled to feed our pets food that we eat because of the begging our parrots do. What's important to remember is that parrots beg because you are eating the food, and they are flock animals.

A few foods that are fine for you, in moderation, can be deadly for your bird. Alcohol or caffeine in any form is toxic to your bird. Chocolate is toxic, too. Even small amounts of these are not acceptable. Cured meats, fatty foods, and salted foods, such as potato chips, are not good for your parrot. Similarly, sugared foods, including cereal, cookies, cakes, and ice cream, are on the do-not-feed list.

Weaving edible leaves, such as lettuce, through the cage bars or laying them on top of the cage encourages your parrot to actively forage.

Vitamin and Mineral Supplements

If you're using a correctly formulated diet, supplements are neither necessary nor desirable. In fact, adding vitamins and minerals could harm your bird. Add supplements like cuttlebone, mineral blocks, and whole minerals only on your veterinarian's instructions. Although most people take some sort of supplement, most people do not eat a well-balanced diet. Because parrots' needs are not entirely intuitive to most of us, consider supplements as drugs and don't add them because you think they might be necessary. Add them only on your vet's recommendation.

Putting Together a Parrot Meal Plan

Providing the right variety of healthy food that your bird is eager to eat is the trick. Most experts agree that the essential nutrition for a companion bird comes from clean, fresh water; a basic diet of high quality pellets; and daily addition of fresh fruits, vegetables, protein, and small amounts of seed. Parrots need food available first thing in the morning and then again in the mid- to late afternoon as they prepare to roost for the night. Clean water must be available at all times.

An uncolored pelleted diet of the appropriate size is one-third of diet volume. One- to two-thirds of the diet should be fresh fruits and vegetables. Less than one-third of the diet should be seed and nuts.

Daily Feeding Routine

Feed your parrot twice each day and provide clean, fresh water morning and night. Parrots prefer to eat in the morning, after the sun begins to rise. In the afternoon, parrots will be ready to eat a couple of hours before sunset. Although companions cannot always stick to exactly this schedule, feeding close to these times is ideal. If you're not going to be home in time to feed in the evening, be sure that enough food is available that your parrot does not go hungry. However, the twice-daily routine is closest to what parrots in the wild do; also twice-daily feeding keeps your birds from picking at their food and eating only the choicest bits.

In the morning, feed the pellets and hang greens and other low-sugar foods for your bird to snack on during the day. After a night of fasting, pellets in the morning will likely be eaten completely if you do not overfeed. In the evening, provide a mix of vegetables and fruits. Once pellets are consumed, then offer fresh foods as entertainment and as a supplement. With 60 to 70 percent of the day's nutrition coming from a pellet diet, your parrot has 30 to 40 percent of a balanced and varied diet to look forward to each afternoon.

The question of how much to feed is always a concern. The best solution is to take this question to your veterinarian when you have your first appointment. Your veterinarian will be able to recommend

The Special Needs of Lories

Lories and lorikeets are nectivores, birds that feed on pollen, nectar, flowers, soft fruits, buds, berries, and some seeds and insects. For many people, the watery droppings that result from this diet suggest that these birds are better suited for the aviary outdoors instead of for the birdcage indoors. For others, the lories' active, often clownish personalities and fantastic colors allow them to overlook the mess.

Nectar products formulated specifically for lories and lorikeets are a key component in their diets. Fresh fruits are also important. In addition, a rich source of protein is important. Notice that the first ingredient on the list of foods for these charming birds is "pollen," a source of protein and critical to maintaining the health of your parrot.

Some keys to successful lory keeping include:

- Change food often to prevent spoilage. The food should be changed and the feeding vessel cleaned at least twice a day. During warm weather, wet food should be changed every four hours.
- It's a good idea to provide flowers and trees from the native habitat, such as grevilleas (*Grevillea* spp.), bottlebrushes (*Callistemon* spp.), and banksias (*Banksia* spp.), around your garden. Other edible flowers, such as hibiscus, should be offered as well.
- Lories enjoy fruits such as apples, pears, strawberries, grapes, melon, peaches, and cherries.
- Offering nectar formula for one to three hours once or twice a day will allow your lorikeet to eat sufficient quantities.

Consult your veterinarian about the specific diet that you plan to provide to your lory or lorikeet; however, here are some tips from long-time keepers of these species. You might consider these points and look very closely at the commercial diets formulated just for these birds.

- Sugars that are complex carbohydrates are important for maintaining healthy bacteria populations in the gut. Fruits and vegetables also contain complex sugars. Make sure the diet includes these.
- Although vitamin A is essential for healthy skin, eyes, gut, and reproductive and urinary tracts, an excess of vitamin A can be harmful. If you feed precursors to vitamin A, your bird converts only as much vitamin A as he requires, thus lowering the risk of toxicity.
- Choose a nectar diet with low iron content.
- Ask your veterinarian about the proper calcium-to-phosphorus ratio.
- Your bird's diet must contain fresh bee pollen.
- Consider mixing nectar with fruit and vegetable puree to add any nutritionally excellent but less preferred foods.
- Occasionally, the purees can be supplemented with a bit of wheat germ, live mealworms, or an insectivore diet.
- For variety, replace the fruit/vegetable puree with cooked brown rice, lentils, and split peas mixed with chopped fruits and vegetables and softened parrot pellets.
- Large chunks of favored produce, such as an ear of corn, an apple, or a completely new item can be both nutritious and enriching.

some amounts of different sorts of food that will work well for your bird's age, health condition, and expected living conditions. For example, a bird who has a large flight cage may burn more calories each day than a bird who does not fly or exercise much.

In addition, good-quality pellet manufacturers will always tell you how much diet to feed. For example, for cockatiels, 1 ½–3 tsp. (2–5 g) of pellets is recommended. For an Amazon, 1 ½–3 Tbs. (15–30 g) is recommended.

For other types of foods, including vegetable mixes or cooked mixes, the old adage, "never try to eat anything larger than your head" works. For a cockatiel, 1 Tbs. (14 g) of mix is quite a meal. For an Amazon, perhaps 2–4 Tbs. or ⅛–¼ c (28–57 g) is plenty. If you look at a measuring tablespoon, you'll see that it is about the size of the cockatiel's head. The same is true for a quarter-cup measure and an Amazon's head. This is not science, but a way to remember how much food is reasonable to expect your bird to eat. However, if your bird is always eating everything, something is wrong. Either you're not feeding enough, you're not feeding the right foods, or your bird is losing his nutrition through activity, keeping warm, or fighting illness.

Home-Cooked Diets

For variety, many bird keepers make home-cooked diets that include fresh-cooked beans, rice, corn, and pasta served with vegetables and poultry. When feeding cooked food, remember that bacteria can grow quickly. To ensure your bird is safe, especially in hot conditions, remove uneaten cooked foods before bacteria can grow.

One of the best home-cooked diet people is Pamela Clark. Ms. Clark, a veterinary technician and an authority on companion parrot nutrition, makes several points about the types of cooked and uncooked homemade foods that she uses. You have only to look at her birds fed in this way to see that they are both emotionally and physically healthy, with gorgeous plumage. The keys to her results are balance, variety, and freshness. In addition, she chops the ingredients so that the mix always looks the same, even when new ingredients have been added. This allows birds to continue to accept a wide variety of nutritious fruits and vegetables.

Pamela Clark's Chop Mix

Chop is a mix of cooked whole grains, cooked beans, and finely chopped vegetables. Using this to supplement your parrot's formulated diets is easy because a batch can be made ahead and frozen. The recipe can be

Grit: Unnecessary

Many people believe that feeding grit to birds is crucial for digestion. This idea comes from raising poultry. Chickens eat whole seeds, requiring small bits of grit to grind off the coating. Parrots, who remove the hulls and eat only the soft inner matter, do not crush seeds in their digestive tracts. So, they do not benefit from grit in their diet.

To confuse matters further, reference books encourage the feeding of grit to parrots. Many avian veterinarians in the United States advise against feeding grit, believing it is at best unhelpful and at worst harmful for psittacines.

modified as you like, although the final mix should contain approximately 40 percent whole grains, 10 to 15 percent beans, and 50 to 60 percent vegetables. The exact proportions don't matter, but the overall goal is to create a foraging mix that provides excellent nutrition without throwing the parrot into increased hormone production due to increased carbohydrates. Therefore, the type of grains you use is important. I recommend sticking to kamut and quinoa, although others can be included in moderation and for variety.

Many parrot species occasionally eat insects in the wild. You can buy mealworms and other feeder bugs at most pet stores.

1. Soak one or two types of beans overnight and then cook until tender (not mushy). Suggestions include pink beans, red beans, or pinto beans. Drain these well and allow to cool. Garbanzo beans are a favorite with parrots, but take longer to cook. I usually use canned and rinsed garbanzo beans and add these to my chop right before serving.

2. Cook whole grains using a rice cooker or the appropriate proportions of water to grain on the stovetop for the time suggested for each grain. Recommended grains include brown rice, kamut, farro, hulled barley, wheat berries, and quinoa. Don't overcook. Fluff to separate grains after cooking and allow them to cool.

3. Finely chop a variety of fresh vegetables. A food processor can be used for this. You can use almost any vegetable but avoid using vegetables that contain a lot of water (cucumber, chayote squash) because your final mix will be too wet.

4. Mix whole grains, cooked beans, and vegetables together thoroughly and package in serving-sized portions. Freeze for up to three months.

5. Variety is the spice of life. You can vary this mix to keep your parrot interested by adding any of the following: spices (cayenne pepper, cinnamon, curry powder, chili powder, ginger, or turmeric added to the grains while cooking), whole-grain pasta (helps soak up some liquid), raw and uncooked oat groats (added right before freezing or right before serving), a few pieces of fruit (added before serving), pieces of vegetables that don't freeze well (beets, cucumber, sweet potato, or winter squash added before serving), seeds (chia, flax, hemp, milk thistle), and other items (dried goji berries, frozen corn or peas, or pomegranate seeds, sprouts.)

Another great source for information on making chop for parrots, which is more extensive than these instructions, can be found at: http://lovinglifefromscratch.blogspot.com/2013/07/chop-all-things-good-for-birdie.html.

Obesity

The amount of food your bird eats each day doesn't vary much. Whether your bird eats properly or whether you provide a breakfast of seeds full of calories and fat (the equivalent of donuts for birds), birds consume a set number of calories. If your bird focuses on the high-fat foods first, he may absorb all the calories needed with the poor nutritional value food and leave good foods in his dish.

Unlike wild birds who fly many miles each day to forage, most companion birds get relatively little daily exercise; accordingly, their caloric requirements are lower.

After a short time with your parrot friend, you'll realize his preference for fatty foods. Sunflower seeds and millet make delicious snacks, and sometimes we overindulge our friends. What we may not realize is that we are creating their obesity problem. If you love your parrot, use some tough love on yourself—give your feathered friend fruits and vegetable treats rather than seeds.

Pamela Clark's Cooked Grain Mix

The second mix Ms. Clark regularly feeds to her birds in late afternoon, every second day, and she removes the uneaten portion before bed because cooked foods will grow bacteria.

The basic mix:

1 cup quinoa (a grain high in calcium and protein that is found in health food stores)

2 cups water

2 cups grated yams (or other vegetable high in vitamin A)

fresh corn kernels cut from two cobs corn or 1 cup frozen corn

1 cup grated green vegetables

½ cup grated nuts (Brazil, almonds, walnuts)

½ cup unhulled sesame seed

½ cup canary seed

Bring the water to a boil and add quinoa. Bring back to a boil, cover, turn heat down and simmer for 5 minutes. Add yams; cover again and cook for 10 minutes longer or until liquid is absorbed. Turn into a bowl, add other ingredients, and mix gently. Serve warm, but check carefully for hot spots that could burn your feathered friend.

Pamela Clark's Corn Muffins

About twice a week, Ms. Clark feeds a cornbread muffin prepared with a standard cornbread recipe, using whole grain cornmeal and whole-wheat flour. An endless number of nutritious additions can be added to a basic mix, thereby once again increasing the variety your parrot gets in his diet. Ingredients Ms. Clark frequently adds to this mix include grated vegetables and fruits, sesame seeds, pumpkin seeds, raw sunflower seeds, creamed corn, grated low-fat cheese, diced green chilies. These freeze well and will thaw in the refrigerator overnight. If you cook in small muffin tins with a paper liner, you minimize the mess and provide a fun addition for your bird—the paper on the muffin.

Organic Produce: Necessary or Not?

The use of organic produce is not just a matter of conscience. Rather, the use of organic produce is about keeping herbicides, pesticides, and other chemicals meant to prevent or disrupt insect growth out of the mouths of the vulnerable. Because of the size of birds and the relative amounts of anything required to create a problem, a bird keeper might consider using organic produce for anything that he does not intend to peel. In addition, purchasing organic produce is a way of voting with your dollars, supporting those producers who farm in a less intensive and more sensitive way.

Parrots enjoy eating with their people, but it's best to feed yours on a play stand near the table rather than actually on the table.

One way to determine when it's most important to purchase organic produce is to use the Environmental Working Group's (EWG) assessment. The *EWG's Shopper's Guide to Pesticides in Produce* will help you determine which fruits and vegetables have the most pesticide residues and are the most important to buy organic.

Listed below are the "Dirty Dozen"; you can lower your pesticide intake by avoiding these most contaminated fruits and vegetables and instead choosing the least contaminated produce, which are listed below as "Clean Fifteen." Alternatively, always eat organic produce.

EWG expanded the Dirty Dozen with a Plus category to highlight two crops—domestically grown summer squash and leafy greens—which did not meet traditional criteria but were commonly contaminated with pesticides exceptionally toxic to the nervous system.

Dirty Dozen		The Clean 15	
apples	nectarines	asparagus	kiwi
bell peppers	peaches	avocado (despite being "clean," never feed your parrot avocado. This food is toxic for them.)	mango
cherry tomatoes	potatoes	cabbage	onion
celery	spinach	cantaloupe	papaya
cucumbers	strawberries	corn	peas
grapes	kale and collard greens	eggplant	pineapple
hot peppers	summer squash	grapefruit	sweet potatoes

This information is adapted from http://www.ewg.org/foodnews/summary.php, as well as background information from the author's book, *Pets and the Planet*.

Preparation Time

Putting information about parrot diets into practice seems as though it might take forever. On the contrary, with a little practice and a routine, you will feed your parrot in fine style in an average of ten minutes a day. The keys are establishing a routine of purchasing a small amount of a wide variety of fruits and vegetables; washing, drying and chopping vegetables and fruit so that you have enough for up to four days at a time; and having enough food and water dishes so that one set is always clean.

Getting Your Bird to Try New Foods

When a parrot has been raised on a limited diet, several problems present themselves when you try to get your bird to try new foods: (1) your parrot does not recognize the other "foods" as food, (2) his habits in eating a limited diet may be deeply entrenched, and (3) broadening the diet can cause both confusion and weight loss, serious problems for your new pet.

The effort you spend broadening your bird's diet will be worthwhile, but the process requires time and patience. Consult your veterinarian about when and how you can start the conversion.

Several methods can help you help your bird to recognize these new "foods" as food and overcome his reluctance to try something new. Dine with your picky eater. You eat the food. Offer him the food. Birds learn what is good to eat from their families. Use this natural search for guidance to your advantage by eating new foods in front of your bird, making clear how much you enjoy the food. Offer to share some with your bird and continue eating the food yourself.

Incorporate the new diet into the plate with your bird's normal diet. Although your bird may choose the bits that look familiar, he will become accustomed to seeing the new foods.

Stir pellets or other new foods in a favored soft food, such as strained carrots or applesauce. This is a way to entice your bird to sample the new pellets, learn that they are food, and make the desired switch. Although this method is not a good long-term solution because of spoilage, pureed fruits and vegetables or fruit juice-soaked pellets trigger learning and will eventually work with even the most stubborn eater

Press small amounts of millet or other beloved seed into a warm vegetable mash, banana, or other new, soft food. In the process of eating the preferred food, your parrot may develop a taste for the surrounding food as well.

Place the new food on a mirror. Some companions have had success with this method. Your parrot sees another parrot eating the same food!

The Importance of Fresh Water

A bird's body is about eighty percent water. Although water is a simple nutrient, it is so important that a loss of 10 to 15 percent of the body's water content can result in death. Water keeps your parrot's body systems working. Without water, he can't digest his food to release energy, move nutrients around his body, or regulate his temperature. Although you may rarely see your bird drink, he does so several times each day. Most birds drink in the morning and again at night before sleep. Clean, fresh drinking water should be available to your bird at all times.

What Are Probiotics and Are They Important?

Probiotics are recommended as one of the "Integrative Therapies" in *Clinical Avian Medicine*. In particular, they are suggested as a way to repopulate a parrot's intestinal tract with bacteria naturally found there to aid in the digestive process. After the use of antibiotics or a chronic digestive disease, probiotics, especially avian-specific products, are recommended. It is possible that parrots can benefit in some ways from an active yogurt culture. However, like any sort of "therapy," discuss the use of these products with your veterinarian on your annual well-bird visit.

Probiotics are cultured forms of the bacteria that are normally found in the bowels of healthy nonstressed animals; these cultures are prepared as a medication. The probiotics reintroduce these bacteria to an animal's digestive system after times of stress, disease, or the use of antibiotics, when the normal bacterial population is disrupted.

Other uses of probiotics include in young birds to help stimulate appetite and to help produce digestive enzymes and B vitamins. These effects help the birds to get the maximum nutrition from their diet. There is some evidence that probiotics stimulate general immunity.

Other uses for probiotics suggested by the producers of these remedies include just before and just after stress of transport, and during molting, breeding, and young birds' fledging.

How Much Water Is Enough?

A bird the size of a dusky-headed parrot or a cockatiel drinks at least three teaspoons (15 mL) of water each day. A larger bird, a Patagonian conure, for example, might drink more than twice that—7 teaspoons (35 mL) or so each day. An increase in exercise or room temperature or a lowering of humidity will prompt your bird to drink more water. Although your bird could survive a day without food, a day without water might cause irreversible harm. For that reason, some parrot keepers always double up on the water vessels, keeping both a bottle and a bowl of water available for their parrot.

More About Water's Functions

Inside the body's tissues, water is a major component of blood that transports nutrients and oxygen to the cells. Water is required for the chemical breakdown of food into energy and into the components your parrot needs to build his body. Water is also major component of the urine and feces that eliminate toxins and food waste from the body. Water also provides lubrication for the joints and tissues, especially the lungs.

5

BEHAVIOR, TRAINING, AND LIFE WITH A PARROT

nderstanding behavior and communicating effectively is a difficult proposition even within a species. For example, think about how easily a simple request to a family member to be quiet for just a moment can escalate into a major incident. Or, how often has an act of kindness been misinterpreted as romantic interest. Now, imagine trying to communicate across species, where not only the vocal language is entirely foreign, but also the body language is different. Some communication experts say that 85 percent of communication is body language. Fantastic. What does that raised crest mean? Does it mean curiosity, alarm, or romance?

This is the challenge that parrots and their people have in establishing a long-term relationship of mutual trust. Not only do the parties speak different languages, but they also have different species tendencies, genetic conditioning, and environmental conditioning—and one has feathers that are raised and lowered in a series of signals that seem more complicated than a cryptographic master code. What gets the people and parrots through the miscues and misunderstandings is the value they place on the relationship.

What Is Behavior?

Basically, behavior is what an animal does. In this case, behavior is what your parrot does. The words we put to what an animal does often are interpretations of an animal's state of mind rather than simply a description. Behavior is a blend of genetics and environment, with the environment contributing the learning portion of behavior. As you and your parrot spend your life together, you and he are learning all the time.

Understanding your parrot's body language will help you build a relationship with him.

Parrots are perfectly adapted for their wild environments: they follow innate behaviors such as perching, climbing, and flapping wings. Parrots have a language all their own that works for them in the wild. However, in our homes, we are not such good interpreters of parrot language. And parrots, not being "people pleasers," are not motivated to do what makes us happy by learning our language. So, that leaves us to learn what the eye, head, and feather movements really indicate.

Many parrots, including Amazons, spread out their tail feathers as a display of excitement or aggression.

The Difference Between Behavior and Training

Parrot parents want to understand their parrots' behavior, in the same way that parents want to understand their children. Part of this desire is to make life together easier, and part of this desire comes from the rewards that a caring relationship provides. Like children, parrots are individuals. No book can teach you how to handle your parrot in your specific situation, although some basic principles of parrot handling are helpful. In addition to the basics, quiet, patient observation and experimentation are the best teachers. And, when you're feeling rushed, curtail your decisions and your physical interaction with a parrot. Set a timer for fifteen minutes and relax. Instead of picking up your parrot or squeezing in a training session that will not end well, spend a relaxing fifteen minutes; you with your eyes closed, sitting in your favorite chair, and your parrot in his cage on his perch, listening to your description of a favorite restful place or some soothing music. You'll both be the better for it.

In human relationships, unfailing courtesy is often cited as what keeps marriages together for thirty or forty years. You might think of consistent asking for and rewarding behaviors in parrots as a form of unfailing courtesy. Your reacting appropriately to your parrot's signals is an important part of this courtesy. When you pay attention to his body language, and he works with you as you do your daily parrot-care things, reward your bird with soothing praise when he does something well—this is the basis for a successful relationship.

Although we speak about training as if it is solely about your parrot, training is about both parrot and person. Training is a learning to communicate. Training is a way to develop a relationship that will last a lifetime. Training is also a way to get beyond the difficult times that you will have together. If your parrot is well trained, and if you are conditioned to ask for and reward desired behaviors from your bird, the training will supersede the daily ups and downs in your emotional and physical states.

Normal Parrot Behavior

Parrots communicate through contact calls and feather position. Parrots often tell us to back away or that they are frightened by something that we are doing, but we often mistake their signals for something else. Rather than biting, parrots do try to back off intrusive beings by raising their feathers, staring, raising a foot, or growling. However, when these signals are not respected, the next move is a slashing strike with the beak. One very important skill for a new bird parent is to learn parrot body language.

Another important skill for parrot parents is to learn the importance of contact calls. In the wild, parrots keep in touch with their family members through contact calls. Birds expect an answer to their calls, and when calls go unanswered, this often escalates to screaming. These natural behaviors are "built in" to the parrot. No amount of training will cause parrots to give up their contact calls or their feather posturing to back off those who come too close.

When, as a parrot parent, you can't interpret the contact calls and feather positions, you may need help. Experts who understand natural parrot behavior can observe the interactions between a bird and his companion and then give suggestions to help parrot parents eliminate unhelpful behaviors in their parrots. Behavioral analysts teach parrot parents what a certain behavior means and useful ways to respond to it. At the end of this book are resources available to help you with your parrot behavior issues. However, there is much you can do to educate yourself to understand the fascinating language that parrots use to communicate their needs and desires.

A nervous or frightened parrot usually stands tall and flattens his feathers against his body.

Parrot Body Language

Parrot body language is a "must-learn" for companions. Think about it: Without lips and other mobile facial parts or meaningful tone of voice, birds say it all with their bodies. The trick is learning the subtleties, which is where the beak hits the skin, so to speak.

The Comfortable Parrot

Comfortable parrots do not perch with the slick, feather-tight vigilance of prey animals. A relaxed and confident parrot allows his feathers to relax just enough to give your parrot a slightly pudgy look. Other signs of a happy, contented, or sleepy bird include preening, tail shaking, stretching, beak grinding, and standing on one foot. Parrots often engage in these behaviors just prior to taking a midday nap or roosting for the night.

The Aggressive or Excited Parrot

Parrots show aggression with threat displays that include standing tall, spreading wings, raising crest or nape feathers, and swaying back and forth. Open-beak lunging or lunge biting is very aggressive behavior. Before a parrot moves to this phase, he will show more subtle, smaller displays of each characteristic. If you ignore these signs, he will escalate his behavior. If you learn the signs and back off at the

Socializing your parrot makes him fun to handle and interact with, and this in turn allows him to have a full life.

beginning of a threat display, you'll find the posture returns to that of "the comfortable parrot."

The difference between the fluffed feathers of a relaxed bird and the erect feathers of aggression is clear if you know what to look for. Fluffed feathers blend, while erect feathers stand out individually or in groups. When aggressive, birds normally erect the feathers on the crest and the nape of the neck. Excited birds also flash colorful parts of the body, such as wings or tail, as warnings. When excited or aggressive, parrots narrow and expand their pupils, sometimes called *eye-pinning*. In birds with irises lighter than the pupils, you can see pupil dilation. In parrots with irises as dark as their pupils, you do not.

Excitement sometimes looks similar to aggression in parrots, but an excited parrot is more likely to be very vocal. With the aggressive or excited bird, the best approach is no approach at all. Let the bird, overloaded with one stimulus or another, calm down in the same way you would give a small child a time-out to let his emotions settle.

The Stressed or Fearful Parrot

Fearful parrots stand stiffly, feathers flat against the body. The parrot may hold his head high and his wings away from the body, sometimes quivering. Repeatedly raising one foot or shifting weight from one foot to another is another sign of a parrot frightened or confused about what to do.

To prevent the problems that result from long-term stress, parrot parents need to discover the cause of the stress and eliminate it. If the stress is caused by something that should be normal in a companion parrot's life, then get some help from a professional to first remove and then reintroduce these factors so that they no longer cause negative reaction.

Socializing and Bonding with Your Bird

Socialization is the process by which a bird learns the life skills necessary to be a companion parrot, and these skills include learning about food, language, and acceptable behavior. Young parrots are socialized by their parents and their flock. Since you are (or should be) the leader of your bird's flock, it is up to you to teach your bird life skills after he leaves his avian parents.

Like a well-socialized child, a well-socialized companion bird can and should lead a full life: he should be accustomed to traveling by car, willingly interact with and go to a variety of people, eat a variety of foods, behave pleasantly during cage maintenance, and know how to have fun and let loose at playtime.

Socializing Requires Some Training

Beginning with a well-socialized baby parrot is a good start. You've avoided starting with a disadvantage. A well-socialized baby parrot is confident, fledged, and fully weaned, willingly eating an excellent diet. This terrific start needs to be followed up with the next level of socialization.

Baby parrots should be trained in daily short sessions; however, there's no reason the training shouldn't look and feel like play. Out of sight of the cage and play gym, work with your bird to get him to step up onto different persons' hands, to step onto a perch held in the hand (sometimes called stick training), and to step onto various surfaces so that the baby becomes accustomed to as wide a range of surfaces as possible. Take your baby parrot to various locations in the house. Have him ride on the laundry basket and step onto the top of your clean washer; let him watch you fold the laundry.

The training needs to be consistent, and it lasts for the parrot's lifetime, not just for a few weeks. Continued training and consistent handling keeps your parrot well-socialized. Without reinforcement, the parrot forgets what he's been taught. Using verbal commands and reinforcing occasionally with a treat or other favored reward ensures that your basic training remains fresh.

This pattern of training, including stick training, will make future problems easier to handle. If your bird goes through an aggressive period (and he will), the stick training will keep him interactive and your fingers from being sore from bites. Consistent expectations and training, as with a child, serve a bird very well and allow him to be a delightful companion.

It's best for everyone in the house to handle a parrot so he doesn't become bonded to just one person.

Why Parrots Need to be Well Socialized

Well-socialized parrots are adaptable to new circumstances and flexible in dealing with change. Parrots need some amount of routine, such as their twelve hours of darkness at night, a safe environment, and the diet and companionship they crave. However, parrots need some variability to remain adaptable to change. Variety in the diet, variety in the routine, and variety in handlers are examples of excellent and interesting changes that can help keep your parrot adaptable.

Because of their long life spans, parrots will experience change. Most people move several times during their life, take vacations, run out of the favored pellets, or have to change the routine because of a change in family circumstance. Your parrot needs the ability to make those changes. This is why most parrot lovers suggest that you include your bird in as many sorts of safe activities as possible.

A greater change comes when parrots need to move to a new home, given that they often outlive their caretakers. If basic behaviors such as easy entry into and exit from his cage have been taught and your parrot has been socialized to interact successfully with other people, he can make a transition to a new home with great success. Of course, this is rarely a planned transition. However, like a well-behaved pet of any sort, the quality of the pet's manners and the pleasantry of interaction make finding a new home for a pet in need much easier.

Avoid letting your parrot dominate your life, to the exclusion of other people. This results in a parrot who does not tolerate being handled by others. Most birds interact best with people who make them feel secure and safe. A bird's trust is earned through consistently gentle, accepting, and patient handling.

If you are the bird's favored person, you have the responsibility to help him have rewarding relationships with others in the home. Would you rather have a bird you can take anywhere and who can be fed by anyone, or a bird who looks beautiful in his cage but is impossible to handle? Socialization makes the difference.

Family Socialization Zen

Whatever your parrot's level of socialization, there you are. Don't sweat what you haven't accomplished. Set aside a few minutes each day on improving your bird's socialization skills. (These

---

Keeping Training Fun for You and Your Bird

Training is fun when sessions:

- are short, such as 5–7 minutes or less
- take place during times when you both want to be together
- begin with an easy request
- end with an easy request
- present the most difficult request in the middle
- take place in a private place so they are successful

Keep your voice light and cheerful throughout the training session. If your parrot gets distracted or frustrated, give him an easy command or two and end the session quickly.

In short, training sessions are successful when you both feel successful and happy.

activities are useful at any time, but if you're exhausted or nervous, don't decide to do a training session. Select another sort of activity that is less hands on.)

Sit near the cage while you read aloud to your kids or watch television. When the bird shows interest, repeat the phrase or sound that stimulated him.

Spend a few minutes feeding your bird through the cage bars. Choose a food he enjoys, but not your training treats. Talk with your bird using a quiet, calm voice.

If your bird is not confident with all members of your family, have the "less favored" person try one of these activities:

- Take your parrot to a different room of your house each day. Point out interesting sights, including mirrors, pictures, or windows.
- Perch the parrot nearby while the "less favored" person works on a project (peeling vegetables, working a crossword puzzle, or answering e-mail). Strike up a conversation. Perhaps provide a few treats.
- Parrots are flock animals, and they learn through imitation. Give your parrot the message that everyone in your home is safe. Hand your bird to others as often as possible. Provide the new person with your bird's favorite toy or a treat to reward and occupy him.
- Play a quiet, gentle game that behaviorist Sally Blanchard calls "warm potato": Pass birdie to a family member. Take him back. Pass him to another family member. Let parrot learn he's safe in the hands of any family member or friend.

As you try these activities, watch your parrot's appearance. The position of his feathers, his body posture, and his vocalization reveals your parrot's state of mind.

A small piece of food your parrot loves, such as a bit of nut or seed, makes a good training treat.

Why Train Your Parrot?

Each time you interact with your parrot, either you are training your bird or your bird is training you. Training is a system of reaction and reward. Just as with your children, if they whine and you give in, you're teaching them that whining works. If you preempt the whining with some exercise followed by a quiet period, then you're doing a good job with your training. Not only are you preventing the whining, but you're also avoiding rewarding bad behavior. The process works in a similar manner with your bird. If you know she gets agitated at 4:30, then, at 4:15, take her to get a bit of exercise and a change of scenery. Immediately afterward, offer her dinner. Similarly, when you ask your bird to return to her cage and she does it, reward her. You won't believe the fun you and your parrot will have.

The benefits of doing even a small amount of training with your new parrot are enormous. Because your bird is trained to step up, you are able to bring him in and out of his cage and move him around your home easily. The benefit to your bird is a more interesting life.

For you, training means that you have a pleasant time as you go about your bird's care and seek his companionship; the benefit for your bird is that he has a companion who enjoys spending time with him. Training sessions keep your bird mentally stimulated because he is engaging his mind during the session. An intelligent animal needs stimulation of his mind as well as his body.

Training also helps you vary your bird's daily routine. Not only can training be stimulating and fun for your bird, but training also enlarges your bird's horizons. As a result of training, your bird is able to accompany you to more places and participate in more activities. *Target training* takes an anxiety-producing activity—like putting your bird inside his carrier—and turns the activity into one that feels more like a fun game.

Other benefits from doing some training daily include:

- helps to maintain the sweetness of your young bird
- helps to build on the positive aspects of an older bird's behavior
- gives you a way to handle your bird in stressful circumstances
- helps maintain the handler's awareness of reward timing
- reinforces handler's commitment to make success easy for his or her bird

Training Techniques

To emphasize the necessity of positive reinforcement, you should know that punishment is not a concept that parrots understand. There is reinforcement and lack of reinforcement—a reason to comply that makes sense to the parrot and no reason to comply. Because of your parrot's intelligence,

Why Punishment Doesn't Work

Parrots are not like dogs. Parrots don't care whether they please you or not—they want what they want. The trick is understanding what your parrot wants and using that to your advantage. You could think about bird handling as a game of tactics.

It is critical to realize that punishment is never a part of training your parrot. You can't spank a bird. You can't make him feel ashamed. Terrifying your parrot will multiply his behavior problems exponentially. Punishing him will only make him afraid of you, and that fear will eventually make him aggressive.

If parrots are new to you, you must develop the skill of thinking like a parrot: parrots use the same rules as two-year-old children. If you have it, I want it. If I have it, you can't have it. If you want it, it's mine. This is how parrots think. They don't understand the concept of punishment. They don't understand shame. They do understand the concept of "mine" and "no" to whatever it is you want. To avoid behavior problems and encourage good behavior, you have to think like a parrot—use two-year-old logic.

For some parrots, head scratches work as well or better than food treats as training rewards.

you must think strategically to enlist cooperation, just as you have to think strategically to get cooperation from a small child. You offer a choice of complying or not complying. Complying earns him a positive reward. Not complying earns him nothing. Trainers and parrot parents using these training techniques try to construct situations that will help the parrot choose to comply. Before any training can occur, the companion needs to set the parrot up for success. This means that training must occur in a place that is not one the parrot needs to defend. In addition, parrots need a quiet and private place to be able to focus exclusively on the lesson that you will present and work on.

Training is a continuous process, one that you could think of as being a series of linked steps. A parrot parent allows familiarization with objects or places so that they are not frightening to the bird. A behavior is broken down into very small steps that are taught sequentially and in a patient, unhurried manner. Consistency in training is a key attribute to success. The parrot parent must ask for a behavior in the same way each time. The small step that is being asked must be either rewarded immediately or marked immediately and then rewarded. Training sessions must be kept short, upbeat, and positive. You may train two or three times each day. The more fun your parrot has in training, the more he will look forward to your short, daily or several times daily sessions.

Use Positive Reinforcement

Positive reinforcement means praising the bird immediately when you see the behavior you want and ignoring the behavior that you don't want. The concept of positive reinforcement and the basic steps of training are not difficult. What is difficult is to remember the primary basic truth about training: every interaction is training. Either you are teaching your parrot good habits, or you are teaching poor habits. Teaching your parrot good habits means that you do three things.

First, think before you ask your parrot to do something. Put your parrot in a situation that helps him decide to cooperate with you. In other words, set him up for success.

Second, approach your request in a relaxed, positive manner instead of in a hurried, tense manner.

Third, provide an immediate positive reinforcement for complying with what you've asked.

The Bridge

To highlight the desired behavior, create what behaviorists call a bridge. Saying "Good job!" is a common bridge. Some people also use, "good bird," or "yes." The important point is that the word needs to be unique enough so that the bird doesn't hear you use it in conversation. This is the reason few people use "yes" anymore. (Think of how many times you say that during a telephone conversation in front of your bird's cage.) The first part of the training is to establish the bridge. In other words, your bird needs to associate the words you choose as a bridge—whether it's "good job" or "Vulcan"—with a reward, which is a tiny treat.

You need this because you cannot always get the treat to the bird fast enough to let him know which of the various behaviors he did is the reason for his reward. It is important to be consistent, always offering a reward for the desired behavior.

Reinforcers

Positive reinforcement helps your parrot associate complying with your request with a pleasant consequence. A positive reinforcer can be anything from your bridge—"Good bird!"—to a scratch on the head, a piece of nut, or being allowed to chew a favorite toy. For example, if Parrot steps onto your hand willingly, reward him with a scratch on his head (assuming he enjoys a good head scratch). Or, stepping onto your hand could mean that he gets to go to his play gym, which is somewhere he wants to go. In that case, maybe returning to the cage needs a stronger positive reinforcement, such as a piece of apple or an almond.

What creates positive reinforcement, and the necessary strength of the reinforcer, depends on what your bird, at that time, views as desirable and not desirable to do. For example, in training a new behavior, strong reinforcement is needed at the beginning. As your parrot understands what you want and perhaps finds the behavior itself rewarding, the reinforcement can be given periodically, and the reinforcement can be a progressively weaker reward. For example, you might reward a well-established behavior, such as stepping onto your hand, with a treat reward very infrequently—once in every ten times, for example. However, when you are teaching a new behavior, you need stronger and very frequent rewards. When a parrot does something that you regard as a breakthrough,

Good Training Treats

What makes a good training treat is something your bird is crazy about, something small, and something that can be eaten quickly. To be a good motivator, a training treat needs to be a highly preferred food. For some parrots, this is a peanut or a piece of sunflower seed. During a training session, you won't want to give a whole peanut or sunflower seed. First, removing the shells takes too long. Second, an entire peanut or sunflower seed is too much. Even if the food is a favorite, your bird will fill up on this quickly. Break the peanut halves into very tiny pieces, and break a hulled sunflower seed in half at least once. If your bird is a parakeet, a single millet seed might be enough. If your bird is a cockatoo, a half a sunflower seed is plenty.

Training your parrot to step up onto a perch or stick is one of the most useful behaviors you can teach him.

then it's time to give a very fine reward. Think about it. When you ask for something that your bird is disinclined to do, but he does it—even a bit, even hesitatingly—you want him to remember that when he did it, he got a great reward. So give him the whole dang nut! You won't do that every time, but the size of the reward should vary with the size of the accomplishment. Make sense?

Consider Boundaries

Life with your parrot will involve training, whether you train your parrot or whether your parrot trains you. What usually happens is that, when you're not paying attention, you're being trained. For the new parrot parent, the temptation is to allow any behavior that appears cute or affectionate. The trouble is that, as with any creature, once the barriers to behavior have been breached, it's difficult to repair them. In other words, consider the behavior that you believe you'll be willing to live with and set the boundaries inside. You can always allow things to be "looser" in the future.

Training Useful Behaviors

There are many behaviors you might want to train your bird to do. Start with two simple and necessary behaviors; these can serve as a basis for everything that follows. Stick training and step up/down are useful behaviors every parrot should know, and you should reinforce them periodically.

Stick Training

Having your parrot willingly step onto a stick you present is important. Although many birds know how to step onto a hand, most of them have never been taught to step onto a stick; for some birds, this is a daunting prospect. Why a stick and not just your hand? When your parrot is frightened or injured, you can ask him to step onto the stick instead of your hand; this limits the probability that you will be bitten. Another common situation occurs when someone unknown to your bird needs to move him. If your bird will step onto the stick for the stranger, that person can work with your bird productively and confidently.

To do any type of training, the best beginning is to move your bird to a space out of sight of his cage or any frequently used space. I suggest a guest room or bathroom as neutral places. These spaces also allow you to close the door so that you are not disturbed or distracted.

Set Up for Training

Training should be done from a T-stand or from a similar sort of perch. Allow your parrot to settle onto the stand. Keep training sessions short—five minutes or so. Be sure to stop on a positive experience.

Training requires a reward. If your bird will work for food, then take tiny pieces of his favorite treat. Put those in your pocket, so they are readily accessible to you.

Your goals for stick training are twofold: (1) to acclimate your bird to the stick and (2) to entice your bird to stand comfortably on the stick.

Step-by-Step Stick Training

Holding the stick in one hand by your side, give your bird a treat. Say, "Good job." Feed a treat. The words "good job," should be said immediately at the time you see the behavior you want to reward. In this case, you are rewarding the bird for remaining calm in the presence of the stick.

Move the stick closer. If your parrot remains relaxed, say "Good job." Feed another treat.

Show your parrot the stick. "Good job." Feed another treat.

If your parrot shows any concern about the stick, continue to work with the stick, but keep the stick away from him until he relaxes. Depending on his experience with sticks, he may be relaxed from the beginning, or he may take weeks to relax.

When your parrot shows no concern about the stick, place it slightly higher than the T-stand and have your parrot stretch toward the stick to claim his treat. Always use "Good job" (or your chosen bridge) before you give the treat.

Always have your bird work a little harder for the next treat. Keep the stick higher than the t-stand, as parrots prefer to step higher, not lower.

Continue moving the treat back each time until your parrot must step onto the stick to take the treat.

Training your parrot to do a few tricks, such as playing dead, is fun for both of you.

Once your parrot has done this, place the stick lower than the t-stand and have him step onto the t-stand. "Good job." Give the treat.

At this stage, reinforce the behavior for one or two sessions. For future sessions, present the stick and say "Step up." When he steps onto the stick, say "Good job." Give the treat.

As you continue training, perhaps mixing in some other behaviors, reduce the frequency of treating to every second or third time.

Once the behavior is learned, reinforce this behavior with practice in fairly frequent training sessions. Once your parrot hits a cranky stage in development, you'll be happy that moving your beloved hormonal parrot via stick is an option.

Step Up and Down

The most frequent request you will make of your parrot to step onto and off your hand. As before, use a T-stand for your training sessions. As you train your bird to step onto your hand, you want him to step off easily. Once he steps on and off your hand easily, you can alternate this behavior with the analogous behavior involving the stick and stepping from one hand to the other.

If you have succeeded in stick training your parrot, this training should be easier. The goal is that when you say, "Up," no matter where your bird is, he should raise his foot to step onto your hand or the offered stick.

The trickier part of this exercise is to have the bird willingly leave your hand. I use the command, "Down." In the beginning, have your parrot step onto your hand, step onto the stick, and then step down. Your parrot will probably prefer leaving the stick to leaving your hand.

Use the same principles as in the stick training. Train for five minutes or less, up to several times each day, if you like and if your bird is willing. Treat with the preferred food every time until the behavior is established; then gradually reduce the treat for compliance to an occasional event.

If your parrot reliably steps up onto your arm, you will be able to interact with him much more than if he does not.

Step-by-Step Step-up Training

At the T-stand, place your hand, index and third finger parallel to the ground and parallel to the T-stand crossbar, at the level of your parrot's lower chest. Say, "Up." If needed, touch your parrot's chest with your extended fingers but don't press his chest; pressing his chest is a negative stimulus and can make the parrot fearful of hands. Most parrots will step onto your hand willingly. Say, "Good job." Then, remove the treat from your pocket and reward your parrot's behavior.

Use the stick, or if that seems too complicated, use the T-stand and place your parrot so that the stick or crossbar is just above your extended fingers where he is perched.

Say, "Down." If necessary, use the treat as a lure to move him in the proper direction. Say, "Good job." Give a reinforcing treat.

Most birds require very few sessions to learn these commands. Be consistent. Work a few minutes each time, and always end on a success. Congratulations. "Good job!"

Other Useful Behaviors

In addition to "Step up/down" and stick training, many useful behaviors can be trained. Here are just a few:

- target
- stay or station
- go willingly into a crate, carrier, travel cage, or night cage
- tolerate nail clipping
- tolerate toweling restraint for grooming and vet exams

To train these and other behaviors, watch the videos from GoodBirdInc.com and begin with targeting. If you can train your bird to target successfully, you'll be able to translate that learning into many other useful behaviors, as well as into behaviors that are simply amusing tricks.

A list of the steps for teaching "target" and "station" appear are described next.

Target

The target is located at the end of a specific stick or a special commercially available wand. Some of these wands come with clickers attached, if you like the idea of using clicker training. A target stick has to be something unique, such as a chopstick or a stick with a knob on the end. The end result you want is for your bird to walk to and orient his beak toward the wand and then gently touch it. To accomplish this, work in small increments, being sure to ask what your bird will likely be able to do. Once you teach the bird to target, subsequent training can build on the "target" command, thus enabling you to

Parrots can learn complicated tricks with patient, positive training.

direct your bird using the wand. For example, you can target him into his cage, onto his play stand, or to any place you need him to go.

- Time your training before a meal.
- Place your bird on a T-stand in your quiet training space.
- Gather up a pocketful of tiny treats for which your bird will work.
- Present the wand in a nonthreatening manner.
- In the beginning, if your bird looks at the wand, click (or give your verbal bridge) and reward.
- As you progress, make the criteria for clicking and treating higher. you're your next criterion is to require the bird to turn his head to look at the wand. Click and treat.
- Ask your bird to reach toward the wand. Click and treat.
- Ask your bird to walk along the T to get to the wand. Click and treat.
- Build up the length of time your bird has to follow the wand before getting a treat; keep building in small steps so he doesn't get frustrated.

Station

The point of the station command is to teach a bird to move to a place, orient his feet in a particular direction, and stay there. If you train your bird to a portable place marker, then stationing becomes a very useful command. For example, if the station is a mat that can be moved to a scale, a transport cage, or some other location, the station command will help you move your parrot less stressfully from one place to another. Some commercially available station mats are color coded so that you can work with multiple birds at once. In other words, you can station one bird on red while working with another on blue.

What is the meaning of the command "Station?" Station is a request for your bird to spend a reasonable interval on the station location. Begin by selecting the station. Have your bird approach the station by using targeting. Reinforce your bird's approach to and then standing on the station. Then, reinforce intermittently as long as your bird remains on his station, so that he isn't sure when the next treat is coming. You want your bird to realize that treats come often when he goes to and stands on his station. So long as the bird remains on the station, he receives treats. When he leaves

You can train your bird to station on his play stand, T-stand, cage top, or any safe place of your choosing.

Resources for Going Further with Training

The places to start are http://www.goodbirdinc.com and Barbara Heidenreich's YouTube channel. Her conferences and seminars are well worth your time as well. Ms. Heidenreich has an easily understandable approach and provides enough information for a relative newcomer to have success.

Beyond what Ms. Heidenreich offers, parrot people might consider either the more technical approach of Susan Friedman or the less technical approach of Steve Martin.

Susan Friedman's science of behavior for parrot caregivers is located at http://behaviorworks.org/. Susan G. Friedman, Ph.D. is a psychology professor at Utah State University who has presented on animal learning and behavior to a wide variety of audiences including the Association of Avian Veterinarians, the European Association of Zoos and Aquaria, the American Federation of Aviculturists, and NASA's Goddard Space Flight Center.

This introduction to Dr. Friedman's materials, including a Yahoo! group called Parrot Behavior Analysis Solutions (http://tech.groups.yahoo.com/group/ParrotBAS/), provides thread leaders with information to help solve specific problems. The group's goal is "to provide a practicum to Susan Friedman's LLP students and anyone else who is interested in improving their Applied Behavior Analysis (ABA) skills to prevent and solve behavior problems with their companion parrots." Many of the participants have attended Dr. Friedman's online class. The files section includes valuable articles that show how some problems were successfully resolved. This group also offers "Living and Learning with Parrots," Susan Freidman's 8-week online course.

Steve Martin's website http://www.naturalencounters.com/ has some wonderful articles and information about his week-long workshops in Florida.

In addition, Pamela Clark has some excellent information about behavior and diet on her website at www.pamelaclarkonline.com.

the station, you walk away, and your bird loses his opportunity for treats from you. After a break, use targeting to return the bird to his station. The key is to make it clear to the bird that so long as he stays on his station, he can and will receive treats. When he leaves his station, that opportunity goes away.

Stationing can be used to keep your bird inside his cage while you remove food bowls, install clean perches and remove the soiled ones for cleaning, or remove soiled paper. You can also station your bird outside the cage and do these things. As you learn to use station, you'll find that you can keep your bird successful: station him in a place he enjoys while you do things that annoy him. With behavior training, success is about thinking how to keep your bird feeling comfortable and acting sociably. Sometimes you need a distraction. Stationing is one tool in your growing box of parrot cooperation methods.

Trick Training

Teaching your parrot a few basic tricks is enjoyable for you and your bird. Intelligent creatures, they seem to enjoy learning and the attention they get from you for performing a trick. If you are a patient and kind trainer, your bird will be excited to participate in training sessions.

Before trick training, your bird must be willing to step onto and sit on your hand; he should also take food politely from your hand. In other words, you and your bird must have some trust to allow learning to occur.

Train in a quiet place used only for training so your parrot will understand that when he is at this location, it is time to work. Birds must have an incentive to work, and usually food rewards work best. Good training requires positive reinforcement, in which you immediately reward behavior you are trying to teach and ignore any bad behaviors. The reward is the reason your bird will repeat a behavior.

The first tricks to teach include turning around, waving a foot or wing, shaking hands, kissing, rolling over, playing dead, and taking a bow. Different species of birds seem to prefer different types of tricks. For example, the more gymnastic species, such as lories, caiques, and cockatoos, often easily learn to hang upside down.

The key to training any trick is to break the

The African grey is one of the best talkers of all the parrots.

behavior down into steps your bird can learn easily. Reward the first step as many times as it takes for your parrot to learn it. Then move onto the next. When he knows that part, move onto the next step, and so on. Once he knows all the steps, put them together and start rewarding him only for the completed trick. (See the upcoming section on clicker training.)

One of the best trick training video series features Tani Robar. Because you can see the trainer's order of instructions and methods of encouragement, you can learn quite a bit from watching a video that shows how to teach simple tricks. Other trick videos are available from Barbara Heidenreich.

Introduction to Clicker Training

For training tricks, clicker training is a very helpful method, but you can use it to train any behavior. With clicker training, you can easily teach one of these tricks very quickly—perhaps in a day or two of several daily sessions of about five to ten minutes each. With training, short and more frequent sessions are more helpful than longer training sessions.

Clicker training is a combination of communicating with and motivating your parrot. The communication is the sound of the clicker—it serves as the bridge—and the motivation is the positive reinforcement, usually a preferred food offered as a treat. What clicker training can help you do is modify your parrot's behavior using something called *successive approximations*.

This method of teaching rewards your parrot for doing something that gets him closer to doing whatever it is that you want him to do. That's the goal; for example, going into a carrier.

Clicker training is used to teach zoo animals to stand on scales for weighing, to come to a position for an examination, and to take a medication or other type of treatment that is not a natural behavior. Because parrots are so intelligent, exercising their minds as well as their bodies is good for them. And, the training for parrots gives us an excellent way forward to a lifelong accommodation of parrot and human needs.

Clicker training relies on positive reinforcement that rewards successive approximations to shape behavior. For example, teaching your bird to touch a target with his beak begins with rewarding your bird for looking at the target, then turning his head toward the target, then moving closer to the target. The clicks and rewards teach the bird exactly which behavior is the desired one.

The click marks the behavior for which the bird is being rewarded. The reward is something you've paired with the clicker sound. This is the *motivator*, the treat the bird will work for. You should eliminate the motivator from his diet and use it only for training.

Target Training Using a Clicker

Training from a T-stand is always the best way to begin. In one short session, your bird will understand that when he hears a click, he knows a reward is on the way. Select as a target something that doesn't look like a perch. You might try a spoon or a knitting needle, for example. Some trainers suggest dyeing the end of a wooden spoon with food coloring so that the target is easy for the bird to see and identify.

You'll click and reinforce your bird for each movement toward the target. Once your bird moves toward the target and "beaks" it, click and reinforce. As soon as your bird follows the target back and forth, move the target up and down. When your bird understands he should follow the target wherever you place it and gently beak it, then you don't need the clicker anymore. However, you should continue to give reinforcement with praise or a pet, if your bird enjoys that.

Targeting is an excellent way to teach stepping up onto your hand or a perch. If you hold the target so the bird has to stretch, and you place the hand-held perch between his body and top of his legs, the bird will have to step up. What you want is for the bird to move his foot. Click and reward. Shape the bird's response to putting his foot on the perch and eventually to stepping on to the perch or your hand. Once taught, you'll maintain his step up onto your hand and a perch because you will have uses for both of these behaviors. Remember to continue to reinforce good behavior and to keep the association positive.

In a similar fashion, you can teach waving, shaking hands, turning around, hanging upside down, and so forth.

Talking

A frequently asked question is "Does your parrot talk?" People are fascinated that birds can imitate human speech. What perhaps should be more fascinating is that parrots and other animals kept as companions can learn to understand human body language and can teach people what they need.

Among the smaller species, budgies are the champion talkers.

Nevertheless, the ability to imitate speech is what fascinates people; what is less well understood by most people who visit your parrot is that these birds have a complex communication system that serves them in the same way that language serves humans. Research done by Karl Berg in 2011 was the first done to prove that parrots in the wild use communication to identify family groups. Parrot nestlings learn their unique contact calls from their parents. These contact calls serve as the parrotlets' names. Because bird vocalizations are so complex and fast, human ears do not distinguish the details; rather, sophisticated sound technology is needed to unravel the aspects that make these individuals' calls distinctive (*Science Magazine*, 22 July 2011; Vol. 333).

Dr. Irene Pepperberg and Alex, an African grey parrot, have become famous through books and

Birds are most likely to learn to repeat words you say frequently and those you say enthusiastically.

television programs about their remarkable scientific partnership. In one of the most famous experiments in comparative psychology, Dr. Pepperberg set out to see whether Alex, a grey chosen at random, was capable of understanding complicated concepts—such as number, color, and composition of matter, and of using words to answer questions and make basic requests (www.amazon.com/The-Alex-Studies-Cognitive-Communicative/dp/0674008065). *The Alex Studies* demonstrated that this randomly chosen African grey parrot could learn these concepts and could use words to make requests and answer questions.

The work with Alex spanned many years, involved a planned series of training exercises in learning and producing speech, and consumed the early university careers of many graduate students. In other words, without years and a degree in psychology or linguistics, you will not get the results that Dr. Pepperberg did. Not only did Alex create words and make requests, but he proved that he understood the words and requests in the same way as humans did. In essence, Alex learned a different species' language and culture. Alex produced sound using his syrinx, which is a different vocal mechanism than the larynx that humans have.

An important difference between what Alex was able to do and what most talking birds do is that Alex understood the meaning of what he said. What parrot parents should be clear about is that imitating a word is no different from imitating a car alarm or a doorbell. The sound has no specific meaning to the parrot. Associating meaning with a sound is a different process than teaching the sound itself.

Vocal Gymnastics versus Sounds with Purpose

Although birds produce sound in a completely different way from humans, birds can use sound for some of the same purposes as humans do. This does not mean, however, that teaching a bird a phrase also teaches the bird the meaning of that phrase. Take the case of a famous talking parrot, Disco, the budgerigar. Not only does Disco repeat more than 100 phrases, he also has his own YouTube channel. Disco's ability to talk does not mean that he understands the phrases; rather, Disco is able to repeat phrases that mimic human speech. Another famous talking parrot is Einstein.

This African grey also has an enormous talent for clear mimicry. He performs on late-night television, but he follows a routine that never varies. His mimicked, or imitated, answers to questions do show an excellent memory as well as good training. What owners often seek is the ability for a parrot to associate words with actions or objects.

Unfortunately, this type of training—the type Alex and his successors have received—requires a small squad of trainers following a highly regimented and consistent

If your bird learns an undesirable sound or word, the best bet is to ignore it and reward the words you prefer.

method of training on a small and focused group of concepts and words over a period of years. However, what parrot parents do find is that some birds consistently ask for things they want, basic things such as to go back to their cage or a particular treat, using a sound they associate with the object.

In a study of a single parrot, a University of Georgia psychologist showed that the bird used specific sound units to investigate the whereabouts of her owner and used spontaneous sounds to ask for her owner's companionship. She was also able to request objects or activities such as peanuts, a shower, water, and grapes. In addition, the vocalizations changed based on whether the companion was in the room and answered the vocalizations. The conclusion was that the parrot learned to create sounds in a context-appropriate manner; in other words, the parrot learned to ask for what she wanted, at least some of the time, given that she had been raised and lived in an environment with a responsive human companion (Colbert-White, E. N., & Covington, M. A. et al. 2011, March 7. Social Context Influences the Vocalization s of a Home-Raised African Grey Parrot. *Journal of Comparative Psychology*. Advance online publication. doi: 10.1037/a0022097).

What Might You Expect to Achieve

People who have kept parrots for years would not be surprised by the finding that parrots can ask for what they want. Parrots are excellent at communicating their needs to us in all sorts of ways: body posture, vocalizations, body movements, and feather movements. The key is that parrot parents do not always recognize what the parrot is indicating through his combination of body movements and sound. Nevertheless, if you want to teach your parrot to mimic or imitate phrases for fun, you should.

Diane Grindol, *Bird Talk* columnist and author of *Teaching Your Bird To Talk*, advises that, if talking is important as a characteristic of your pet bird, you become familiar with the types of birds who are most likely to talk. Next, decide what type of talking is important and then encourage the bird to talk through lots of interaction and practice. Which birds talk? Some species are more likely to talk than others, although some individual birds never talk. You might get an individual bird who simply doesn't talk. The only way to ensure that your bird will talk is to adopt an older bird who talks.

The smaller and more inexpensive parrots who can talk well are cockatiels and budgies. Although the sex of the larger parrots does not seem to matter, many small-parrot experts believe that males are more likely to talk than females. However, only a few birds develop extensive vocabularies, and, when it comes to vocabulary, budgies rule: a male parakeet named Puck from Petaluma, California, holds the world record vocabulary of 1,700 words since 1995.

Other readily available companion parrots who often talk include African greys, Indian ringnecks, and Amazons, particularly the double-yellowhead and blue-fronts. That eclectus parrots talk as well as greys is a secret. Among these larger parrots, females talk as well as males. Remember that not every parrot will talk, and that different parrots have differing skills with talking and mimicry of sounds.

Different Kinds of Talking

In the five years of research that preceded her book, Ms. Grindol identified three types of companion bird talk. Birds can be taught to mimic or repeat phrases (imitation), to ask for what they want (functional or context talking), and to speak on cue (trick training). When you think about your parrot talking, consider which of these is most important to you. In this book, the focus is on mimicry or imitating and repeating phrases. To learn about functional talking, consult resources listed at the end of this book. Likewise, intensive training is required for a routine like the one that Einstein does on television and YouTube. Training resources at the end of this book will help you become an expert.

The Technique of Teaching Talking

Ms. Grindol suggests that enthusiasm and energy are the keys to getting parrots to talk. Teaching new phrases is an activity children enjoy, and who can muster more enthusiasm and energy than small children?

To encourage your bird to repeat a phrase, follow this sequence of steps:

* Decide on a phrase.
* Repeat the phrase several times.
* When your bird tries to repeat the phrase, give the training bridge words "good job."
* Teach one phrase until your bird continually tries to use it. Then move to the next.

What you might experience is hearing your bird rehearse the phrase or word as a part of his morning and evening parrot jabber. First thing in the morning and again in the late afternoon, many parrots spend a period of time vocalizing. These vocal torrents, especially from budgerigars, include portions of words or phrases that the parrot seems to be rehearsing.

Pros and Cons of Potty Training

Veterinarians will tell you that potty training your parrot is asking for trouble. Some behaviorists will tell you that potty training is a key to happiness and a lot less cleaning. The key is to understand the definition of potty training.

According to his website, Einstein, the famous African grey parrot, is potty trained. However, what Einstein's people mean is that he poops at will in his cage and on his play stand, but when he's on a "trip" across the home or elsewhere, his people have him poop before he leaves on his "trip" and then wait to poop again until he returns home.

Birds can hold their poop. As you will have learned, parrots do not defecate at night. Rather, the poop in the morning is a very large one. However, what veterinarians warn against is teaching your bird to defecate only on command. Because parrots are very intelligent, they can learn to wait for the command. Because of this, many parrots have had problems with *prolapsed cloacas* as a result of trying to hold their waste for too long.

The pros of a limited sort of potty training can be helpful: in other words, if your bird will defecate on command, you have about another 20 minutes or so before he'll want to defecate again. And, given that he prefers to defecate in one location, you can encourage this behavior.

However, the risk of teaching your parrot only to defecate on command is serious injury that requires surgical repair.

Another way to encourage communication is to respond to your bird's communication. In the wild, birds vocalize to communicate with the flock; one part of the flock language is vocal and the other contains visual components, just as human speech and body language work together. When your bird communicates either with vocalization or with body language, your response will encourage him. For example, if your bird whistles at you in the morning, whistle back and say "Good morning." Over time, the bird will recognize "good morning" as your greeting in the morning and will likely say it when he sees you. Say "hello" when you come in and "goodbye" when you leave. Talk to your parrot as if he were a young child, with simple phrases about your comings and goings, your preparing and providing meals. Over time, key in on phrases that will enhance your communication. For example, if you always say, "Want a bath?" when you place the large, shallow bowl containing bath water on the play gym, your bird will associate "want a bath" with the bath water. Again, you may hear portions of this phrase in the morning or evening jabber, but, at some point, you will likely hear it when your bird actually wants bath water. This is the time to drop what you are doing and provide a bowl of bath water.

Another way that mimicry begins is in hearing household sounds. Unlike dogs, who want to please you, birds are wild animals trying to take care of their own needs. Their actions appear selfish in human terms. Your attention is important to them. They notice that the telephone and the microwave get your attention, so they imitate those sounds. They will also imitate other sounds that get your attention. As you hear those sounds, be careful about which ones you react to. If you react to unpleasant, harsh, or very loud sounds, you are encouraging their use. Remember, with sound as with any other sort of training that reinforces an action, either you are training your bird, or your parrot is training you. Your attention is a *very powerful reinforcer.*

Playing recordings for your birds won't teach them to talk. Playing lively music and asking "Wanna dance?" then dancing with your bird will work over time. Birds get excited about what you get excited about. Anything you say with emphasis or excitement is likely to get your bird's attention and may someday be repeated back to you—possibly and embarrassingly in front of company, so be careful what you say within birdie earshot.

What Birds Say

Grindol collected stories about talking parrots for *Teaching Your Bird to Talk*. A most unusual story Grindol reported was on the occasion of a pair of eclectus parrots in their veterinarian's examination room. One parrot of the pair watched while the other was being examined and said, "Pray to God. Say your prayers." One part of the fun at bird clubs is listening to the stories of parrot parents and their birds' various verbal antics.

A very common story is about birds putting the family dog through his paces. Overhearing family members work with the dog on basic commands, the parrots will often use these commands to amuse themselves when no humans are at home. Many of us have witnessed a dog's confusion when the parrot calls him and then puts the dog through his paces: "Sit. Stay. Good dog." Many parrots are said to toss their kibble through the cage bars as rewards. A few parrots are reported to call the dog and, when he comes, rebuke him: "Bad dog." Some parrot parents have had to go through agony with their dogs before they discovered the source of their real problem—their parrots were playing with the dog to amuse themselves. The parrots' game caused the dog to stop responding to commands.

Parrots will say what they like in order to get along with others in their flock, which might include people and other animals. Some birds sound an alarm call when they are afraid, as in seeing a stranger or a cat. Birds will call for food or for attention: "Wanna peanut"; "Wanna go upstairs"; "What are you doing?"; "Wanna bath"; "Fruit."

The Cursing Parrot: What to Do

Talking birds are charming until they aren't. Most bird guardians have experienced the humiliation of a super-sized "breaking wind" sound followed by maniacal laughter or a singsong "oh s%&$!" as background to the follow-up call for a job interview. As the big finish to the enchanting talking bird act, there's ceaseless screaming at decibels equivalent to a jackhammer on concrete.

Guess who taught the bird the bad words? That's right: a human in the bird's life. And how do we get the bird to stop? First, we need to figure out how we caused it. Make a list of the words and other vocal behaviors you don't like. For a day or two, also jot down the time and what was happening when the word or behavior occurred. Remember, birds respond to energy, enthusiasm, and attention. Now, strategize before you take action. Many times, eliminating the curse words is difficult, but an excellent solution can be changing bad words into good ones. Next time you hear an unacceptable word, react as if you do want to hear it, but change the word. Instead of "Mandy," the old girlfriend's name, you could say, "Dandy. Dandy yes, I like it too!" or, "candy," or any other word that sounds similar. Use the same strategy with curse words.

Similarly, the volume of the curse can also be the problem. This may be opposite to how you've handled this in the past, trying to "out talk" the bird. Whispering intrigues most birds. Your bird may learn to whisper and love it.

This is a time to employ the most basic tool in the trainer's tool box: Ignore unwanted behavior and praise good behavior. When your bird makes an undesirable word or sound, the worst approach is to shout, "Bad bird!" In seconds, you will have trained your bird to repeat the word and then shout, "Bad bird!" He'll be laughing while you rage. Ignore bad behavior, encourage good. Using this strategy, ignore the swear word or the unseemly sound. Bridge and reward the words and sounds you want to hear. Cue your family members to do the same.

Solving Behavior Problems

Whenever noted behaviorist Liz Wilson had opportunities to address avian veterinarians and behaviorists, she emphasized that whenever an adult human lived with young medium or large parrots, the odds were good that no matter how much human companions love their parrots, the parrots would move to another home at some time in their lives. Because of parrots' long potential life spans, they often outlive their caretakers. When owners become too old or sick to be able to provide the care they deserve, the future becomes grim for parrots who are unpleasant companions, especially for aggressive biters and nonstop screamers.

Wilson believed that parrot companions, to be responsible to their pets, should find assistance to solve behavior issues that no reasonable person would tolerate. Not only does tolerating outrageous behaviors create problems for the parrot's current family, but tolerating these behaviors means that your parrot will likely not find another family when his current family can no longer care for him.

Behavioral problems in parrots usually arise because, as companions, we accidentally reinforce bad behaviors. Once we reinforce a bad behavior, the smart parrot tries the bad behavior again.

Owners often create behavior problems by giving their parrots attention when they misbehave.

The more often we reinforce a bad behavior, the more frequently the parrot practices the behavior because he is getting a satisfying result. The most frequently reported behavioral problems include screaming, aggression (including biting), fearful or phobic responses (including biting), begging, food-related issues, and self-destructive behavior (such as feather plucking).

Natural Behaviors Sometimes Create Problems

When your bird exhibits a problem behavior like these, take a few minutes to consider what problem the disturbing behavior solves for the bird. The secret to preventing problem behaviors is to preempt them: to stop them before they start. A key to coping with problem behaviors is not to obsess about them but to treat them as a normal periodic occurrence in your life with a parrot. The prepared companion has done some reading and some thinking and will have decided in advance what to do and not do in response to these often distressing developments. In case it's not obvious, Murphy's Law applies to bad parrot behavior. At the times when you can least afford the time or the patience to deal with parrot issues, that's when the issues arise. This is in part due to the sensitive nature of parrots. They do know when you are stressed, and this stress creates stress for your parrot. You, as a flock member, must have a reason for your anxiety. If you are anxious, your parrot will be too.

Parrots seemingly have nothing to do but bend you to their will, unless you give them important jobs to do. On average, wild parrots spend 50 percent of their waking hours looking for and eating food, 25 percent of the time interacting with a mate or other flock members, and 25 percent preening. Most problem behaviors arise either because a bird does not have enough to do, or because the exercise the bird is getting is insufficient, or both. One very important way to reduce or prevent problem behaviors is to make sure that your bird is receiving enough exercise and enough stimulation during the day so that he has a restful night.

How We Accidentally Encourage Bad Behavior: Drama

Here is a sequence of events that is all too common in parrot–companion relationships. In this example, the companion is rewarding the parrot's undesirable behavior by providing interesting interaction when he screams.

This is what not to do:

1. Your bird screams.
2. You shout, "Bad bird!"
3. Your parrot thinks, "Fantastic! I bet I can get her to do that again." As a result, he screams like a serial killer is attacking the cage.
4. You up your volume. "Bad bird!" If you're having a bad day, you'll stamp your foot and scream back, "STOP!"
5. Your parrot thinks, "Awesome. If I scream really loudly, she screams. Excellent. I can do this all afternoon because we're having a great time. She loves to scream too!"

For a parrot, nothing is more exciting than drama. Do you see how the parrot is training the human companion?

How to Avoid Rewarding Bad Behavior: No Drama

Although each type of poor habit has its own beginning, you want to avoid rewarding the bad behavior. As when someone asks you a question that you consider rude or acts badly, your best tactic is to change the subject or walk away. No matter how much you want to punish your companion bird for bad behavior, this never gets you very far. Remember, your bird is not a domestic animal, selectively bred for generations for its people-pleasing behavior. Your parrot is essentially a wild animal. Your only recourse is to reinforce good behavior and either prevent or ignore bad behavior.

For problems that seem impossible to solve, don't be embarrassed about asking for help. And spend the money for a behaviorist sooner rather than later.

Screaming

We know that punishment doesn't work. A common and badly considered prescription for screaming is to use a squirt bottle to interrupt and punish screaming. Ms. Grindol cautions companions not to fall prey to the concept of the squirt bottle to punish birds who vocalize loudly. Birds need baths. If you use the squirt bottle for punishment, imagine how your bird will react when you go to bathe him. And some parrots like being squirted!

Instead, ignore the scream. Walk away until the screaming stop. Then, change the subject. Sing your bird's favorite song. Get your bird to sing with you. Gradually, lower the volume of your voice.

Alternatively, think about your bird's needs. Think about why he might be screaming. Do you answer his contact calls? Does he need some time with you? After the screaming stops, go and get your bird. Take him on a tour of the house, talking about the various pictures. Distract him and spend time with him. Or, if you wanted to watch the news when the screaming started, move the training perch into the den and put newspaper underneath. Talk with your bird in a normal tone of voice. "What do you think about this?" During the commercials, mute the sound and have a good talk. Give your bird attention, but not in a way so that he can link his screaming with the attention.

In summary, walk away from the screaming. When it stops, find something to do with your bird so that you meet his needs but do not

Screaming often starts because your bird is bored and not getting enough attention.

reward the screaming. Instead, reward the quiet. The moment your bird is quiet, grab a peanut, take him from his cage, and go on a tour of the house, looking at his favorite things. Give the peanut. Reward the quiet with attention and with little unexpected treats—a scratch on the head or stroke of the beak—whatever your bird likes. In other words, give positive reinforcement for good behavior and no reinforcement for bad behavior.

If you simply cannot stand the screaming, one way to change the behavior is to whisper. Most parrots seem fascinated by whispering. If your bird is screaming, put in your earplugs. If and when he takes a breath, from the point of the cage furthest from him, try whispering something to him. Odds are he will stop and come to see what you are doing. At that point, you have interrupted the behavior. Begin rewarding the good behavior.

Another suggestion is to consider the noise level in your home. Does your bird have to talk over the surround-sound system for attention? Reducing the volume will benefit everyone's hearing.

If nothing else works, before your last nerve snaps, consider the cover up. Like an overstimulated child, your parrot may need to lower his energy level. After a few minutes of shouting, you do too. Make sure the cage cover is thick and dark. Don't treat this as a punishment; consider this as a time-out. It's a change of environment. Set a timer for 10 minutes. When the timer goes off, do something interactive with your bird before the cycle begins again, and find reasons to use lots of praise.

Favorite tips for prevention of screaming include the following:

When your bird talks to you, answer. Birds are engineered to communicate over long distances to their social partners, so make sure you answer contact calls.

When he needs attention morning and night, give it. You'll find your bird gets quieter and you get happier the more you interact.

When you know that your bird tends to scream at a particular time, preempt the behavior by including your parrot in some activity that he enjoys. Then, when it's time, put your bird to bed in a safe, quiet, dark room and proceed with whatever it was you were going to do.

Aggression

Aggression and related biting can occur when your parrot becomes overloaded with excitement. A bird who has been battering a toy does not calm when you put your hand up to remove him from the play stand. He bites in a continuation of the roughhousing he started with the toy. Before you decide it's time to put your bird back in his cage, give him time to calm down. Put on some relaxing music. Sing together or talk. Give him time to return to perching and even to grinding his beak, the sign of a relaxed bird. An excellent way to make returning to the cage a pleasure, rather than something your bird doesn't want to do, is to use his out-of-cage time to clean and straighten his cage, change the water, and refill a foraging toy with a favorite food. As your bird watches you do this, he'll be more interested in returning to the cage once he's calm and sees that there is a pleasurable reward for his doing so.

By the way, if your bird is being aggressive and you must handle him, use either the stick he's been trained to climb onto or use a towel to move your parrot gently to the necessary location.

Avoidance Biting

Another reason your parrot learns to bite is to avoid what he doesn't want to do. This type of biting can be trained away with determined effort. This particular bad habit is easier to solve if your bird is stick trained. Many birds will refuse to go back into their cage when they're not getting enough time out of it. Or, some companions ask their birds to leave the cage at times when they are sleeping or about to sleep. Or, they ask their birds to go to a place that frightens them. Your normally compliant bird, when you give the step-up command to leave his current location—whether your hand or the cage—will strike out and bite. Once this strategy works, which reinforces the behavior, you know this is going to be an issue the next time you ask your parrot to do something he doesn't want to do.

When you know that your bird will not want to comply, you have several choices. First, you can take a different approach. If you're returning your bird to his cage, make it worth his while to return. What does he love that you can put there as an enticement? Put a special treat in his bowl or hang an especially loved toy in the cage.

Second, you can move your bird to a location he wants to go to, avoid the confrontation, and reapproach the unwanted location at a better time. If stick trained, you can use the stick to transfer your bird to the cage and offer a treat in a manner so that your bird must step off the stick and onto a cage perch in order to take the treat through the bars with his tongue.

However, the long-term solution to this is to look at what you're asking your parrot to do. If he's spending all his time in a small cage, of course he doesn't want to go back. Make it a point to have

Many parrots learn to bite to avoid doing something they don't want to do, like return to their cage.

him spend lots of time out of the cage. Have a few training sessions. Make sure that he gets plenty of exercise with flapping and perhaps flying. Dance together. Do an aerobics or Pilates routine together. What your bird is telling you is that you're not spending enough time together.

A parrot who has become fearful of hands will resort to biting.

Young Bird Biting

Chewing on fingers is a case of putting your fingers where they should not be. Finger chewing is a stage young birds go through. From the beginning, teach your bird that chewing toys is fine, but fingers are not fine to chew.

If you are not diligent in giving your bird a toy when he wants to chew something, the bites become harder and what was once an amusing game with a baby parrot becomes a painful game with an adolescent parrot. Improper handling of this situation has caused many parrots to lose their homes.

Fearful or Phobic Responses

When your parrot is fearful, he will bite. Fear often arises when a bird is approached too quickly or is confronted with something new without time to acclimate. Parrots will often bite or strike out at people who are very nervous about handling them. Or, if a bird has had an unpleasant or painful experience with one person, he will not want to step up on that person's hand.

One particular type of fearful parrot is the one-person bird. Sadly, sometimes we encourage this because it can become a point of pride that our parrot prefers us. Although this might be good for our egos, this is very bad news for your parrot. This means that no one else can create a good relationship with your bird. If you become sick or injured, your bird suffers. Keep in mind that, in the wild, parrots are social animals who interact with others, not just their mates; psychologically, it is unhealthy for a parrot to only interact with one person. The situation needs correction.

Behaviorist Sally Blanchard's "Warm Potato Game" is an excellent way to demonstrate to your parrot that all the humans in his environment are important members of his flock; this game is equally useful for introducing new people, like a new neighbor or pet sitter. The weekly use of this game can also help prevent psittacine birds from becoming so overbonded to one person that no one else can handle them.

Working in a neutral room, the humans form a circle and slowly pass the bird around from person to person. Each circle member steps the bird onto her hand with the step-up command, then

Once a parrot is fearful of hands, it will take patient, careful training to resolve the problem.

interacts positively with the bird before passing him to the next person. In this way, the bird will understand that each person in the circle is important and that he should be polite to all.

Encouraging your companion parrot to develop friendships with other people and spending time visiting with other people is an excellent way to keep your parrot learning and growing emotionally, to keep him interested and challenged, and to keep him flexible and excited about life. The more positive experiences your parrot has, the more accepting he is of new experiences. This is the hallmark of a parrot who will succeed in life long after you are gone and he is in his new home. Isn't this what every parent wants?

Some birds seem to become fearful or phobic about any handling at all. Consider the idea that your bird may have suffered an injury from a fall, for example, and he may find leaving the safety of his cage frightening. If your bird becomes suddenly phobic or fearful of being handled, a first step is to have him examined by a veterinarian. If there is not a physical cause, you will need to look more deeply.

When you need help, ask your veterinarian or your bird club for a recommendation for a bird behaviorist. Especially as a beginning parrot parent, understanding things from your parrot's point of view is not always easy. Getting a knowledgeable professional to assist you in identifying and correcting a problem is no more a shame than taking your dog to a puppy training class. This is simply a normal way to learn how to do something new.

Food-Related Issues

Begging is a habit that birds develop because we assist them. In other words, we respond to the begging. If you never, ever feed your bird from the table or between his scheduled feeding times, you have a bird who does not beg. This is a simple habit to break. The problem is that the habit is a human one.

Self-Destructive Behavior

Self-destructive behavior is seen for a variety of reasons, including health problems. If your parrot begins barbering—chewing off part of his feathers—or pulling the feathers out, the best approach is to eliminate a health cause before the barbering becomes a habit. Barbering is not to be confused with preening. Normal preening includes the zipping of every feather every day. Barbering is breaking off the feather at the shaft. You will find pieces of feathers with breaks in the long, flexible central shaft. Bring the pieces along with your bird to the veterinarian.

The one reaction that you do not want is to correct the plucking or barbering. If there is a behavioral cause rather than health or environmental reason, coming to the cage and yelling, "Parrot! Stop Plucking!" provides attention, which may be what your bird is seeking.

If you are able to eliminate a health reason for this new behavior, then examine the environmental causes next. Look at cage position and humidity. Could the air be too dry, causing your bird's skin to itch? Have you recently changed his diet? The new diet could include an ingredient that causes your bird some distress. Finally, have you rearranged your furniture, brought a new pet into the home, or made any other changes that, while insignificant-seeming to you, could be causing your bird to react in a negative way?

Several approaches you might try include making sure your bird has enough opportunities to bathe; enough full-spectrum light (not light through a window); and enough food, playtime, and chewing materials, such as cardboard, paper, and toys to destroy. Make sure to supply these, along with lots of healthy foods and plenty of time together. Along with these actions, it's wise to consult an avian behaviorist. Plucking is a difficult problem to remedy without professional help.

Some birds periodically pluck or barber their feathers. Most companion birds who are psychologically healthy and who have enough foraging opportunity and a good diet do not pluck to a dangerous extreme. If neither your veterinarian nor a behaviorist can find a cause, the best way forward is to consider that you will love a parrot who plucks. If you begin to obsess about the plucking, your bird will pluck more. That's a guarantee.

Chewing

Chewing on wood is normal for your parrot. This is not a behavior problem. In the case of your parrot, keep your bird away from treasured objects. Ask yourself how many blocks of pine do I need this week to keep my bird whittling happily? If your feathered friend has enough of his own items to chew, he is less likely to chew on yours.

Self-plucking is a challenging problem to solve.

When and How to Get Professional Help

Because parrots and people have different expectations about behavior and methods of communicating, parrot–person relationships can result in misunderstandings, especially at the beginning of your experience with parrots. Before your frustration escalates, call an avian behavioral consultant. Not only can behavioral consultants help you understand your bird's body language, they can also help you with your handling skills, which may be causing some of the miscommunication.

Some companions engage a behavioral consultant before or shortly after acquiring a bird, before trouble arises. Although a breeder can help you get started, the expectation that she will be able to help you solve problems indefinitely is an unrealistic one.

Finding a consultant who can help you is not difficult if you're willing to be somewhat flexible in your expectations. Many behavioral consultants work by telephone. Still others can help you via Skype or other Internet services that offer picture transmission. If you prefer in-home consultation, some behaviorists offer this service when the distance is not prohibitive.

Find a behavioral consultant by contacting local bird clubs, reading bird publications, and talking with local bird shops. You can also try the Internet, being sure to search on "bird behavior consultants" and not "bird behaviorists." The first is what you need; the second is a degreed person with university research experience. One organization that features a parrot division is the International Association of Animal Behavior Consultants http://iaabc.org/.

How can you determine if a behavioral consultant is right for you? Request a conversation about her experience with your type of bird and your specific problem, at no charge. Ask for references. Your best consultant will have hands-on experience with both your species and the problem.

Parrots do best when they have a regular bed time and get about twelve hours of sleep.

The Daily Routine and Why It's Important

Daily cycles of day and dark affect an animal's biology. Biological clocks, called *circadian rhythms*, match the daily twenty-four-hour cycle of the earth's rotation on its axis. Birds have a rhythm of metabolism, body temperature, and alertness that follows the rhythm of the day.

As a result, birds become active as the sun rises, gather food, drink, bathe themselves, and attend to flock business until midday, when they rest. Birds become active again about 3:00 PM, gathering food, drinking, and preening before the twelve hours of darkness during which they sleep.

A Short Introduction to Training a Flighted Parrot

Training a flighted parrot is a lot more complicated than letting the flight feathers grow out and opening the aviary door. The parrot's recall training has to be 100 percent reliable. A bird's flight muscles need to be built up, along with his endurance. Parrots who have never flown in large facilities need to become familiar with the area, learn about perch selection, understand how to deal with wind and the distractions of other birds or predators in the area, and how to land safely. This all sounds automatic, right? Birds can fly, right?

Birds who have successfully fledged and been coached by their parents can fly, certainly. But for birds who have spent their lives in cages that are not built for flight, flying is a new skill and one that does not come quickly.

People who are parrot free-flyers have worked successfully in training birds under the tutelage of a mentor either as a full-time animal trainer, as a falconer, or as very successful amateur trainers. For example, Chris Shank of Cockatoo Downs has been free-flying her parrots for many years. Shank hosts biannual workshops with Barbara Heidenreich, at which you can observe her cockatoos flying freely and gain some appreciation for the training that she has invested in her flock.

You may have heard of Chris Biro, who holds free-flight trainings, and you may know or have been fortunate enough to attend a workshop by Biro or other trainers who are skilled in the art of training birds in free-flight for shows or in aiding parrot owners to teach their birds the skills to fly either on long leashes called creances or in free-flight inside large aviaries. Yahoo groups devoted to free-flyers, including Biro's freeflight@yahoogroups.com, can provide some information to get you started.

If free-flight is your aim, read and consult with some experts before taking your bird out for a flight. As many trainers will tell you, there's nothing worse than losing a bird who won't survive in the wild because you've prepared inadequately.

Companion bird experts suggest supporting your birds' natural timetable as much as practical for the happiness of both human and bird companions. A simple way to do this is to make use of full-spectrum lighting and to set the timer on a twelve-hour cycle. This mimics the twelve-hour equatorial light cycle, and, after all, most parrots are from somewhere near the equator.

In addition to the daily cycle of light and dark, parrots do have their daily routines. Like most creatures, parrots enjoy a certain amount of predicability.

Many parrot parents let their birds out in the morning while they make breakfast or get ready for work.

Establishing Routines

As his human caregiver, it is your responsibility to establish your parrot's routine while taking into account his normal circadian rhythms. As much as possible, especially in the beginning, you want to establish routines that help your parrot cooperate with you, the same as you would do with a child. In the morning, feed and provide clean paper at a regular time. Turn on a video or the radio. Maybe you change these out and use one on some days and the other on alternate days. Or, use timers to change things up during the day when you're not around.

Like people, birds appreciate routine: we want to know that we'll be fed about on schedule and that we will be able to get enough sleep in the evening. For example, if you know that by 6:30 PM your bird is cranky, then plan around this. Feed the evening meal early, before he's cranky, and put him to bed by 6:15. Establish a routine that makes bedtime fun, like a special treat and a song after you turn out the light and before you cover the cage at night. Use the same phrase every night. Like children who find comfort in nursery rhymes, parrots like repetition. But it's fine if you come home one night, and let Parrot share your dinner, and let him stay up to watch a movie with you past his normal bedtime. If he's sleepy, let him sleep there on his perch, and take him to bed when you're ready. In other words, you don't want so much routine that he can't adapt to sometimes having things different. What works well is a slightly different weekday and weekend routine.

When you leave the house, say "bye-bye." When you return, go over to his cage immediately and say "Hello." Spend a few minutes before you sit down to rest in talking with your parrot. When you do cage maintenance, tell him what you are doing. Your parrot does not understand what you're saying. What he does understand is that you're focused on him, and that's the point.

For busy families, keeping a parrot happy can be a challenge. After all, from his point of view, it should be all about the parrot, all day, every day. If you establish a routine that allows your parrot reassurance that he is the center of attention at certain times during the day, and you provide for his amusement when you're not there, your life together will be much happier.

A Busy Parrot Is a Happy Parrot

While you are at work and the kids are at school, your bird is home alone. Building on the daily routine just described, you need to plan ways to keep your parrot happy and entertained while the family is away.

Morning Fly-Out Routine

Before family members fly the coop, heap some attention on birdie. While fixing breakfast and bag lunches, hand feed a snack or two to your parrot—a little peanut butter, a little carrot stick, a piece of shredded wheat. Talk with the bird, using his name, and share the morning bustle. Who knows? Birdie might provide comic relief for those hectic morning launches.

Diane Grindol, author of *Cockatiels for Dummies* advises bird companions to set up a radio or mp3 player for day-long bird entertainment. Since birds communicate through calls, voice or music of any kind is company for your avian friend. A random play of different music types gives the bird variety. Slow, sleepy songs contrast with country western up-tempo tunes; classic show tunes and arias give birds a chance to sing along or provide syrinx accompaniment. Public radio, where a mix of

Greet your parrot when you come home. Remember, he's been waiting all day to spend some time with you.

conversation and music is available, is fun. Birds also like nature sounds, although certain animal calls can be upsetting to individual birds. If you leave your birds with talk radio, be prepared to live with the vocabulary your bird will acquire. Music, sounds, a video of parrots doing their daily activities—all of these will keep your bird's physical activity up and his brain busy processing the sounds, responding, or choosing not to respond. A busy brain is a contented brain ... and it's a brain that is not waiting for you to provide all the stimulation.

Mattie Sue Athan, noted avian behaviorist, recommends visual stimulation for birds left home alone. She suggests using an aquarium, video, or windows onto an active location.

Recess Time: a Change of Pace

When you dash home before soccer practice or on a lunch break, grab a leafy celery stick for your avian kid and spend just a moment talking to and feeding him. Ask him questions. Pet him, kiss him, and say, "Bye bye."

Returning to the Roost

When the family returns to the roost in the evening, your companion bird will want to be a companion. But you want a few minutes to yourself. Be an adult and save yourself some heartache. When you arrive home, go first to your bird, greet him, and chat a moment. If you're comfortable with your bird out of the cage, take him into the bathroom while you wash your face and brush your hair or to the bedroom while you change clothes.

Keep birdie out for an indoor stroll as you check your messages. Use the speaker phone so he can hear the messages, too. Involvement in what you are doing is what your bird wants. At dinner time, feed your bird some fresh veggies while you eat, so he gets to participate in this important flock behavior.

After dinner, especially as it gets dark earlier, your bird will be content to sit on a perch near your recliner or on your knee while you watch television or do homework.

Changes in routine are tough for everyone, including your parrot. Keep in mind that your bird is a prey animal, and he sees change as increasing his chances of being eaten. When your parrot looks to you for comfort and support as routines change, provide it, and life at your roost will be good!

Taking a Parrot Outside

Remember the first day you could walk outside this spring—after the bad weather was over? Like you, your parrot can benefit from the stimulation of fresh air, the sounds of nature, sunlight—all those things we miss indoors in the winter. For parrots, in addition to elevating mood, sunlight converts precursors from his diet to vitamin D, which is responsible for feather, bone, and skin health.

Safety First

The first rule of outdoor adventures is safety. Pet parrots outdoors must be (1) caged or leashed, (2) have a wing clip, and (3) be supervised. If you can't do all three, don't take them outside. Otherwise,

For safety reasons, only take your parrot outside in his carrier or in his harness.

expect it will be your bird on the sad poster, "Lost: Pete Parakeet, blue and white, owner frantic." Parakeets and cockatiels are excellent flyers and can sometimes fly even with proper primary feathers trims. So, let me repeat: leash or cage and clipped wings.

Keep it Simple

If your goal is a trip out of doors, start by feeding your bird in his travel crate. After the bird is comfortable eating in the crate, take a sandwich and the crated bird and head to your balcony or patio. (Remember, birds must be crated or harnessed out of doors to be safe.)

One quiet afternoon when you and your parrot are alone, take the cage he lives in outside. If his cage is too large, use his smaller travel cage. Plan in advance where you'll position your bird. Keep the cage up, off the ground. Use a table or other sturdy surface. This helps ensure that cats, dogs, or snakes do not overturn or stalk the cage, frightening or injuring your bird (or worse!).

Remember that the sun moves and temperatures change over a few minutes. Monitor this closely. If you are able to sit next to your bird comfortably while you are wearing a short-sleeved shirt and shorts, your bird will be okay with the temperature. That range is no lower than 60°F (15.5°C) and no higher than 90°F (32°C).

Before moving the cage containing your parrot outside, cover the entire cage with a towel. Once the cage is outside and positioned, fold the drape back to cover only a portion of the cage top. This helps your bird feel secure. Birds assume that trouble can come from any direction, and they hide from trouble as a defense. Denied this opportunity, they become frantic.

Think of the process you went through with your children or that you went through as a child. You traveled in a baby carrier. Then by stroller, then walking while holding hands. Then short supervised play dates followed by longer unsupervised play dates. Then an overnight trip. Then camp for the summer. Same thing for a bird. You can't take an adult parrot who has never been out of his cage to your favorite café for nuts and expect him to do tricks to amuse your friends while you drink your coffee. He'll be scared out of his wits! As with all training, go gradually and make sure your parrot is totally at ease before moving on to the next step. And, reward your bird so he sees being outside as fun.

Travel: With Parrot or Without?

The decision to travel with your parrot or without should be based on the amount of time you will have to spend with him and the difficulty of the travel challenges.

If you are going on a family vacation to Disneyworld, leave your parrot at home. You'll be away all day, and there's no time for your bird. In addition, not all hotels want birds left in hotel rooms during the day. Obviously, you won't take your bird on a cruise or on a plane trip. The logistics are substantial. Instead, take the opportunity to take a break from each other. Board your parrot or have a pet sitter come in. You'll both be very glad to see each other when the vacation is done.

If, on the other hand, you're taking a car camping trip to a place with a moderate climate, perhaps you will want to take your bird along. If you're exploring the local area, spending a lot of time reading under the trees or visiting with friends, what better way to spend time with your favorite bird?

For trips like those, do be sure to carry a first-aid kit and the numbers of local twenty-four-hour veterinary centers. And, of course, carry your bird's medical records. Some states require that birds have health certificates to enter the state. Be sure that your paperwork is in order.

Check ahead that your hotel, campground, or other accommodations will allow you to bring your bird. DogFriendly.com gives great information about traveling with pets, including those hotel chains that accept pets, rules for various parks and campgrounds, and local veterinary resources. Start with DogFriendly and then narrow your questions to be parrot-related. Also, www.birdchannel.com/bird-travel gives tips related to bird-specific questions.

Checklist for Finding a Good Parrot Sitter

A good bird sitter is not easy to find. The best sources of information about sitters include the following:

- Your veterinarian
- Breeder
- Local bird club
- Pet Sitters International (www.petsit.com)
- National Association of Professional Pet Sitters (www.petsitters.org).

Parrot Escape Kit Checklist

Prepare a kit with the following items and have it on hand at all times. If your bird takes off, it's an emergency. You have no time to assemble these things then. Most of these items can also be a part of your emergency evacuation kit.

- Take a picture of your bird for your flyers and cards.
- Microchip your parrot.
- Take video for posting on the internet.
- Make at least 250 lost-bird flyers.
- Make 250 lost-bird business cards.
- To enable others to help you search for your bird, make sound files you can distribute to others that can reproduce your bird's call. This can sometimes help a bird feel confident enough to emerge from hiding or descend from a high place. Purchase a small digital recorder or mp3 player and a portable battery-operated speaker.
    - Have fresh batteries for the speaker, recorder, or player.
    - Record your bird's call.
    - Make 25 CDs of your bird's call.
- Write down and photograph your bird's band number.
- Prepare a small portable travel cage or crate with several pillow cases, a long rope, a few of your bird's favorite treats, some toys, and a bottle of water.
- Print out a map that includes a five-mile radius around your home.
- Binoculars.
- Dowel rod to retrieve your bird from a high place.
- Phone numbers and e-mail contact list for search helpers.

There are a number of behaviors you can train to make it more likely that your bird will return if he escapes. These include the following:

- recall
- enter a crate or travel cage
- step onto a long dowel rod
- contact call using words, whistles, or other sounds
- step up onto other people
- saying your name, address, and/or phone number (if your bird talks)

Checklist for Finding a Lost Parrot

Despite our best efforts, sometimes our companion parrot escapes an open door or window, and our worst nightmare begins. If you are prepared, you can increase your chances of finding your parrot considerably. The best collection of information on how to locate a lost parrot has been assembled by Barbara Heidenreich, a well-known bird trainer and the provider of indispensable information at her website, *Good Bird*.

The following list of information is adapted from her website, GoodBirdInc.com and used with the kind permission of Barbara Heidenreich.

Bird Is Flying Away

- Call to your bird loudly; your voice may help him find his way back to you.
- Do not take your eyes from your bird. Note the last place you saw him, the height of his flight, how tired he looked. He may have landed in that area. Radio or phone a group of people to help you search.
- Create a group of people, spread out, and circle the area of last sighting.
- Continuously call him with words or sounds he mimics. He may call back. Most parrots are located by their screams.

If he has a parrot friend, cage that parrot and bring her to the area of last sighting. Walk away from the cage to encourage the parrot friend to call. Your lost bird may call back. Keep quiet to listen for the scream.

Look within one mile in the early stages. Unless blown by the wind, chased by a bird of prey, or extremely frightened, your parrot is unlikely to go far.

Your parrot may see you before you see him. When this happens, parrots are sometimes very quiet because they are relieved to see you.

Despite bright colors, parrots are very difficult to see in trees. Look for movement as opposed to your whole bird perched prominently on the tree.

You Have Located the Bird, but He Is out of Reach

Once you find your bird, relax (unless your bird is in immediate danger). Let him sit while you create a strategy. Do not try to grab the bird or scare him down.

If he has just landed, he will probably not fly again (if at all) for a while.

Bring the bird's favorite person and favorite bird friend (in a cage) to the area.

Bring favorite food items, favorite toy, familiar food bowls, and the bird's cage if possible. If not, bring out his T-stand.

Be careful not to ask your bird to fly from a great height or a steep angle. Position yourself, bird buddy, or cage to allow short flights or short climbs to lower places.

Lure your bird to fly or climb to branches/objects that are similar to those upon which he is sitting. A bird may be too frightened to climb onto a distinctly different perch, such as a fence.

Expect the process to be slow; be patient as he builds confidence. He may also fly again if he touches the new perch and is frightened by it.

Do not raise unfamiliar objects up to your bird to have him step onto them. If you have a familiar item, your bird may step onto it. Ladders, cherry pickers, and tree climbing may frighten your bird. If you must resort to using these items, stop if your bird looks like he wants to fly away.

Call your bird when his body language indicates he is ready to try to come down. Do not constantly call.

Try hiding from your bird to create anxiety, which may cause him to try to come to you once you reappear. Usually, birds will scream and or start moving when they are ready to try to return to you. If you notice this activity, come out from hiding.

If you hear your bird screaming or relieve himself, he is ready to fly. Be alert for this. Be ready to run to see where your bird flies.

The Sun Is Setting and Your Bird Is Still Out

Parrots will usually fly again shortly before the sun starts to set. This is probably your last opportunity to get your bird back before he roosts for the night. Try to get the bird pumped up by yelling and creating a level of excitement. This may encourage one last flight.

As the sun sets, your bird will fluff his feathers and roost for the night. Allow him to sleep. Keep an eye on him until the sun has set completely. Remember his exact location.

Before the sun rises the next day, return to that location. Your bird should still be there, unless he was frightened in the night (owls can cause this).

By 8:30 or 9:00, your bird will be ready to fly or try to get to you. Repeat the steps described in the previous list.

Your Bird Has not Been Spotted After a Full Day of Searching

Contact the following and let them know you are looking for your bird. If a person finds your bird, they may contact one of these organizations:

- animal control
- local police
- local veterinarians
- pet shops
- SPCA/local animal shelters
- zoos

Place an ad in the classified sections of local newspapers for a lost bird.

Check the classified sections of local papers for a found bird. Answer all ads. A Congo African grey may be mistaken for a red-tailed pigeon by a person unfamiliar with parrots.

Post "Lost Bird" fliers in the areas where you last saw your bird. Offer a reward as incentive for people to call.

Note: Don't give out the bird's band number. If your bird is recovered by a dishonest person, this could lead to removal of the band.

The key to getting your bird back is perseverance. Do not accept that you will not get the bird back once you have lost sight of him.

GROOMING

rooming a parrot is nothing like grooming a poodle—no clippers, brushes, coloring, or shampoos required. However, grooming—and providing the materials for your bird to groom himself properly—is a part of keeping your bird healthy and safe, as well as with claws blunted so as not to puncture your skin during handling. Like any other aspect of parrot parenting, your first experiences with grooming should involve a professional. In the same way that you wouldn't take your child to a doctor of doubtful qualifications, you shouldn't leave your bird's grooming to an amateur. Although a nail and wing trim doesn't seem a big event, this is a very important procedure that affects your pet's balance, self-confidence, and ability to glide safely down from heights. Amateur services for wing and nail trims is a mistake that new parrot parents make. These grooming procedures are not like getting a haircut; they are more analogous to minor surgery.

Restraining Your Bird

For the new bird person, it's probably best get someone else to do grooming and restraining unless no other options are available. This is because, first, you want to engage in trust-building activities only. If your bird does not enjoy being restrained (what creature does?), don't be involved. Second, without instruction, restraining isn't going to be your forte. In other words, restraining doesn't hurt a bird, but it needs to be done quickly and firmly. For a novice, this is not possible. When you add the stress that the bird being restrained is your new companion, this is usually too much for some people to handle.

It's important that you learn how to do a restraint, however. Restraint is essential in the event that your bird breaks a blood feather, becomes entangled in a toy, or needs to be examined if you see any evidence of injury. This is especially true if your veterinarian is more than a few minutes away.

Some parrots are enthusiastic bathers and will hop into any available water.

Videos are available that can help you learn to train your bird to allow wing and nail trims without restraint. This is an ideal situation. And, if you have a baby bird who has been trained to allow this sort of handling, you must keep working with your bird to reinforce this behavior. Find a veterinarian who will support this approach.

Although professionals use a variety of methods including clamps on towels, tubes, or other devices to complete grooming alone, having one person restrain and reassure the bird and another focus on the grooming is the best procedure. Most professionals prefer this approach. If you are alone and you need to restrain your bird, some options that are safe for you and for your bird are available; do consider in advance what method you will use and learn to use that method from a professional.

Small parrots can be restrained with one hand for grooming tasks, but having a helper is still recommended.

How to Hold the Bird

In the event that only you are available to do the restraint, the general idea is to hold the bird's head in position with two fingers of one hand. If you feel the bony points of your own skull just behind your ears, you'll have your hands in approximately the same position that you need your fingers to be on the bird's skull. The second area of restraint is the wings and feet. You want to restrict the movement of the wings with your body and a towel while you restrict the feet with the fingers of your second hand. If this sounds a bit complicated, it's not. However, practice at restraint is important. You want to hold just firmly enough to immobilize the bird but not so much that he feels more stress than necessary; in addition, restrainers need to be conscious of the importance of allowing air to flow freely through the bird's body. Because of the stress created by restraint, air flow is very important, and the air sacs, located in various parts of your bird's body, need to be able to function properly.

Using a Towel

For small birds, a smooth cotton wash cloth is of sufficient size and thickness as a tool of restraint. For medium-sized birds, a hand towel no larger than a dish towel is enough. For a large bird, you may need a small bath towel. Wrap the towel around the back of your bird, grasping the back of the skull between thumb and forefingers to control his beak. Wings or feet are accessible from the front of the towel. Towels also serve to keep oils and other materials from your hands off your bird's feathers.

Training for Restraint and Grooming

Alternative methods are available and can work well. Keep in mind that restrained parrots will use their beaks first to free themselves. Sometimes having a piece of the towel or a small toy to chew on relieves some of their stress. However, the best stress reliever is either a quick procedure or a combination of a quick procedure and a bird trained to tolerate wing and toenail work without restraint.

If you are dedicated to training, GoodBirdInc.com's website offers a video for sale that explains and

Using Grooming as a Health Inspection

One of the reasons to have a veterinarian do your grooming is that she can use the visit as an opportunity to do a health inspection. Most veterinarians do not charge much more than a groomer to perform a wing trim as well as a toenail trim. At the same time, practiced eyes are observing your bird's ability to withstand stress and his physical condition, as well as the condition of his skin and feathers.

Your veterinarian's trained observation could spot an illness that is developing, a parasite, or an indication that his diet is not working before the situation becomes serious (and expensive) to resolve. This practice of using your veterinarian as a groomer is an inexpensive form of insurance that many long-time companions recommend.

demonstrates how to train your bird to accept nail and wing trims without restraint. If we all trained according to the video, our birds would benefit through much reduced stress. This sort of training, although it can be accomplished with an older bird, is best begun when a bird is very young.

Bathing

Birds in the wild bathe in water that collects on leaves, by hanging upside down during a rainstorm, in dust, or in puddles and small rivulets, depending on their species and location. Birds bathe to maintain their feather and skin condition, to help remove parasites, and—seemingly—to enjoy themselves. While bathing, many birds call, screech, flap, and show extreme excitement.

For companion birds, bathing opportunities are especially important because of the drying effects of heating systems and indoor living. Not only does bathing help keep your bird's skin and feathers in excellent condition, but the moist air is good for his respiratory system, and the stimulation of flapping and the excitement of this activity is exercise for body and mind. Flapping during bathing is exercise. Daily bathing is ideal for companion birds.

How Companion Birds Bathe

A parrot bathing in a collection of water dips his beak and then his head into a shallow pool. Then the parrot may get into the water, flutter his wings, and scoop water over his body. Other birds enjoy a soaking mist, mimicking droplets dripping from the leaves. These birds are good candidates to take with you into your morning shower. Even if your parrot does not enjoy a very, very gentle direct spray from the shower, he probably will raise his contour feathers and his wings and let the warm, moist air reach his skin. Other birds prefer to be spritzed with a gentle mist from a spray bottle. Aim your sprayer above the bird, letting the mist settle on his feathers, creating the same sort of moistening that walking through a damp fog might. Birds such as budgerigars and cockatiels might prefer bathing in damp lettuce or other green leaves, mimicking their most frequent sort of bathing in the wild.

Different species of birds, as well as different individuals, have their bathing preferences. As a companion, experiment until you find the methods that your bird prefers.

Encouraging Your Bird to Bathe

The best of all possible worlds is that your bird can be persuaded to jump into any shallow bowl filled with lukewarm water intended for his bath. Make sure that the bath container is large enough for your bird to put his whole body in but shallow enough so that when he stands he is only tummy-deep in water. The best time to offer a bath is morning to midday, so that your companion is completely dry before it's time to roost for the night.

The best circumstance is that your bird always has a bowl of water large enough to accommodate a bath at any time he feels the need. On the cage bottom, use an earthenware bowl too heavy for your bird to overturn. He might be intrigued if you place floating toys, ice cubes, or leaves in a shallow pan of water. If you have a small cage and a bird who enjoys being misted, try spritzing your bird in the morning before you replace his cage liner paper. Some birds prefer a warm gentle spray from a water bottle. Spray the air above the bird: Think perfume atomizer instead of power washer for the spray setting. Spray the water on yourself to demonstrate and habituate the bird to the sound, as well as to gauge whether the power of the spritz is too strong.

This female eclectus seems to be really enjoying her misting.

A shower perch lets your parrot come right into the shower with you.

Some birds like bathing in wet branches or leaves. Place fresh greens on a plate at the bottom of the cage. Weave branches with leaves into the cage-top bars. Spray the leaves until they drip with water. Your bird may come down and rub his feathers against the leaves or climb up and let the water drip onto his body.

Using the Shower

For a bird who might enjoy showering with his favorite person, clear the bathroom counter and allow him to perch there to observe your delight in your own shower. Observe your bird's reaction, so that you know how long the familiarization process may take. Some birds are anxious to join you on the first day, but most birds are more comfortable perched outside the shower for a couple of weeks, just watching. After that, you might install a shower-perch and continue the familiarization process slowly.

Avoid battering your bird with the full spray from showers. In addition, some birds have been disciplined with spray from a water bottle, and these birds should not be sprayed for bathing purposes. No bird should be allowed unsupervised in water deeper than his feet. Be vigilant that your bird cannot get into shampoos, soaps, body washes, and other similar materials; also be sure you don't get any on him accidentally as you shower.

Your approach means a lot in how your bird will react. Integrate the water into something fun, a morning ritual that you have with your bird. Talk enthusiastically about the experience. "Isn't this fun? I love baths. Wanna shower?" If you have fun, chances are your bird will too.

Soap and water?

Unlike humans, birds don't need soap or shampoo. Never add anything to your bird's bath water. The exception is if your bird meets with something oily or soils his feathers in a substance that needs to be removed. Then you need to bathe your bird immediately, using up to ½ teaspoon (3 cc) of mild detergent (Dawn brand dish soap is what wildlife rehabilitators use to remove oil from birds) in 1 cup (250 cc) of water. Ensure that you blot your bird as dry as you can with a towel. Some birds do not mind the heat and noise from a hairdryer. Others are terrified by it. The point is to be sure that your bird does not become chilled during the drying process.

Molting

Feathers are not permanent structures and periodically they must be shed and replaced. This process is called *molting*. Wild birds' flight feathers are worn by flying. You can see the wear on the edge of the feathers where repeated rubbing against the air dulls them. (Seriously, you can.) Because mating requires brilliant, well-conditioned feathers, most birds molt at least once each year. Unlike birds who migrate, parrots do not "wear out" their feathers on long flights. However, parrots do molt in new feathers to create their brightest appearance for the mating season. Most birds have one complete molt each year and a second molt just before the breeding season. In other words, expect heavy molts twice each year. In addition to these molts, there is a steady and progressive turnover of old feathers. In parrots, each feather is normally replaced once each year.

Light provides cues for this seasonal behavior. At the beginning of the breeding season, hormones induced by the seasonal variations in daylight hours stimulate molting and breeding. This process of feather development benefits from highly effective nutrition and metabolism that is the result of a bird consuming a balanced diet in the presence of adequate sunlight.

Birds do not molt all at once. Over about six weeks, feathers drop in an orderly pattern. The flight feathers molt one at a time, usually the same feather position, on left and right wings. The powder down is produced on the thighs of many bird species, especially cockatoos and African grey parrots. This shows itself as a fine white powder. This is normal throughout the year, not just during molting times (Proctor and Lynch, *Manual of Ornithology,* p. 104; Harrison and Lightfoot, *Clinical Avian Medicine.* p. 177).

You will notice during the molt that the energy your bird requires is substantial. He is producing new feathers, the feather sheath, and the feather *pulps*. In the process, your bird is replacing 3 to 10 percent of his total body mass (about 20 to 30 percent of the lean body mass). Accordingly, expect

Never Trim Your Bird's Beak

Parrot beaks are complicated, powerful, and delicate, all at the same time. The beak is the parrot's substitute for teeth and lips and is the entrance to his mouth. Used for a variety of purposes including climbing, grasping, processing food, preening, and display, it contains bones that underlie the horny covering that you see. The upper bill is hook-shaped and covered in a keratin layer that is lost through wear and replaced by new growth.

The lower bill has a sharp, chisel-shaped surface that pushes against a ridge in the under surface of the upper bill. This shape allows the crushing of seeds and nuts, as well as the efficient processing of other foods before they move into the mouth.

The growth of the bill is moderated by the wear it receives, as well as by your parrot's diet, so *never* attempt to modify or trim your bird's beak. Beneath the keratin layer is bone and tissue that is well-supplied with blood vessels. In trimming or shaping your parrot's beak, you could, without meaning to, create a medical emergency that could result in permanent damage.

If your parrot's bill seems overgrown or misshapen in any way, contact your veterinarian and ask for an appointment. If your companion's bill needs shaping or is growing incorrectly for a medical reason, your veterinarian will be able to correct this in a safe and efficient way.

your parrot to be consuming more food during these periods. However, the food needs to be a balance of protein, carbohydrate, and fat. In other words, don't change the diet, but be sure that your bird has sufficient food and water during these very physiologically stressful times (Harrison and Lightfoot, *Clinical Avian Medicine*, p. 87). During the molt, birds need extra protein and are not as resistant to disease.

A bird living as a companion needs help in grooming the feather sheaths on his head and neck. This process can be a source of bonding between you and your bird. *Gently* preen the end of the feather, working back toward the skin. If the sheath does not disintegrate naturally, *leave it alone*. The feather is not completely formed, and the sheath should remain in place.

Blood Feathers

During the molting process, new feathers poke through the skin wrapped in a cuticle-like sheath to protect the feather's structure during development. The process can be uncomfortable, as you can imagine, especially before the feather has completely emerged. To nourish the feather as it grows and develops, a blood supply flows through vessels contained in the feather shaft. As long as the blood supply continues to flow, these blood feathers remain fragile; touching them hurts.

During this time, any manipulation of the feather not only is painful, but you risk breaking the feather and opening the artery and vein that provide the nutrients and remove the wastes of metabolism. If a blood feather breaks, it bleeds prolifically, requiring flour or styptic powder applied to the central feather shaft to stop the bleeding. In addition to the powder or flour, companions must watch to be sure that the bleeding does not restart through further trauma or your bird worrying the feather. Sometimes, to stop the bleeding, the feather has to be removed at the follicle. This should be done by your veterinarian, or, if in an emergency situation, with your veterinarian coaching you through the process.

Once feathers mature, blood no longer flows to them. At that point, your bird will be anxious for your preening help to remove the remainder of the waxy coating that helped the feather grow through the bird's skin.

Wing Clipping

When grooming is said to include wing clipping, this does not mean the main structure of the wing is in any way affected. Wing clipping or trimming should more correctly be considered a trimming away or shortening the length of some flight feathers. The purpose of wing clipping is to provide your bird with a way to make a controlled short flight or a seamless and gentle glide to the ground from his play stand or any elevated perch while preventing him from actually flying up and away.

Although there is a substantial community that does not believe in trimming the flight feathers, the experience of veterinarians and bird behaviorists is that most pet homes are not equipped to provide a safe environment for a fully flighted parrot. Mattie Sue Athan, author of *Guide to a Well-Behaved Parrot,* claims untrimmed wings are often at the root of loss and death in companion birds. According to Athan, companion parrots taking flight out open doors and windows or drowning in toilets with lids raised is a heartbreak prevented with proper grooming and trimming. Athan is only one of many professionals who advise their clients to take care with the fully flighted bird. Dangers include not only escape and accidental death through investigation of unsecured locations (open toilet lids), but also death through frightened, full-powered flight into windows. Clipping the flight feathers reduces most parrots' ability to gain altitude and enough flight speed to cause accidental deaths by striking a window or other object.

Importance of Experienced Grooming

Dr. Marli Lintner, Avian Medical Center, Lake Oswego, OR has seen significant injuries following wing trims. "I've seen birds with their keels split open from falling after wing trims that are too severe. This is not just a grooming problem." She performs wing and toenail trims on her avian clients herself, with her veterinary technician restraining the bird in a gentle, safe manner.

Dr. Lintner suggests bird companions have a veterinarian

Checklist for Flight Feather Trims

- Trim only as many primary feathers as you need to keep your parrot from rising when he flies.
- Trim wings symmetrically.
- Only cut primary flight feathers, never secondaries.
- Never trim the feathers shorter than the coverts. Primary feathers clipped too short can result in complications as they regrow.
- Trims should be the least necessary to keep the bird out of trouble.
- Good trims must be frequently maintained because a bird trimmed in this way can regain flight with a few new wing feathers grown in.

monitor or perform all grooming procedures. Most veterinarians specializing in birds offer grooming; in most cases, the grooming at the vet's office is done by a veterinary technician. An advantage of having the veterinarian himself groom your bird is the opportunity he has to observe your bird's general health. If he sees a reason for concern, the problem can be discussed and addressed on the same visit. Most veterinarians' rates for grooming are comparable to those of professional groomers.

Using Professional Groomers

Many people advertise professional bird grooming services, but there are no accreditations or professional guidelines for bird groomers. The companion must determine whether the groomer has the experience to do a good job. Sally Blanchard, noted parrot behaviorist says, "The basic rule applies—are they working with the parrots in a trust building, gentle manner?" Blanchard suggests that parrot companions can be taught to groom their own birds by capable professionals.

What Does Wing Clipping Look Like?

Trimming flight feathers is an art. Trim just enough to keep the bird from rising flight. Birds should be able to make a controlled glide from a high place to the floor. The primary feathers are the ones to trim. Your groomer should inspect the wing for blood feathers. Blanchard's explains, "When a bird loses the long-shafted feathers on his...wings..., the follicle receives a hormonal message to grow a new feather. These emerging feathers continue to receive a blood supply from the follicle until they are mature." When they are mature, the blood supply is stopped through a natural process. Once this occurs, the feather can be trimmed.

It's best to have your avian veterinarian clip your parrot's wings.

If, during grooming, you feel uncomfortable about what is happening to your bird, speak up. Your bird may be annoyed by grooming, but should not be terrified. The stress of a poor grooming experience can kill birds. In advance, discuss with the groomer her procedure for capture and restraint of your bird. You should also discuss the tools and the extent of the grooming. Good grooming is a companionable collaboration, and individual birds require different treatments. The most important aspect is planning your grooming goals, selecting a competent groomer, and asking questions until you feel comfortable with the process.

Grooming Hazards and Prevention

When grooming goes wrong, "clumsiness" can result. Especially in heavy-bodied birds such as African greys and Amazon parrots, it is important to ensure that your companion bird has been properly fledged—taught to fly—before his first flight feather trim. In addition, in longer-lived birds who are somewhat slow to mature, the young birds need a little extra care to allow them to develop their physical skills and coordination at their own pace. If this means moving perches closer to the bottom of the cage and delaying flight feather and toenail trims, then follow your breeder's advice and delay these grooming procedures.

"Clumsiness" in your bird is typically the result of three common and ill-thought out practices: premature trimming of baby birds' flight feathers, excessive wing trimming, and severe toenail clipping.

The routine features of even the safest homes, such as mirrors, windows, open toilets, and spaghetti pots, present life-threatening hazards to flighted birds. However, trimming babies' wing feathers before they have learned to fly can have negative impacts on the bird's physical and psychological well-being. The process of learning to fly provides the essential experience from which babies learn lifelong body awareness, control, and confidence. Body awareness and control prevent clumsiness. Once learned, this knowledge is never forgotten and is critical to the personality development of a well-adjusted companion bird.

Even birds who have mastered flying can be seriously injured and traumatized as a result of a severe or improper clip. An appropriate clip allows birds to land on their feet by gliding gracefully to the floor with balance and control. Custom clipping is necessary to adjust for the strength and determination of each individual bird. If too many feathers are clipped, a bird will have no lift and will hit the floor like a brick. Clip one feather at a time on each wing until a 15-foot (4.5-m) glide path, with no gain in altitude, is achieved.

Only the very tips of the nails should be clipped. Toenails that are too short hamper natural balance and footing when perching and climbing.

Nail Care

Nails should remain sharp enough so that your bird can grip perches, but not sharp enough to hurt you or poke holes in your skin. Like your nails, birds' nails also have a blood supply. After clipping the nail to reduce the length, the natural shape of your parrot's nail needs to be restored so that he can grip properly. Many vets use emery boards with a conical tip to restore the concave surface on the back of the nail.

Although the best approach is professional nail clipping, knowing what a good nail shape looks like is helpful. Harrison and Lightfoot describe nail trimming as not only shortening the length of the nail, but also making sure the two sharp ridges on the sides of the nails are smoothed toward the end of the nail. Although this honing makes handling your bird more comfortable for you, it decreases the bird's ability to maintain his balance. This is why a dialog with your veterinarian as he does the grooming is important. In addition, your veterinarian will probably use an emery board rather than a rotary grinding tool. Although the grinding tool can be useful for heat cautery if a nail bleeds during trimming, the heat generated by the grinding can be uncomfortable for your bird. In addition, many vets feel they get a more precise result using emery boards, in just about the same amount of time.

Should You Use a Groomer, and How Do You Find One?

Finding someone who knows how to trim your bird's feathers and nails properly is essential. Clipping flight feathers requires consideration of the individual habits, body type, and conditioning of your bird. As an example, African greys and eclectus, both sensitive species, need to be protected from excessive feather removal. As heavy-bodied birds, they need quite a bit of wing area to be able to fly successfully to a controlled descent. When these birds' wings are clipped unevenly or too much, significant damage can result beyond the trauma to the breast muscles. These birds can become unconfident; thus, anything but the mildest wing trim for these birds should be a point of much discussion in advance.

Your parrot's claws need will need regular trimming.

Often, the best resource for bird grooming is your veterinarian. She and her technician can trim flight feathers appropriately so that your bird avoids the significant injuries that frequently result from incorrect wing trims. Her veterinary technician will restrain your bird in a gentle, safe manner while the vet does the actual trimming.

Another advantage of having the veterinarian groom your bird is the opportunity she has to observe your bird's general health. If she sees a reason for concern, the problem can be discussed and addressed at the same visit. Most veterinarians' rates for grooming are comparable to professional groomers.

What to Do If You Clip a Nail Too Short

The first aid for a too-short nail clip is styptic powder or flour packed into the bleeding nail. One good reason to have someone else do your bird's grooming is that the chance of trimming nails too short is less in a well-lighted environment with a technician and/or a veterinarian doing the procedure. Nevertheless, clipping a nail too short happens to everyone, including vets. The flour or styptic is packed into the nail to close off the vessel with a blood clot that will hold while healing takes place. After packing, watch your bird carefully. Stress or physical exertion increases blood pressure, which can dislodge the clot. Check on your companion every few minutes, and be sure that the paper or towel he's standing on is clean so that you can discern any sign of rebleeding immediately. A drop or two of rebleeding might be expected after 10 minutes. If your bird bleeds more than that, repack the nail. If this doesn't slow the bleeding to a drop or two within five to ten minutes, get your bird to his veterinarian. The blood volume of birds is surprisingly small. Continuing to bleed freely after ten minutes is a bad sign.

Another reason to use a veterinarian is that no accreditations or professional guidelines exist for bird groomers. You, then, must determine whether a groomer has the experience to do a good job. If you are a beginning bird person, this is difficult to do without the experience of seeing proper feather and toenail trims. This is another reason to start with your veterinarian and have him or her teach you the principles of good wing trims.

Discuss in advance with the groomer her procedure for capture and restraint of your bird. Also discuss the tools and the extent of the grooming. Individual birds require different treatment. The most important aspect is planning your grooming goals, selecting a competent groomer, and asking questions until you feel comfortable with the process.

The delivery and configuration of the companion bird's trim should leave the bird comfortable, confident, and recoverable. Wings are trimmed symmetrically. Only primary flight feathers are trimmed because only the primaries enable the bird to gain altitude. All other wing feathers are for protection or maneuverability. Primary feathers clipped too short can result in several troubling complications as they regrow.

Long-feathered and light-bodied birds cannot be grounded by even the most severe of wing feather trims. These birds usually require all flight feathers to be trimmed at about one-fourth to one-half inch beyond the coverts—enough to allow comfort and confidence indoors. However, you must be aware that no parrot can be trusted not to fly away, no matter how short the feather trim. Take your parrot outside only when secured by harness or in a travel carrier.

7

HEALTH CARE

Although some people feign illness to avoid tasks they don't want to do, birds are the opposite: a bird fakes being well. By the time that you notice a bird looking a bit disheveled, perhaps with his feathers fluffed or sleeping more than usual, it's time to get to the veterinarian right away. Birds have evolved to hide weakness; in other words, parrots are very good as masking their illnesses.

Because parrots can become very ill very quickly, being prepared is important—perhaps more important than for any other sort of companion animal. You need to know the signs of illness, have a first-aid kit and hospital cage ready to be used, and have the number of a 24-hour emergency clinic and the number of your veterinarian handy or on speed dial.

Not only that, but you must get into the habit of weighing your birds regularly and taking him to his veterinarian for grooming. Another pair of eyes seeing your birds is an excellent idea. Because we see our birds each day, seeing change can be difficult. This is why we need objective measurements, such as weight and stool samples to help us see the first signs of illness.

Feathers cover a multitude of problems; they are like a costume our birds wear. Weight loss, lumps and bumps, as well as weight gain can all disappear under a bird's feathers.

If you're a new bird companion, you don't need to be alarmed, but you do need to be made aware that if you suspect that something is wrong, you're probably right. And, once something begins to go wrong, a bird's delicate physiology needs immediate attention.

A sick bird may sleep more than is normal and may sleep during his usual activity times.

Spotting a Sick Bird

Two tools will help you spot a sick bird: newspaper at the bottom of your bird's cage (and some knowledge about what normal poop looks like) and a postal scale. In the same way that new parents of human babies never believe that their lives will revolve around preparing meals and examining poop, companion bird people can't believe it either—yet, this is your new life. Parrot poop is free, frequent, and informative. However, some instruction is required; *Clinical Avian Medicine* by Harrison and Lightfoot is the reference avian veterinarians rely on as one source of information, and it is the source of our descriptions here.

To know what unusual droppings look like, being familiar with usual droppings is helpful. Parrots droppings are made up of feces, urates, and urine. Birds release these wastes

Emergency!

Consult your veterinarian immediately if you see any of the signs listed in this table. If your bird is showing these signs, he is potentially very ill.

Abnormal droppings	Possible causes
diarrhea	sudden diet change, parasites, ingestion of foreign object, egg binding, stress, over-treatment with antibiotics
bloody feces (red or black)	intestinal inflammation, egg binding, tumors, poisons
undigested food	poor nutrition, intestinal infection, pancreatic disease, oil ingestion
increased volume of feces	egg laying, egg binding, poor digestion
decreased volume of feces	appetite loss, shortage of food, intestinal obstruction
increased urine output	normal with increased stress and diets high in fruits and vegetables; abnormal with infectious diseases, poisons, drug reactions
decreased urine output	dehydration
abnormally colored urates (anything except white or beige is a serious problem)	liver problems, failure to eat
green or yellow	liver disease; anorexia; changes in diet including seed, eggs, or other yellow-pigmented fruits and vegetables.
brown or red	lead or zinc poisoning; intestinal bleeding; kidney or liver disease; change in diet to include pellets, beets, artificial colorings.

simultaneously through one orifice, the cloaca. In a healthy bird, the feces or solid wastes should be well formed, look the same throughout, and have little or no odor. The color will be brown when pellets are fed. Seeds give a more greenish color; fruits and vegetables, especially those with strong pigments, can affect feces color, as can colored pellets. Urates should be very white and somewhat moist. The diet, species of parrot, and stress can change the ratio of urine to feces. For example, lorikeets' liquid diet produces large amounts of urine and a less solid fecal component.

Once you know what your parrot's normal droppings look like, you can quickly identify any differences that might indicate problems. A change in the appearance, color, or quantity of droppings is one of the earliest signs (and may be the only sign) of a sick bird. This is one reason that frequent cage cleaning is not only a neatness issue but a health confirmation issue. This is, of course, the reason that loose beddings should never be used. Aside from their other disadvantages, substrates other than a flat sheet of paper make evaluation of wastes impossible.

Most veterinarians suggest that companions take a moment to look over their bird's droppings daily. Signs of trouble include a change in the color and amounts of urine and feces and a change in the color of the urates. Diarrhea in birds is not simply more liquid in the bird droppings, but is a clear lack of feces formation.

The second tool in spotting a sick bird is the scale. Weighing and recording your bird's weight weekly is an excellent practice. Many bird people weigh their birds even more often. The daily or weekly weight gives you a baseline from which to discover a trend. Keep the weight records with your scale or your emergency first-aid kit for ease of access.

If you find that your bird's weight is decreasing and you haven't noticed a corresponding increase in your bird's stress level or a drop in the temperature of the area in which he is kept, look more

The best veterinarian for your parrot is an avian specialist.

It's best to take your parrot to the veterinarian for a well visit yearly.

carefully. Typically, birds who are ill will appear sleepy, slightly fluffed, and may even perch on the bottom of the cage. Any of these signs mean that you should immediately call your veterinarian and bring your bird to the clinic. By the time that you see outward signs, an infection or some other condition may be very advanced.

Weighing your bird is also an excellent way to prevent weight gain, which is detrimental to your bird's health. If your bird's weight is rising, this may be an indication that he is not receiving enough exercise or he's ingesting too much high-calorie food. Birds should always have abundant food available. The mix of greens along with fruits and other higher calorie foods, however, can be adjusted.

Finding a Good Parrot Vet

Certified avian veterinarians are veterinarians certified as Avian Diplomates by the American Board of Veterinary Practitioners. Certified veterinarians have a specialty certification similar to a surgeon's or cardiologist's. This certification requires five years of specialty practice to achieve specific levels of competence in avian medicine and the successful completion of the avian board exam.

Many avian veterinarians are not board certified by the American Board of Veterinary Practitioners. This certification only recently became available, and there are still only a few more than 100 such certified vets worldwide. At the time certification became available, many highly qualified avian veterinarians were already established. Those individuals did not need to become board certified to attract clients. In many cases, these older, established veterinarians can be significantly more qualified than newer graduates.

The best way to find a good veterinarian for your parrot is to ask your breeder, local rescue groups, and members of your local bird club. The goal is to find a veterinarian who sees lots of birds. If you live outside a large city, you may have to drive quite a few miles to find someone who does see lots of birds. However, the effort is worthwhile.

The Well Visit and Why it's Important

Having your parrot seen annually for a well visit is important for several reasons. First, you must have grooming done at least twice each year anyway. You might as well have the most educated person possible doing the grooming. This includes nail trimming and trimming or shaping of the beak, if necessary.

Second, having baseline blood work and a fecal exam done annually is good preventive care. In the same way that you should have an annual checkup to record your baseline weight, blood pressure, and blood test results, your bird needs a similar consideration. Some long-term problems can be discovered and treated at an early stage as a result of the annual exam. Also, any reputable facility that accepts birds for boarding requires a recent health certificate.

Finally, the relationship that you have with your veterinarian is an important one to develop; likewise, the discussions that you have over behavior, feather condition, and diet can be very helpful, either to set your mind at ease or to help you make a decision about changing your bird care routines. In addition, if you have an ongoing relationship with your bird's vet, emergency situations can be more easily handled. Recent fecal and blood test results show what is normal for your bird. In addition, the communication and trust that you need during these difficult situations is there for you.

Vaccines for Parrots

The topic of vaccines for companion parrots is a difficult subject. Although vaccines do exist for poxvirus, paramyxovirus-1, and salmonella, the vaccines are indicated for birds raised outdoors. In addition, the herpes virus vaccine, as of this writing, is effective only against one type of the virus. A broader vaccine, one that protects against other similar diseases, including Pacheco's disease and internal papillomatosis, is wished for but not yet available. A related situation exists with the West Nile vaccine, for which the risks of side effects to an individual bird outweigh its relative value. In other words, protecting your bird with adequate mesh screening from potential carrier mosquitoes is a more effective and safer form of prevention for this particular disease.

Research into vaccines to protect our companion birds from illness continues. As of this writing, most companion bird veterinarians do not recommend vaccinating pet parrots.

Checklist of Signs of Illness

Because your bird cannot tell you when he doesn't feel well, you have to look for the signs. As you become familiar with your bird, you will be able to detect changes in his activity level and appearance.

Changes in activity that you might recognize include being less active, sleeping more, and decreased responsiveness to things that usually excite him. Changes in appearance could include fluffed feathers, listlessness, drooping wings, closing of the eyes at midday, and a leaning posture.

Other signs include:
- change in droppings
- change in food or water intake
- damaged feathers
- flaking of skin or beak
- lumps or bumps under the skin
- nasal discharge
- noisy breathing
- rubbing of eyes
- straining to eliminate
- vomiting

Injuries and First Aid

First aid is emergency treatment given to a sick or injured companion bird before transporting him to the veterinarian. The goal of first aid is to stabilize your bird so that the time and movement required to get your bird to the veterinarian does not worsen his problems. In other words, first aid is the first step and not a substitute for veterinary care.

Gary Gallerstein, DVM, in *First Aid for Birds* explains first-aid priorities. There are life-threatening emergencies; painful, but non-life-threatening injuries; and minor injuries. Severe bleeding or blood flowing from a wound must be attended to immediately. Stop the flow of blood before calling your veterinarian. This is a life-threatening emergency. Non-life-threatening illnesses or injuries, such as fractures, diarrhea, or vomiting, cause distress and pain. The goal is to prevent the injury or illness from worsening and to transport your bird to the veterinarian as quickly and as comfortably as you can. Minor injuries include superficial abrasions. For small scratches or scrapes, you can care for your bird at home if you know how, and then take him to be seen by his vet if the injury does not improve.

Knowing what to do for the most common emergencies can be a comfort. The most common companion bird emergencies include animal bites; bleeding from broken nails, beak, or blood feathers; broken bones; oiled feathers; and poisonings.

It is important during an emergency situation to keep your bird calm, keep him warm (between 80 and 85°F [26 to 29°C]) to help prevent severe shock, and get your veterinarian on the telephone as quickly as possible to help you assess next steps. The last step is especially important if transport will take more than a few minutes.

Animal Bites

Bites from animals are life-threatening emergencies. Not only can there be obvious or hidden puncture wounds from a bite, but also internal injuries and fractures can result from the crushing power of the animal jaws. In addition, infections develop from bites and scratches, particularly from cats. These puncture wounds can be difficult to see without a thorough physical examination under powerful lights. The first twenty-four hours after the bite are critical. Even if your bird appears bright and alert, have him seen by your veterinarian immediately.

Beak injuries always require veterinary care.

Broken Nails, Beaks, and Feathers

Bleeding from a broken nail or beak can be quite serious. With as little commotion and stress to your bird as possible, catch him and apply direct pressure to the injury using a towel or your finger. If a minute or two of pressure doesn't stop the bleeding, apply cornstarch or flour and watch the injury until the bleeding stops. Be sure to observe your bird once an hour for several hours after bleeding stops. If a piece of nail or beak is cracked or dangling, it will need to be removed. Call your veterinarian right away for instructions.

Sometimes birds break feathers before the feather is fully developed. Because these developing feathers have an active blood supply, they are called *blood feathers*. When blood feathers break, blood drips without stopping because the blood vessel has been opened. The first step is to try to stop the bleeding with flour or cornstarch packed into the feather shaft. Often this does not work or bleeding recurs because your companion will worry the painful feather. Call your veterinarian for coaching. To stop the bleeding, you may have to remove the feather shaft from the follicle, where it attaches to the wing. This procedure is best done with two people, one to restrain the bird, and one to remove the feather. If you cannot find help, restrain your bird using a towel and vet wrap and remove the broken feather without delay.

Use sturdy tweezers or needle-nosed pliers to grasp the feather as close to the skin as possible. Support the wing as you pull out the feather to avoid breaking the wing bone because bird bones are easily broken. (This is why you want coaching from your veterinarian.) After removal, apply pressure directly on the follicle for one to two minutes using a cotton ball or gauze. Once you control the bleeding, observe the bird for an hour. Bleeding can recur.

Fractures

Fractures are painful, but also a sign your bird could have additional more serious injuries. Pet birds fracture legs more commonly than they fracture wings. The signs of a fractured leg include the bird not standing on the leg or the leg hanging in an awkward position. A fractured wing will hang lower than the other, and the bird will be unable to move the wing. If you suspect a fracture, confine your companion to a small carrier padded with a towel. Keep him warm. If possible, immobilize the wing by binding it to the body, either with a stocking with a hole cut in the toe or with a towel draped over the bird like a cape and encircled with masking tape. For a fractured leg, get aid in immobilizing the leg by wrapping it onto to a flat rigid object cut to the correct length. Let your veterinarian do the rest.

For unknown reasons, cockatiels are especially prone to night frights.

Night Frights

Some birds, particularly cockatiels, experience thrashing episodes when noise or vibration causes them to awaken suddenly in the night and they try to take flight. During these night fright episodes, your bird can seriously injure himself. If this happens, assess your bird for bruises, cuts, broken feather, or other injuries. Calm and comfort him. Sometimes night frights can be reduced by installing a small night light near the cage so the bird can orient himself. Thus far, no one seems able to explain the origin of night frights, nor why cockatiels in particular seem to suffer from these upsetting episodes.

Don't Wait

Once a bird exhibits any sign of illness, he needs to be seen by a veterinarian immediately. Birds, because they evolved as prey animals, never show signs of illness until they are too ill to mask the signs. So, by the time you notice, your bird needs immediate help. Call in to work and say you'll be late. Call your veterinarian and say you're coming in. If your regular avian veterinarian cannot see you, find out who can. Repeat: do not wait.

Exposure to Oil

Oil-soaked birds are a serious emergency because not only do birds lose their ability to regulate their temperature when feathers are oiled, but also because, in attempting to remove it from their feathers, they ingest the oil, which can damaging or fatal. Contact your veterinarian as soon as you discover the situation. Cleaning an oil-soaked bird requires multiple steps, best done by an experienced person.

If you cannot reach your veterinarian, dust oiled feathers with cornstarch or flour to soak up excess oil, taking care to keep your bird's eyes and nose clear. Wrap him in a towel to reduce heat loss and prevent him from trying to remove the toxic oil from his own feathers. After thirty minutes, fill a sink with warm water and add a minute amount of soap. (See Chapter 6, for proportion.) Wet all affected feathers, handling gently and following their contours. Dip the bird slowly for one or two minutes. Rinse the feathers well with fresh warm water. Repeat as needed. Blot feathers dry. Put the bird in a box and keep the temperature at about 85°F (29°C) until he is dry. Steps may need to be repeated several times for thorough cleaning.

Poisoning

A poisoned bird may suddenly regurgitate, develop diarrhea, go into convulsions, or show signs of redness or burns around his mouth or on his body. Birds can be poisoned by inhaling fumes, eating a poisonous plant or chemical, or coming into contact with poison on the skin. If your bird is overcome by fumes, open all windows and move him into fresh air. If the poison is a contact poison, flush the skin with water. Call your veterinarian and ask to be seen immediately. Bring the poison in the original container with you. If you are unable to reach your veterinarian, call the ASPCA National Poison Control Center at (888) 426-4435, open 24/7, 365 days each year. Have a credit card ready. The charge is $65, and well worth it if it gives your bird a chance to survive.

Any of these situations is frightening for your companion. Your best focus is on taking care of the accident or emergency, staying calm, keeping your bird as warm and calm as possible, and later, having your own moments of stress. Your bird is depending on you to handle the emergency.

Supportive Care for the Sick Parrot

The best supportive care for your sick parrot can be provided by your veterinarian or emergency animal care clinic. However, assuming that you have to travel some way to reach this facility, you should first telephone the veterinarian for advice on supportive care during transport.

Key aspects for care include minimizing stress; providing a quiet, dark place for your bird to rest; and providing supplementary heat to help your companion maintain his body temperature. The best source is a heating pad set on a low setting, positioned under a portion of your bird's transport cage. Alternatively, heat can be provided through a hot water bottle covered with a towel. If neither of these is available, try filling a small jar with hot water, securing it to the side of the cage with duct tape, and covering it with a towel so that your bird is not burned.

Offer a perch, but also offer a soft towel for your bird to stand on, rather than the perch. If your bird seems too exhausted to perch, fold a towel into a U shape and offer it as a support for your bird to rest against, with his chest set into the rounded portion of the U.

Unless your veterinarian suggests that you do otherwise, do not attempt to feed or hydrate your bird. Birds who are ill need to be fed and hydrated carefully. Unless you have skills in gavage (tube) feeding or injecting subcutaneous fluids, leave this to the professionals. In trying to help, you can easily compound the problem.

Outfitting a Hospital Cage

A hospital cage needs to provide a warm, dark, moist, and quiet environment for a recovering bird. As your bird responds to treatment, in consultation with your veterinarian, you can reduce the

Some trainers advocate training parrots to take liquid from syringes. This makes it easier if you ever need to medicate your parrot.

amount of support provided. However, in the beginning, you need to do the following:

Set up a small cage or carrier with at least 50 percent of the cage bottom resting on a heating pad set to low. Provide a clean, soft towel for your bird to stand on. Also offer the option of a low perch. Provide a small saucer of water, shallow enough so that your bird can drink easily, but not so large or deep that a tired bird could drown in it. Provide a ready supply of high-calorie, high-nutrient foods that are favorites of your bird (assuming your veterinarian has not put your parrot on some other diet). Make it easy for him to eat and then to rest.

Having Your Parrot Sexed

Having your parrot sexed can be done in one of several ways. First, your parrot may be of a species that has feathering differences. This, of course, is the easiest way to tell male from female. A second way, and one which occurs more frequently than you might imagine, is that a bird (usually one assumed to be a male!) lays an egg. This is the definitive sign of a female bird.

Two additional ways include an internal examination and DNA testing. For the DNA testing, only a drop of blood is needed, and the cells are examined for the presence of the male or female sex chromosome. The test is inexpensive, and reports can be had in short time. The blood can be collected as part of your baseline blood work at the time you purchase your bird. The final method is surgical sexing, which is done under anesthesia by your veterinarian. The avian veterinarian will pass an endoscope into the body and look for an ovary or testicle.

Wrap the cage or carrier in a towel to help hold in heat and to create a calming, dark atmosphere while making sure that adequate air exchange is possible. You might keep a thermometer inside the cage. A moist environment of 80 to 85°F (26 to 29°C) is optimal, unless your veterinarian recommends otherwise.

If your bird has an injury that makes standing difficult, provide a towel rolled and bent into a U shape, so that your bird is propped up comfortably.

Make sure that your bird has plenty of quiet and is not bothered except when necessary to ensure that adequate water and food are supplied. If your bird requires medication, be sure to provide this at the same time as the food and water, so that your bird gets as much rest as possible.

Clean and sanitize the area so that your bird is not exposed to other pathogens while he is recovering. In particular, be sure that no other pets or small children are in contact with your bird at this delicate time.

Common Health Problems

Common health problems in companion birds come in many different forms. Gallerstein, in his *Complete Bird Owner's Handbook,* discusses the seven major forms of problems that can arise based on their causes. These include the following types of diseases:

Infections: caused by bacteria, viruses, and fungi. Although bacteria and fungi live on "dead tissue," viruses live protected inside living cells; this, Gallerstein, explains, makes them " very difficult,

The First-Aid Kit

It's wise to keep your first-aid kit for birdie well-stocked and accessible. You never know when you are going to need it. Check the contents a few times a year, replacing items that have been used up or have expired. A tool kit or fishing tackle box works well. Make sure it is clearly labeled, and, if you use a bird sitter, make sure she knows where you keep the kit.

First-Aid Kit Contents

- apple juice and eye dropper for fluid and quick energy
- appropriately sized towels for catching and holding your bird
- basic bandage materials, including gauze squares and rolls
- blunt-tipped scissors
- cotton swabs to clean wounds
- eye irrigation solution (like saline) to flush wounds and eyes
- flour or cornstarch (instead of styptic powder) to stop bleeding and remove oil
  - half-inch masking tape
  - heating pad and/or hot water bottle
  - hydrogen peroxide as an antiseptic and disinfectant
  - nail clipper and nail file
  - small flashlight
  - small pad and pencil for notes about your bird's condition
  - tweezers or needle-nose pliers to remove blood feathers
    - vet wrap
    - veterinarian and closest emergency hospital name, number, address, and directions

if not nearly impossible, to treat." Some vaccines are available for viral diseases common to pet birds.

Metabolic diseases: Diseases such as diabetes, allergies, and thyroid problems come from abnormal chemical processes that affect the production and use of energy.

Nutritional diseases: These result from either too much or too little of essential nutrients, such as vitamin A deficiency. Alternatively, these problem can be caused by a metabolic malfunction that prevents the body from using the nutrients; hypocalcemia in African grey parrots is one example.

Parasites: Parasites are animals, such as mites or worms, that live on or in your companion bird at the expense of your bird's health.

Toxins: Poisons can irritate, damage, or weaken the body's systems.

Cancers: This uncontrolled cell growth invades the body and destroys surrounding tissues, causing organ damage, bleeding, obstructions, and opportunistic infections.

Developmental and degenerative diseases: These diseases signal problems related to growth or the aging process as tissue deteriorates and loses function.

These sorts of diseases are indicated by signs and symptoms in various body systems. The following are common problems that you might see and that indicate a need for a visit to your bird's veterinarian.

Eye Problems

Any eye problem requires immediate veterinary care. If you see discharge, rubbing, or swollen eyelids, call your bird's veterinarian. This could be an indication of conjunctivitis or a scratch on the cornea.

Respiratory Problems

Symptoms such as noisy breathing, difficulty breathing, open-mouth breathing, or discharge around the cere could be signs of a respiratory infection, a metabolic problem, or a parasite. These signs are consistent with sinusitis, vitamin A deficiency, pneumonia, air sac infections, aspergillosis (a fungal disease), mites (a parasite), and psittacosis (also called chlamydiosis).

Digestive Problems

Digestive problems are indicated by vomiting; a loose stool that may contain blood, mucous, or undigested seeds; straining to eliminate; or droppings that contain urine and no feces. These signs can be consistent with oral cavity problems such as *Trichomonas*, a parasite found in the mouth. Most digestive problems are caused by infections or parasites. Crop problems especially occur in young birds and are often caused by bacteria and yeast infections. The proventriculus or stomach of the bird is affected by proventricular dilatation

Feather plucking can be caused by physical problems as well as mental ones.

syndrome (PDD), suspected to be caused by a virus. In the intestines, "good" bacteria sometimes escape into the bloodstream and cause widespread infections. Also in the intestines, parasites, including single-celled ones such as *Giardia* and organisms as large as worms, cause weight loss. In addition to weight loss, look for the passing of undigested food or diarrhea. Treatment may include a course of drugs to clear up the parasite after diagnosis is made through a microscopic examination of the feces.

Another serious problem you might recognize is when the cloaca, a sac where feces and urine collect, protrudes through the vent or muscle that controls elimination. When an organ falls out of its normal place like this, the medical term is *prolapse*—a *cloacal prolapse* in this case. This can result from straining with diarrhea, constipation, or egg laying. A prolapse is an emergency requiring immediate veterinary care, usually in the form of surgical repair.

Two diseases that cause digestive symptoms and that deserve special mention are psittacosis (chlamydiosis) and tuberculosis. Both these diseases can be transmitted to people. Psittacosis, also called parrot fever, is a bacterial disease. Signs include light green feces, watery urates, and loss of appetite. A specific test for psittacosis should be done on all newly acquired birds. A treatment using the antibiotic tetracycline must be continued for at least 45 days.

Tuberculosis (TB) of birds is related to the TB known in humans, but transmission to human beings is rare. The disease usually shows itself in birds as prolonged diarrhea. Also called mycobacteriosis, this cluster of diseases can manifest in several ways, depending on the progression of the disease.

Microchipping

Microchipping is one way to ensure that you can identify your bird should he become lost and then found. These small electronic devices are injected into the body, usually into the left pectoral muscle in parrots. The code, when scanned with a reader, provides identification for the bird.

Most shelters and veterinary hospitals have a microchip scanner. Unfortunately, there are several different code standards, so that one model of chip reader cannot read all microchip types. Nevertheless, if your bird is found by an honest person, a microchip enhances the chances that he will find his way back to you.

Although there is no easy diagnosis, and some forms of the disease can be managed with a battery of antimycobacterial drugs, humane euthanasia is recommended because of the uncertainty of the control of the bacteria and the potential for transmission to immune-compromised people. These two diseases, chlamydiosis and tuberculosis, are reasons to be concerned about the source of your companion bird. Not only can your bird become ill, but you or a family member (especially one with a weakened immune system) can become ill also.

Liver disease is common in pet birds and comes in three most common types: psittacosis, fatty liver (seen in obese birds), and Pacheco's disease, a viral liver disease affecting only parrots. This is another disease more likely to be seen in a recently acquired bird.

Abnormal Beaks and Claws

Normal beaks are hard and symmetrical, and the width and shape varies with each species. If you see overgrowth, rough surfaces, or a chip or crack, this is time to see a veterinarian. Traumatic injury is the most common problem, followed by infection, once the wound is open. Liver problems can also create beak and nail issues.

Most common in budgies, the scaly face mite creates a white, honeycomb crusting on the beak, which must be treated in order to prevent permanent beak deformity.

Bumblefoot

Bumblefoot is an infection of the feet and is caused by unsanitary conditions, trauma to the feet, obesity, and sandpaper perches. Appearing as sores on the bottom of your bird's feet, bumblefoot is a serious problem that will prevent a bird from perching correctly. The treatment requires antibiotics, and sometimes surgery to repair the damage. If you see signs of rubbing on the bottom of your bird's feet, examine your perches, your cleaning practices, and stop the problem before it progresses. Once injured, feet are difficult to heal.

Abscesses and Cysts

Lumps and bumps vary in cause from the not very significant to the serious. Abscesses are collections of pus surrounded by a wall of tissue. The abscess must be opened, the pus removed, and the wound treated with antibiotics. Feather cysts, or ingrown feathers, are another cause of a lump. These can occur almost anywhere on the body. Again, the cyst must be opened, the debris removed, and antibiotics applied. Tumors also can occur anywhere on the body. These tumors can be benign, such as a lipoma, which is common in overweight birds; tumors may also be malignant and spread. Removal and biopsy is usually recommended.

Feather Disorders

Feather disorders and picking can be difficult problems to solve. Some feather picking may be the result of stress, inadequate stimulation, or a medical condition. If the feathering elsewhere is normal, a nonmedical cause is usually the issue. Feather picking is a particularly difficult problem to solve, but is generally improved through changes in the bird's environment to create a more nurturing and interesting lifestyle, as well as increased interaction and exercise to help the bird discharge stress.

Feather disorders may also be the result of serious medical issues. The most serious is psittacine beak and feather disease virus (PBFDV). This disease results in extreme malformation of feathers. Typically a disease of Australian parrots and African parrots, this disease has no effective treatment and no vaccine at the time of this writing, although research continues. This is a disease that should be included in the screening when a new bird is purchased.

More and more parrots are reaching their senior years, and the field of geriatric avian medicine is expanding.

Neuromuscular Disorders

Nerve and muscle disorders are most frequently caused by two infectious agents of serious concern: Newcastle disease and avian polyoma virus. As of this writing, these diseases have no effective vaccines, which is to say that, especially in the case of polyomavirus, there are few circumstances where immunization is helpful in its control. (A similar situation exists with the West Nile virus vaccine that, in birds, remains unsatisfactory.) Birds suffering from exotic Newcastle disease (END) show signs such as a stagger in walking and head bobbing after a period of weight loss and diarrhea. Recovery can occur from END, but a regulatory veterinarian must be immediately contacted because recovered birds may shed virus for months to years, thus endangering other birds. Avian polyoma virus (APV) infects adult parrots as well as nestlings. Many infected birds show no signs, and this is a sign that the bird may also have a PBFDV infection. Testing by blood and swabs examined by polymerase chain reaction (PCR) is required for a diagnosis. A vaccine is available, but its value in prevention is questionable. Control of the virus is through extensive cleansing and disinfection, as well as supportive care for ill birds.

Caring for a Senior Parrot

For many years, the poor diets given to parrots precluded many from reaching a geriatric age. However, with improvements in knowledge about nutrition and other aspects of care, many more parrots are reaching senior status. Senior status begins at different ages for different species of parrots. Cataracts and arthritis are the most commonly seen problems for senior parrots. Cataracts most commonly develop in older birds and appear as a whitening of the lens. They limit your bird's vision as they develop, just as they do in people. As with any senior citizen, adequate diet and assistance in maintaining a comfortable body temperature, as well as awareness of moodiness or tiredness related to age or chronic soreness, are necessary. Aging is an individual and natural progression. The best way to help your bird age gracefully is to notice what seems to be more difficult physically than before and create cage modifications to ease your bird's mobility. If your bird seems to need help in supporting his body temperature, usually indicated by fluffing his feathers, add a heating pad set to a low temperature underneath a portion of the bottom of his cage. Alternatively, a heat lamp could work as well; make sure you position the heat source so that only a portion of his cage is warmed. In this way, he can move out of the heated area if it gets too warm.

A recent article, "Geriatric Psittacine Medicine," by Teresa L. Lightfoot, DVM, DABVP, (*Veterinary Clinics of North America: Exotic Animal Practice*, 13:1, January 2010, pp. 27–49. http://dx.doi.org/10.1016/j.cvex.2009.10.002) recommends that the annual exam for geriatric parrots include several factors not present in the annual exams of younger parrots. Then, of course, the question arises, "When is a parrot of geriatric age?" The true answer is that we don't know. The vast majority of parrots imported or bred in the 1980s through 2000 are no longer living. As our knowledge of nutrition and other caretaking has improved, so the life spans of our companion parrots have also increased. However, a ten-year-old budgie or cockatiel is definitely geriatric. A ten-year-old African grey is an adult but definitely not geriatric.

Special-Needs Parrots

Many special-needs parrots exist today in sanctuaries and rescue organizations across the country. Although these parrots have special needs, many people feel that the extra care they require makes the relationship with these birds even more extraordinary than with a bird who is more independent. These special needs include chronic medical or behavioral problems, handicaps such as malformed limbs, and birds blinded by cataracts. Caretakers of these birds often report forming a very close bond, as if the bird seems to understand that the caretaker is providing exactly what is needed.

Your veterinarian will be a partner in helping you understand the scope and limitations of your bird's capabilities, as well as suggesting modifications to housing, diet, and bathing that may be required.

Of the thousands of birds looking for homes, these are the most difficult to place, but, according to the people who care for them, they are the most rewarding of all companion birds.

Lightfoot recommends the following items be included in the exam of the elderly bird:

- questions about behavior changes that could be manifestations of pain, nervousness, fear, or disorientation compared with previous years
- questions about changes in water consumption or urinary output, food preferences, sexual behaviors, preening habits, preferred perching locations, and sleep cycle
- an examination that includes assessment of weight, muscle mass, grip strength, joint range of motion, mobility, feather condition, and exercise tolerance
- x-rays to examine bone density, arthritic changes, cardiovascular abnormalities, and to screen for organ masses or enlargement
- complete blood count and plasma chemistries, including bile acids, triglycerides, cholesterol, and HDL and LDL levels if indicated.
- an eye exam
- an echocardiogram if warranted

8

SELECTED
SPECIES

arrots originate on different continents: There are Australians, Africans, Asians, and New Worlders (Americans). Each of the more than 350 parrot species has adapted to live in a particular environment. None of these species has evolved to live as a companion parrot. The closest to "domestic" parrots that we have are the budgerigars, cockatiels, and some of the Asian parakeets, which have been bred in captivity for many generations. The other species are essentially wild animals. Their DNA is almost identical to that of their wild forbears. A generation or two of captive breeding does not domesticate a parrot; rather, thousands of generations of breeding for pet qualities are needed. Breeding for pet qualities means choosing temperament over appearance.

The choice of species that you make is the most important decision you'll make in your relationship with a companion parrot. Some species are more adaptable to apartment or suburban living than others. Some species should be kept only by experts in huge cages or aviaries. And there are many different species in between.

The point of this chapter is to help you in your selection. Many of the species most frequently kept as companion parrots are profiled on the following pages. Before you look for an individual parrot, make a list of several species that seem as though they might fit your lifestyle. Then, visit those species to see whether, in person, the birds are what you expected. Always select the species before you begin considering individuals. Although individuals may not conform exactly to a species profile, you will rarely find a large macaw who is a quiet bird. Similarly, although many cockatiels can talk, you won't find one who has a large vocabulary. However, a small, loving cockatiel can be the companion of a lifetime whereas a large talkative macaw who screams can be a misery.

Research carefully. Meet some representative members of the species you're considering. Talk with people who own the species about what they like best and least about their pets. Do these things before you venture into parrot parenthood. This is a long-term commitment, longer in most cases than your human children will live with you. If that isn't a daunting thought, it should be. All of us who live with parrots question whether we would start with another large parrot. Many of us believe that the smaller, more adaptable parrots are a better bet for the modern lives that most of us lead. Start with the facts. Then listen to your gut. If your gut tells you that a particular species might be too much for you, listen. You can always add another bird later. It's difficult to rehome a bird who hasn't fit in—difficult for you and very, very difficult for the bird.

African Greys

Scientific Name: *Psittacus erithacus*

Size: Approximately 13 in (33 cm)

Average Life Span: 8 years; reported maximum is 48 years.

Recommended Cage Size: 24 × 36 × 48 in (60 × 91 × 122 cm)

Recommended Perch Size: 1–1.5 in (2.5–3.8 cm)

Talking Ability: Very good to excellent

Noise Level: Moderate; natural calls are high-pitched, with prolonged whistles. Harsh screeches are the grey's response to alarming situations.

Pet Potential: Good, but not the best parrot for beginners. They are sensitive and do not recover quickly from handler mistakes.

Introduction: These medium-sized parrots have become popular because they have a reputation as excellent talkers. A famous parrot, Alex, the subject of Dr. Irene Pepperberg's long-term studies on intelligence and language of parrots, popularized this notion. Although some African greys are prolific communicators, others prefer to whistle or to imitate sounds rather than to mimic human speech. Some Greys are very quiet and never talk. Somewhat heavy-bodied, Greys are not the most acrobatics of parrots, but nevertheless are highly intelligent, are comical in their interactions, and can make very good companion birds.

    Origin and Habitat: Dwelling most of the time in lowland forests in central Africa, these birds visit savanna woodland and open country to feed. Although they do come to the ground to feed, they

Congo African grey parrots are intelligent and sensitive birds.

prefer to stay high in the trees and move from branch to branch by climbing rather than by flying. As wild birds, they typically live in groups of 5 to 50 of their species; grey parrots in the wild tend to be shy of other species. Males and females are feathered alike.

Physical Characteristics: Adult plumage is pale gray, with the gray head and neck feathers having gray-white edges, a color similar to the face. The abdomen and rump feathers are very pale gray, while the primary feathers (wing) are almost black, as is the bill. In sharp contrast, the bird's tail and tail coverts are bright red, while his legs are gray and his iris pale yellow.

Temperament and Personality: Most African greys are relatively quiet and enjoy companionship without soliciting a lot of petting or physical contact. Some African greys are shy and nervous. Because these birds are intelligent, they are also sensitive to changes in their environment. In addition, because of their heavy bodies, they do not fledge easily. To have the best chance of a confident grey, be sure he is fully fledged and flies well before doing the initial flight feather trim.

Most Popular Subspecies: The two subspecies are *Psittacus erithacus erithacus* and *Psitticus erithacus timneh*. These are called the Congo African grey and the Timneh African grey, respectively. Some authorities view them as two different species. Overall, Timnehs are 10 to 15 percent smaller than the other subspecies, with a darker tail—dark maroon edged with black—and a smaller beak. The upper mandible is a pinkish color rather than the dark color of the Congo grey. The positive and negative traits are usually somewhat reduced in the Timneh subspecies.

Other Information: In the wild, these parrots eat seeds, nuts, fruits, and berries in the treetops. They are reportedly very fond of the oil palm fruit.

Because African greys are intelligent and sensitive, they remember negative experiences and retain associations with people and objects that can develop into phobias and neuroses. Feather picking is a very common problem in this species of parrot. To keep a parrot of this intelligence occupied, the keeper needs to put a good deal of thought into the sorts of toys and foraging challenges that will meet this parrot's needs. Not as bold and playful as some varieties of parrots, nevertheless they need a wide array of activities and changes of toys—in particular, toys to destroy—especially during breeding season.

The Timneh African grey is a bit smaller and darker in color than his Congo cousin.

These birds need both ambient attention as well as direct attention each day to remain emotionally healthy. Behaviorists frequently recommend videos, radio, or television if you are going to be away from home much of the day. Keep in mind that these parrots have the intelligence of a two-year-old child.

To keep such an intelligent creature busy, offer choices of food, activities, and changes of pace to keep your parrot's brain and body exercised. If you don't have plenty of time to spend with your bird, this is not the one for you.

Amazons

Scientific Name: *Amazona*; there are about 30 species

Size: 11–15 in (28–38 cm)

Average Life Span: 5–30 years, depending on the species; reported maximums are 11–66 years, depending on the species.

Recommended Cage Size: 24 × 36 × 48 in (60 × 91 × 122 cm)

Recommended Perch Size: 1–1.5 in (2.5– 3.8 cm)

Talking Ability: Many popular species talk well. Yellow-nape, double yellow-head, and blue-fronts are thought to be better talkers.

Noise Level: Can be very loud, but generally not as loud as macaws

Pet Potential: Best for experienced handlers

Introduction: Parrots of Central and South America and the Caribbean, the Amazons are probably the best-known of the New World parrots. These parrots move in flocks of 5 to 50 or more, sometimes with other species. In flight, these birds have a constant, harsh call. While grooming or feeding in the wild, they are reported to make a soft clucking or purring sound, varying dependent on the species. Popular as pets in many parts of their home range, some species of Amazons are excellent mimics of both words and song.

Origin and Habitat: Most species inhabit moist forests where they can move from fruiting tree to fruiting tree. Difficult to see from the ground, Amazons in the wild are best located by noticing fruits falling from above.

Physical Characteristics: Stocky, medium-sized birds, their bills are short, strong, and heavy. They have slightly rounded tails and broad round wings. Males and females are usually feathered alike, mostly green with yellow, blue, or red shoulders, heads, faces, or lores (the area between the eyes and bill). Many Amazons have a distinctive sage-like odor, which you may or may not find appealing.

Temperament and Personality: Fiercely territorial in the wild, these parrots have big personalities and can be very difficult for a beginner to cope with because of their fast-changing moods. Gregarious and raucous, they can cause novice owners problems, especially when they reach sexual maturity. However, people fall

Blue-fronted Amazon. All the Amazon parrots are best for experienced parrot keepers.

The unusual hawk-headed parrot is similar to the Amazons in size and temperament.

The white-fronted is the smallest of the Amazons.

in love with their antics and with the fact that they are quick learners and learn tricks well (as well as with their beauty).

Most Popular Species: Relatively common species of Amazon include blue-fronted (*A. aestiva*), lilac-crowned (*A. finschi*), orange-winged (*A. amazonica*), red-lored (*A. a. autumalis*), the yellow-headed (*A. oratrix*), yellow-crowned (*A. ochrocephala*), and yellow-naped (*A. auropalliata*). Quieter species include festive (*A. festiva*), mealy (*A. farinose*), and spectacled or white-fronted (*A. albifrons*).

Blue-fronted Amazons can acquire a large vocabulary and are known to be playful but noisy. The species has a blue forehead and lores, and the cheeks, crown, and upper breast are yellow.

The spectacled Amazon is the smallest of the group. It is playful and affectionate and can talk but does not have a large vocabulary. The head is red, white, and blue, with the rest of the small bird green.

Yellow-naped Amazons may learn a large vocabulary and are usually curious and playful. During breeding season, males become moody, even if no female is present.

Although not an Amazon parrot, the hawk-headed or red-fan parrot (*Deroptyus accipitrinus*) is similar in size and temperament. Hawk-heads mainly differ in having a beautiful ruff of feathers around the head that they can expand dramatically when excited. Like Amazons, they are best left to experienced companions who know how to socialize and train birds with a tendency to be stubborn and territorial.

Other Information: Wild Amazons thrive on fruit, berries, seeds, nuts, blossoms, and leaf buds. These parrots need a companion who is willing to spend lots of time on positive training. Otherwise, Amazons are prone to screaming, territoriality, and aggression, including lunging and biting. Despite this, Amazons are popular. Consistent training helps keep the relationship between an Amazon and his family positive. Requiring lots of toys, these big-bodied birds also need lots of exercise because they are prone to obesity. Provide lots of chewables and rotate toys frequently. A bored Amazon is a noisy Amazon.

Bourke's Parakeets

Scientific Name: *Neopsephotus bourkii*

Size: 7.5 in (19 cm)

Average Life Span: 6 years; reported maximum is 19 years.

Recommended Cage Size: Minimum, 24 × 24 × 24 in or (60 × 60 × 60 cm); preferred is an aviary or suspended cage, minimum length 4 ft (1.2 m). Although much smaller cages are used, the exercise your bird gets in an aviary setting translates into better health and softer temperament.

Recommended Perch Size: 1$\frac{1}{8}$–$\frac{3}{4}$ in (31 mm–2 cm)

Talking Ability: None

Noise Level: Low; their flight call is a mellow *chu-wee*; perched, they give a quiet rolling whistle; the alarm call is a shrill, metallic note. Calls are softer and higher pitched than those of the budgerigar, but the calls of the two species are similar.

Pet Potential: Very good

Introduction: In their native habitat, Bourke's parakeets are nomadic, quiet, very tame birds who spend most of their day feeding on the ground or sitting in low bushes. They are endangered in their own homeland of southwestern and central Australia, but they are popular in aviculture, readily available in the United States, and relatively inexpensive.

Bourke's parakeets are quiet and easy-going birds.

The Bourke's parrot has recently been removed from the *Neophema* genus and placed in a genus of its own. Some discussions about this change are still ongoing.

Origin and Habitat: Interior of southern and central Australia. Bourke's parakeets live in dry acacia scrubland.

Physical Characteristics: Bourke's are long, slender birds. The feather colors give the impression of a bird with a light blue forehead and under parts, a rosy-pink belly, and whitish face. They have blue-washed tail, flanks, and thighs, and brownish wing coverts. Females have narrower pink margins in the throat and breast and a wing stripe that is absent in males. The bill is gray-brown, as are the legs; the iris is brown.

Temperament and Personality: These parakeets are quiet, gentle, and unassuming, with very endearing personalities. They are not known to be aggressive with other species, even those smaller than themselves (i.e., finches, canaries). However, their gentle nature may make them an easy mark for more aggressive birds.

Other Information: They do well in planted aviaries; they are not likely to destroy any woodwork. Provide safe, seeding grasses if possible, along with branches for climbing and areas for bathing. Bourke's will breed readily, and this parakeet can be visually sexed. Adult males have blue-brown crowns, whereas adult hens have white brows. Hens and juveniles have a full gray head.

They accept any parakeet nest box, placed as high up as possible to give them some sense of security and privacy. Providing more boxes than pairs will reduce bickering over the favorite boxes. There are several splendid mutations, such as the opaline (rosey), white face pink, cinnamon, fallow, cream, lutino, and rubino.

This species is not very flighty, being most active at dawn and dusk. They are social and do enjoy the company of other birds or people. Young handfed birds make excellent pets and can be kept in medium-sized parrot cages as long as they have ample time out of the cage. A parent-raised bird will enjoy a mixed aviary or the company of its own species.

The wild diet is primarily composed of seeds of grasses and herbs, which they gather on the ground or in bushes. They are known to sometimes eat green shoots.

Be sure to use a small-bird seed mix, such as one containing canary seed, millet, and smaller amounts of oats, buckwheat, safflower and hemp. Offer limited sunflower seeds and millet sprays, along with pellets formulated for small birds.-Rather than feeding a larger proportion of dry seed for these parrots, try sprouting seeds for higher levels of nutrition and lower amounts of fat.

A Bourke's parakeet is good choice for a first-time parrot keeper

Caiques

Scientific Name: *Pionites*

Size: 8 in (23 cm)

Average Life Span: 6–13 years, with reported maximums of 23–27 years

Recommended Cage Size: 24 × 24 × 36 in (60 × 60 × 91 cm); preferred 2 m (6.5 ft) for a pair

Recommended Perch Size: ¾ –1 ¼ in (2–3 cm)

Talking Ability: Not known for talking

Noise Level: Low to moderate; not excessively noisy, caiques' calls can be shrill. The alarm call is a shrill *wey-ak*! Some birds raise their wings and call, *toot*. Other calls are a screaming *heeyah* and *wheech-wheech-wheech*.

Pet Potential: Good for bird-keepers with some experience

Introduction: Caiques exhibit many traits of larger birds in the body of a small bird. With some ability to talk, caiques are high energy and can be loud. Nevertheless, experienced bird handlers enjoy their colorful antics. In summary, these are beautiful and playful small parrot. These species can be somewhat difficult to locate; once you find a good breeder, you may have a wait to acquire a bird. Caiques are social, clownish, comical, very precocious, and fearless.

Origin and Habitat: Forest and savanna birds of the tropical zone, caiques' range spans much of the Guianas, Brazil, Venezuela, Ecuador, and Colombia.

Physical Characteristics: Caiques are sturdy, small parrots with short, square tails, a narrow bill with a notch in the upper mandible, and a featherless cere. Both species have white bellies, violet-blue primaries, and orange vents and irises. The pantaloons of the black-headed caique are orange, and those of the white-bellied are green. The black-headed has a black head, a blue eye ring, black bill, and gray feet. The white-bellied has an orange head, white eye ring, and pink feet.

White-bellied caique. The caiques are playful and energetic.

Black-headed caique.

Temperament and Personality: Confident and bossy, caiques have the peculiar habit of hopping or bouncing. Clownish in appearance and actions, they can exhibit a tough side. Many veterans suggest that caiques are not a good first bird because of their brash and bossy attitudes.

Most Popular Species: Two species are known, and both are found in the pet trade: the black-headed caique (*Pionites melanocephala*) and the white-bellied caique (*Pionites leucogaster*).

Other Information: Somewhat wary in the wild, these birds collect in large family parties of up to thirty and browse the upper branches of trees for fruits, berries, and seeds.

As pets, caiques do well on a mixture of soaked, sprouted, and dry seed, with an emphasis on fresh fruit in addition to a pellet that requires them to chew, chew, chew.

These birds need to be kept busy. Plan for foot toys, bird-safe chewable branches, sterilized pine cones, hanging toys, ladders, vegetable-tanned leather knotted toys, puzzle toys, and overhead misters or shallow water bowls for bathing. Caiques tend to be good at learning tricks, and such training will help divert their abundant energy into positive activities.

Cockatiels

Scientific Name: *Nymphicus hollandicus*

Size: 11–13.8 in (29–35 cm)

Average Life Span: 7 years; reported maximum is 35 years.

Recommended Cage Size: 24 × 24 × 24 in (60 × 60 × 60 cm); if you can provide an aviary-sized cage, your cockatiel's health will benefit from his exercise in flight.

Recommended Perch Size: ½–⁵⁄₈ in (1.3–1.6 cm)

Talking Ability: Cockatiels are capable of repeating a small number of words. However, a more realistic expectation is that your cockatiel will make good use of his mimicry skills. Cockatiels can reproduce tunes by whistling, and they imitate sounds in addition to their natural call, which has been described as sad or plaintive.

Noise Level: Low to moderate

Pet Potential: Excellent

Introduction: An excellent bird for a beginning bird-keeper, the cockatiel is a cuddly companion, with many characteristics of its cockatoo cousin but without the size and noise factor. Generally good tempered and somewhat comical, cockatiels can be kept singly or in small groups, require a moderate amount of exercise, and can be taught simple tricks, whistles, and sometimes a few words.

Origin and Habitat: The cockatiel, also known as the quarrion, is native to Australia; they live in most habitats except for very wet areas. Although these birds prefer open woodland that includes acacia scrub and forests along rivers, they also are attracted to the water and grain associated with agricultural activities in their range. In addition, cockatiels enjoy spinifix grass, containing spiny seeds the cockatiels devour. You can find cockatiels on farms, in grasslands with scattered trees, and along roadsides.

Cockatiels are ideal for first-time parrot parents.

Physical Characteristics: The cockatiel is a very small and slender cockatoo. The normally colored bird (also called wild type) has a yellow face and crest, distinctive orange cheek patches, gray feathers, and white wing patches that seem to flash when this bird flies. The cockatiel's crest, in addition to his orange cheek patches, is distinctive. The crest gives an indication of the cockatiel's state of mind: A cockatiel raises his crest when he's interested, curious, or alarmed. To distinguish which of these situations exists, human beings must pay attention to the rest of the cockatiel's body posture. In general, females have a gray crest, with colors—including the cheek patches—usually duller than those of the male. However, in some color variations, the differences are very slight. In addition, all immature birds resemble females.

Oddly, cockatiels scratch their heads by reaching their leg over their wing. Seeming like a circus trick at first, this strange habit becomes endearing and a fun point of discussion with small children.

Temperament and Personality: A cheerful and somewhat shy bird, the cockatiel has charm and personality. They can be quite affectionate.

Other Information: Basic color mutations include lutino, pied pearl, and cinnamon, but many other mutations exist.

Cockatiels are subject to unexplained night frights; anecdotally, this is especially true of the lutino color mutation. Characterized by sudden thrashing in the night, night frights can result in bruised wingtips and chest and sometimes broken blood feathers and bones caused by the terrified flapping of this normally gentle bird inside his cage. With each collision with cage furniture or bars, the fright increases. Believed by most avian specialists to be a reaction to a noise during the night, night frights and their results can frighten cockatiel companions as well.

If your bird is prone to night frights, reduce the incidence and the resulting damage by being proactive. Create white noise to eliminate sudden disturbances for the bird during the night. Small machines are available to generate an environment with a constant sound level. Next, leave a small night light on so that the cockatiel can see. In addition, for birds prone to night frights, consider removing your bird from his cage and housing him overnight in a hospital cage, one without perches and bars. Line this cage with towels to create soft surfaces and provide shallow dishes for small amounts of food and water so that, if frights occur, there will be minimal damage to your bird.

Some females are prone to chronic egg-laying. See your veterinarian if this problem develops.

Cockatiel preening his human flock mate.

Cockatoos

Scientific Name: Cacatuidae; there are at least 21 species categorized in seven genera.

Size: Pet-suitable species vary from 12 to 20 in (30–50 cm)

Average Life Span: 8 to 12 years; reported maximums are 35 to 75 years, depending on the species. Larger cockatoos tend to have greater maximum life spans.

Recommended Cage Size: For mini-toos, 34 × 24 × 36 in (86 × 61 × 91 cm); for large toos, 36 × 48 × 60 in (91 × 121 × 152 cm)

Recommended Perch Size: For mini-toos 1.5–2 in (4–5 cm); for large toos 2.5–4.0 in (6–10 cm)

Talking Ability: Poor except for Ducorp's, galah, and sulphur-crested, which are moderately capable mimics

Noise Level: Quite loud

Pet Potential: Best for experienced bird-keepers

Introduction: Cockatoos present themselves as snuggly teddy bears with feathers. And sometimes this is an accurate description. However, with their strong beaks and incredible vocal power, cockatoos often become demanding and difficult pets because of their intelligence and ability to read human body language. In addition, cockatoos are birds with an enormous amount of powder down. This creates a problem for people with allergies.

Origin and Habitat: A varied family that inhabits Australia, New Guinea, parts of Indonesia, and nearby islands, cockatoos typically inhabit treed areas in a variety of habitats. Adaptable, this omnivore enjoys not only seeds, berries, fruits, buds, and blossom, but also insects and small animals.

Physical Characteristics: Cockatoos tend to be either white or black (with some exceptions), with brighter colors on the crest, wings, and tail. One species, the galah, is pink and gray. The beaks tend to be large and strongly curved. Most species are medium to large parrots with a stocky build.

All cockatoos have a crest that the bird raises after he lands or when alarmed or excited. In addition to their crest, a characteristic common to a few parrots including the cockatoo is their powder down. This substance allows the cockatoo to clean and arrange

The galah, or rose-breased cockatoo, makes a better pet than most other species.

his feathers properly; powder down makes up the particle cloud you see rise when a cockatoo flaps his wings or rouses his feathers.

Temperament and Personality: Most cockatoos are fast at everything they do. Inexperienced caregivers sometimes create significant behavior problems without meaning to through inappropriately petting and constantly carrying their cockatoo. As a result of their behavior, which is interpreted by the birds as sexual, the birds become very difficult to handle and frequently exhibit screaming and biting behaviors. If you choose a cockatoo, be sure to choose a bird who is parent-reared—one who is aware he is a bird.

Cockatoos usually are extremely affectionate birds, but that affection can transform into overdependence on their companion and severe separation anxiety. Temperament problems well-known among cockatoos include screaming, mate aggression, and unpredictable severe biting episodes, even toward people with whom they are bonded.

Most Popular Species: The smaller cockatoos, including the Ducorp's cockatoo (*Cacatua ducorpsii*), the galah (*Eolophus roseicapillus*), Goffin's cockatoo (*Cacatua goffiniana*), and the little corella (*Cacatua sanguinea*), can be good pets. The citron-crested cockatoo (*Cacatua sulphurea citrinocristata*), lesser sulfur-crested cockatoo (*Cacatua sulphurea sulphurea*), Moluccan or salmon-crested cockatoo (*Cacatua moluccensis*), and white or umbrella cockatoo (*Cacatua alba*) are all best left in the hands of very experienced bird-keepers.

Ducorp's are small white cockatoos with a blue eye ring. These are good mimics and are fast moving and fast learning. These are playful escape artists who are suited to caregivers who can react quickly to reading bird body language.

A Goffin's cockatoo (left) and a sulphur-crested cockatoo (right).

Galahs, with their medium pink and gray bodies, are rather acrobatic and sociable. Known to swing upside down sometimes, they forage on the ground in the wild and love nibbling on bark. These comical birds are fast and extroverted and need a quick response from their caregivers. Galahs have been known to talk.

Little corellas, also called bare-eyed cockatoos, are white with poor potential to talk but playful personalities. As are many cockatoos, this bird is an escape artist who can make you laugh by rolling on his back or hanging upside down from wires.

Goffin's cockatoos, also known as Tanimbars, are small white cockatoos with a bluish white eye ring. Calls are loud screams, with minor potential to talk. This bird is a chewer, requiring indestructible toys (which he will then destroy). He needs an experienced keeper.

The larger cockatoos, including the white cockatoo, the sulphur- and citron-crested cockatoos, and the Moluccan cockatoo require extreme amounts of attention, are inveterate chewers, and need an experienced bird handler because of their lack of suitability as pets. They are large, loud, quick, and hard to handle. Common novice mistakes create an overly affectionate relationship with the cockatoo, which creates a situation in which the bird will not tolerate being left by his person. This situation leads to screaming, plucking, and attacking non-preferred persons and is the root cause of so many cockatoos losing their homes. If you believe that you want one of the large cockatoos, an excellent experience is working as a volunteer at a bird sanctuary so that you can have the experience of caretaking these challenging species.

Umbrella cockatoo showing off his spectacular crest.

Other Information: Bathing is particularly important for these birds who create quite a bit of powder from their feathers. Cockatoos all bathe in wet foliage in treetops or during rains by flying about or hanging upside down. As companions, they enjoy frequent misting and very broad, shallow bowls in which to bathe.

Most species feed both in the treetops and on the ground and benefit from a feeding scheme that requires substantial amounts of foraging to uncover. This allows the cockatoo to exercise his natural instincts for disassembly in a safe and useful way. In addition, these birds in particular need to be kept mentally and physically stimulated to remain emotionally healthy as pets. A large aviary best meets their needs. In addition, provide plenty of wood, sticks, and toys to destroy because these birds have a serious need to chew.

Known as the "engineers of the bird world," most cockatoos can disassemble their cages (and almost anything else that is not made of welded steel) to create unpleasant surprises for the unwitting first time bird-keeper. Equipped with a large bill and a yen to chew, cockatoos are wily, industrious, and comical birds. If you must have a cockatoo, be sure to acquire a sizable aviary for the activities and exercise that your bird will need, as well as a behaviorist who can provide you with the necessary guidance and supervision.

Scientific Name: More than 40 species exist in nature; *Aratinga*, *Cyanoliseus*, *Eupsittula*, *Psittacara*, *Pyrrhura*, and *Thectocercus* are the genera present in aviculture.

Size: 8–18 in (20–46 cm)

Average Life Span: 6–14 years, depending on the species; reported maximums are up to 60 years, depending on the species.

Recommended Cage Size: 30 × 30 in (76 × 76 cm) at a minimum; larger is much better

Recommended Perch Size: ⁵/₈–¾ in (1.6–2 cm)

Talking Ability: Varies by species

Noise Level: From very noisy to relatively quiet; in general, *Pyrrhura* conures are quieter and less shrill than their cousins.

Pet Potential: Varies by species from birds who are best for experienced keepers to ones who are great first parrots

Introduction: Conures are a group of birds to consider, especially if you are a new bird-keeper. Several of the species have terrific pet potential, especially if you are not determined to have a bird who talks. Intelligent and fun, conures can be entertaining acrobats. Conures are particular bathing enthusiasts.

Origin and Habitat: Mostly forests of different varieties in Central and South America

Physical Characteristics: Conures are slender, lightly built birds with a distinctive eye-ring. In most species, the tail is long and slender. The overall green feathering of most species is complemented by a signal color on and under the wing and on the tail feathers. This coloring is visible in flight or in courtship displays. Many species have contrastingly colored heads. Coloration is usually the same in males and females.

Temperament and Personality: In general, these birds offer a big bird personality in a small body, although each type of conure is slightly different. As an example, the dusky-headed

Sun conure (left) and blue-crowned conure (right).

conure is a very shy bird with a very quiet demeanor, and is sometimes known to cuddle; this is in contrast to his *Aratinga* relations, who are known for their shrill voices and independent (read: non-cuddly) natures.

Most Popular Species: There are many relatively common and popular species of conures. These include the black-capped conure (*Pyrrhura rupicola*), blue-crowned conure (*Thectocercus acuticaudata*), dusky-headed conure (*A. weddellii*), green conure (*Psittacara holochlora*), green-cheeked (*Pyrrhura molinae*), jandaya or jenday conure (*A. jandaya*), maroon-bellied (*Pyrrhura f. frontalis*), nanday conure (*A. nenday*), orange-fronted conure (*E. canicularis*), Patagonian conure (*Cyanoliseus patagonus*), peach-fronted conure

The green-cheeked conure is a relatively quiet species.

(*Eupsittula aurea*), red-masked or cherry-headed conure (*Psittacara erhthrogenys*), sun conure (*Aratinga solstitialis*), and white-eyed conure (*Psittacara leucophthalmus*).

Among the conures, you have some choices to make especially if you—or your neighbors—are noise sensitive. The most popular species are not necessarily the ones with the best pet potential. The *Pyrrhura* are quieter birds, whereas the *Aratinga*, *Eupsittula*, and *Psittacara* cousins are noisier. The *Aratinga* conures are beautiful and intelligent birds with loud screams. This group of conures can become very cage territorial. *Aratinga* are not known for their talking ability. The *Pyrrhura* species are smaller and generally quieter than the others and make very nice pets.

Species with the best pet potential include green-cheeked, maroon-bellied, peach-fronted, Patagonian, orange-fronted, white-eyed, dusky-headed, and black-capped conures.

Green-cheeked conures are small parrots with brown throats and maroon on the belly and tail. The primary feathers are blue. Although these are not likely to talk, they are lively parrots, mischievous, and energetic, with moderate voice. Green-cheeks are often considered the best pets of all the conures.

One of the most friendly conures, the maroon-bellies are comical, high-energy pets. However, they're also reasonably quiet. They need lots of toys to play with and enjoy doing tricks and hopping for you. Acrobatic little birds, they can be affectionate and fun-loving. Their primarily green bodies are decorated with a maroon belly and a white eye ring, contrasting with the darker head and beak.

Peach-fronted conures have an orange forehead and blue flight feathers. These birds are good at tricks and likely to talk, but they are strong gnawers who can be cage-territorial.

The Patagonian conure is a large conure with an olive brown and yellow belly and blue flight feathers. With a good potential to talk, they are social, playful, and touchable, as well as enthusiastic bathers. They like the ground rather than perches for feeding and play. Patagonians are relatively quiet conures.

Orange-fronted conures, also called half-moon conures, are small parrots with a bright orange patch on the forehead. They are good mimics and learn tricks well. They like time spent with people but prefer not to snuggle.

White-eyed conures can imitate words and mimic sounds well. Although they are heavy gnawers, they are curious, clownish, and shy, with great pet potential for a sensitive keeper. As the name suggests, the white-eyed has a white eye ring. This conure is mostly green with bright red marks on the shoulders.

Dusky-headed conures, also called Weddell's conures, are gray-green with blue feather tips and black flight feathers. These are very quiet *Aratinga* conures, who are usually cuddly, calm, and steady birds. These conure gems are often overlooked, which is a shame.

Peach-fronted conure.

Patagonian conure.

Black-capped conures are small conures that have a black patch on top of the head and an attractive ring of white-edged black feathers around the neck. Black-caps have a limited potential to talk, but have subdued voices and are quiet for members of the conure family. They seem to have a lively sense of humor but can be somewhat timid.

The sun conure is a brilliant yellow bird with orange and red splashes of coloring. Although the coloring draws many people to the sun conure, his harsh, loud voice is what drives those same people to give up their birds and explains the many sun conures seen in rescue organizations. The jenday is similar in color and personality to the sun but has more green on the wings and is more orange than yellow. It's sometimes confused with the sun conure by less experienced bird hobbyists.

Other Information: Generally, conures are strong gnawers and enthusiastic bathers. Because they are smart birds with energy and moxie, learning tricks and playing with toys help to keep your friend mentally and physically exercised. Conures can be naughty and need a caretaker with a commitment to enforcing behavioral rules. Of course, this is perfect for the person who wants a big bird personality in a small bird body.

Eclectus

Scientific Name: *Eclectus roratus*

Size: 14 in (35 cm)

Average Life Span: 9 years; reported maximum is 41 years

Recommended Cage Size: 36 × 24 × 36 in (91 × 60 × 91 cm)

Recommended Perch Size: 1–1.5 in (2.5–3.8 cm)

Talking Ability: Moderately good talkers

Noise Level: Relatively quiet

Pet Potential: Excellent; eclectus are affectionate pets and learn to talk.

Introduction: If cockatoos and macaws are the party animals of the companion parrot world, eclectus are the stay-at-home with a hobby sort of personalities. Stunning in their looks with male and female completely different in coloring, these parrots make good, quiet companions.

Pair of Solomon Islands eclectus parrots; the green bird is the male.

The feathers of eclectus are glossy and hair-like.

Origin and Habitat: The eclectus parrot is native to a small number of islands, including New Guinea and the Solomon Islands, and the Cape York Peninsula of northern Australia. They inhabit lowland forests or small clumps of trees in a savanna.

Physical Characteristics: This stocky parrot has a short, square tail and long, round-tipped wings. The bill has a notch in the upper mandible. The feathers have a hair-like structure, which produces a glossy plumage noticeably different from other species. These birds have the most pronounced difference in male and female feathering of any parrot species. The male is predominately green with a yellow upper mandible, orange iris, yellow-tipped tail feathers, and red and blue under the wings. The female is predominately vibrant red with a purple lower breast, matching under wing, a black bill, and yellow iris.

Temperament and Personality: Eclectus parrots, generally quiet and more reserved than other parrots, can be excellent companions for those who do not require a cuddly bird. Not only can they talk and imitate noises, but they also are quite happy just to hang out with you while you read or watch television. Males are said to be more docile than females. These parrots are suspicious of new situations and locations.

Most Popular Species: Although there are subspecies of eclectus, including red-sided (*E. roratus roratus*); vos (*E. roratus vosmaeri*), and Solomon Island (*E. roratus solomonensis*), these birds do not show the diversity in plumage that a group like the conures do. The birds do vary a little in size and in the particulars of their plumage, but the general color patterns and personalities are quite similar.

Other Information: In the wild, eclectus eat fruits, nuts, seeds, berries, leaf buds, blossoms, and nectar. Playful and chewers, rope swings and plenty of soft wood to destroy are appreciated by eclectus. Prone to be quiet, eclectus are sensitive birds who appreciate routine, a moderate amount of attention, and toys to occupy their rather large minds.

Lineolated Parakeets

Scientific Name: *Bolborhyncus lineola*

Size: 6–7.5 in (16–19 cm)

Average Life Span: 10 years; maximum 15 years (possibly more)

Recommended Cage Size: Aviary with minimum length of 1.2 m (4 ft) for flight

Recommended Perch Size: ⅛–¾ in (31 mm–2 cm)

Talking Ability: A few words by some birds; others are said to talk well. They learn all kinds of sounds and whistles.

Noise Level: Small flocks are moderately noisy.

Pet Potential: Good; common in parts of Europe, less so elsewhere

Introduction: The lineolated is indeed a good choice for the person who wants a smaller parrot. Their normal life span is about 10 years, but individual birds have been known to live up to 15 years, so they are less of a commitment than the larger parrots who can live up to 80 years. This quiet and relatively social parrot may become agitated on approach, flying and becoming more vocal.

Origin and Habitat: Lineolated parakeets are named for the striped lines found on their back feathers and are sometimes referred to as the barred or Catherine parakeet. Originating from the

Blue mutation of the lineolated parakeet.

high mountains of Central America from southern Mexico to western Panama, they live in flocks of 6 to 30 birds in dense forests.

Physical Characteristics: These small parrots are generally green in color with black barring on upper parts, except for the crown. Flanks and side of the breast are olive green with black-green barring. They have blue-green under wing coverts and undersides of flight feathers with a dark green tail that has the center feathers edged with black. Bill is pale horn color, and eyes are dark brown. Females have narrower black barring than the males. In the subspecies *B.l. tigrinus*, both adults are darker green, with stronger black barring.

Temperament and Personality: Lineolated parakeets—often called "linnies" by their fans—offer the advantages of a parrot without the major life adjustments demanded by larger, more high-maintenance parrots. Lineolated parakeets have a sweet temperament; a hand-fed, single pet linnie often bonds very tightly to its owner and can be defensive of him or her. They are playful and acrobatic. Calls are soft, but far-carrying notes. Alarm call is series of slurred notes. They can emit a high-pitched contact call or an excited loud twittering.

Other information: There are a numerous color mutations of this parrot, including dark green, olive, lutino, blue, and cremino.

Dark greens look similar to the normal greens, except the plumage is a darker green with less blue on the forehead and less yellowing on the underside of the body. Olives' plumage is blackish-green with the under body having mustard tinge.

Blue mutation variations include aqua, cobalt, and mauve. The blue series is marked the same as the green, but without blackish or yellowed coloring. The light blue is sometimes referred to as the aquamarine. Cobalts are a much richer blue with a violet effect. Mauves have a grayish tint. Creminos are soft cream yellow. Whites are similar to creminos, except the eyes are black instead of red, and the body color is pure white instead of cream. Lutinos are deep yellow with red eyes and have light-colored beak and feet. Yellows are the same as the lutinos, but with black eyes.

Lineolated parakeets are playful and usually good tempered birds.

Scientific Name: More than 50 species in the family Loriidae

Size: 6–13 in (15–33 cm)

Average Life Span: 6-10 years, depending on species; reported maximums are 10–28 years, depending on species.

Recommended Cage Size: 2 × 3 × 3 ft (60 × 91 × 91 cm)

Recommended Perch Size: ⅜–¾ inch (1–2 cm)

Talking Ability: Ability is very good; clarity sometimes lacking

Noise Level: Moderate

Pet Potential: Can be tame, but droppings are messy; bites can be painful because of sharp beaks. Not usually a good choice for a first parrot.

Introduction: The Loriidae family consists of lories and lorikeets, which are birds with brilliantly colored, tight, and glossy feathers. They are tree-lovers, flocking in large groups and feeding on pollen, nectar, and fruits. They can be quite tame when hand raised.

Origin and Habitat: Australia, New Guinea, New Caledonia, and many nearby islands. They can be found in forests, plains, mangrove swamps, and agricultural areas—basically any habitat with enough flowers to support their specialized diet.

Physical Characteristics: The startling difference between lories and lorikeets when compared with other parrots is the tongue, which has a brush-like tip for harvesting pollen and pressing it into a form suitable for swallowing. The bill is relatively long and narrow. Lories are heavier bodied, square-tailed birds, and lorikeets are leaner with long tails that taper, but the difference is not a scientifically based one. Both come in an array of brilliant colors.

Temperament and Personality: These parrots are gregarious, fun-loving, and amusing. They are acrobats and often play by lying on their backs and kicking small toys with their feet. By the way, rainbow lorikeets sometimes sleep on their backs.

Red lories are curious and outgoing birds.

The rainbow lorikeet is the mostly commonly kept of the lories.

Dusky lories are among the loudest of the group.

The chattering lory is an excellent mimic but can be aggressive if not carefully trained.

Most Popular Species: The rainbow lorikeet (*Trichoglossus haematodus*) is the most popular species; there are several subspecies that vary somewhat in color. The red lory (*Eos bornea*) and dusky lory (*Pseudeos fuscata*) are relatively common as well. Goldie's lorikeet (*Psitteuteles goldiei*) is a smaller species and makes a good choice for people who've never had a lory before.

Other Information: Lories are not strong chewers, but they do enjoy shredding leaves and edible flowers. Because these birds' diet consists principally of nectar and pollen, their droppings are very liquid, making daily clean-up somewhat challenging. In addition to fruits and vegetables, commercial mixes of properly formulated nectar are available and recommended. Lories and lorikeets should get very little, if any, seed in their diets. More detailed information about the diet for lories and lorikeets can be found in Chapter 4, page 101. Given the specialized needs of these parrots, anyone interested in sharing their lives with one (or more) should do careful research and preparation before making the commitment.

Lovebirds

Scientific Name: *Agapornis*; there are nine species.

Size: 5.5–6 in (14–16 cm)

Average Life Span: About 7 years, depending on species; reported maximums are 16–31 years.

Recommended Cage Size: Minimum, 24 × 24 × 24 in (60 × 60 × 60 cm); preferred is an aviary or suspended cage, minimum length 4 ft (1.2 m). Although much smaller cages are used for lovebirds, the exercise your bird gets translates into better health and softer temperament.

Recommended Perch Size: ⅛–¾ in (31 mm–2 cm)

Talking Ability: Rarely talk

Noise Level: Moderate-low, including loud call notes, shrill whistles, and high-pitched twitter

Pet Potential: Very good, especially masked and Fischer's lovebirds

Introduction: Taking their name from their habit of preening others of their kind, lovebirds are popular and familiar throughout the pet world. Active and mischievous, they can also be fine pets. Hardy, they can learn a few tricks and perhaps say a few words.

The masked lovebird is a commonly kept parrot.

Origin and Habitat: Central and southern Africa and Madagascar

Physical Characteristics: Small and square, these birds have short, round tails and bills that seem large for their faces. Bodies appear mostly green; the rumps, faces, foreheads, and chests often show splashes of colors that include gray, orange, red, blue, purple, and black. Males and females have similar feathering.

Temperament and Personality: Playful, especially when acquired at a young age and handled frequently; they can be very tame and bonded to people

Two different color mutations of the peach-faced lovebird.

or other birds, but they can become aggressive during breeding season.

Most Popular Species: Peach-faced (*A. roseicollis*), Fischer's (*A. fischeri*) and masked (*A. personata*) lovebirds are the most commonly seen bird in aviculture. The peach-face is the most popular and feisty of the lovebirds. The face and upper breast are pink, the rump a bright blue, and the body green. The masked lovebird—sometimes called the yellow-collared lovebird—has a gentle personality. The head is brownish-black, the beak bright red, and the body yellow-green. The Fischer's are pleasing birds, usually not aggressive, and they learn tricks easily. Mostly green, the Fischer's have bright red beaks, orange heads, and dusky blue rumps.

Other Information: In the wild, lovebirds eat seeds, figs, berries, insects, and various grains, including millet and corn. For each species of this bossy little bird, a variety of color mutations is available. For example, peach-faced lovebirds come in colors that vary from dark violet through bright yellow to almost white, while maintaining the basic look and markings of the normally colored peach-faced lovebirds. Similar mutations exist for the Fischer's and masked lovebirds. For more information about color mutations, consult the African Lovebird Society.

Intelligent and energetic, lovebirds need plenty of exercise and hands-on attention. Enthusiastic bathers, lovebirds also enjoy climbing swings, ladders, and ropes, as well as puzzle and foraging toys.

Macaws

Scientific Name: At least 18 species in the genera *Anodorhynchus*, *Ara*, *Cyanopsitta*, *Diopsittaca*, *Primolius*, and *Orthopsittaca*

Size: 24–48 in (60–120 cm)

Average Life Span: 6–18 years, depending on the species; reported maximums are 10–63 years, depending on the species.

Recommended Cage Size: For mini-macaws, 34 × 24 × 36 in (86 × 61 × 91 cm); for large macaws, 36 × 48 × 60 in (91 × 121 × 152 cm)

Recommended Perch Size: For mini-macaws, 1.5–2 in (4–5 cm); for large macaws, 2.5–4 in (6–10 cm)

Talking Ability: Some talk well

Noise Level: Extreme; macaws are at the high end of the decibel range. Two macaws squawking can be literally deafening.

Pet Potential: The large macaws can be poor pets because of their loud voices and abundant energy. Mini-macaws can be good pets, but they are not easy to acquire because few were bred in captivity, and the genetic pool is small for most species. Macaws are not for beginning bird-keepers.

Green-winged macaws (left) are easily confused with scarlet macaws (right). Scarlets have yellow feathers on their wings and green-wings do not.

The noble (top) and the red-fronted (bottom) are two macaws that make fairly good pets.

Introduction: Macaws, especially the scarlet and the blue and gold, are the faces of the jungle. Their brilliant colors and noisy calls are what we see in movies or photographs meant to evoke the tropics. Because of our feelings about these tropical places, people often purchase macaws on impulse—a bird to remind them of their wonderful vacation, for example. Unfortunately, this is a mistake for both the bird and the family. Macaws can be wonderful companions for a few people in special circumstances, but that isn't most of us. Their cage or aviary needs are extensive as well as expensive, and their need for activities to occupy themselves is substantial.

The young birds, which are what you see in the stores, are especially appealing with their tendency to cuddle and make cute sounds. When a macaw becomes an adult, however, that tendency to cuddle turns into a demand, and he has the vocal equipment (as well as the beak) to insist on having things his way.

Origin and Habitat: Macaws are native to Mexico, and Central and South America, and, at one time, they were native to the Caribbean. Most species are rainforest dwellers, but some live in savannas and scrubby forests.

Physical Characteristics: These are generally large birds with long, gradated tails. Beaks are large and strong. The males and females are similarly feathered. The *Anodorhynchus* are predominately blue. *Anodorhynchus* includes the hyacinth macaw (*A. hyacinthinus*), the largest of all parrots at 39 in (100 cm). Most species have a bare ring around the eye and have bare faces as well. The mini-macaws of the genus *Primolius* have fully feathered faces, and the hyacinths only have a small bare patch of bright yellow skin near the beak. *Cyanopsitta* is extinct in the wild and not available in the pet trade. *Diopsittaca* includes Hahn's Macaw. *Orthopsittaca* includes the red-bellied macaw, which is not readily available. *Ara* has the most common large macaws available in the pet trade and includes most of those in pet homes today.

Temperament and Personality: With an experienced caretaker, these birds can be wonderful companions for a few people with the necessary space and isolation from other neighbors. Intelligent and seeming to have a sense of humor, macaws are goofy entertainers for your family. However, these birds can be aggressive, bossy, and intimidating unless expertly socialized and trained.

Most Popular Species: The most popular species of macaws unfortunately are not the ones that make the best pets. These include the blue and yellow macaw (also called the blue and gold macaw, *Ara ararauna*), scarlet

When a macaw gets excited, the bare patch of skin on his face may turn pink, as seen here on a military macaw.

macaw (*Ara macao*), and green-winged macaw (*A. chloropterus*). These are among the largest of all parrot species and are very challenging to keep as pets. The big macaws are physically active and vocal birds who require frequent training and structured play to focus their energies. These birds are loud, and screaming can become a problem. Although these birds learn tricks readily, they require a knowledgeable owner.

The mini-macaws, including yellow-collared (*Primolius auricollis*), noble (*Diopsitta nobilis cumanensis*), and severe or chestnut-fronted (*Ara severa*) can be excellent, affectionate, and intelligent pets.

Other Information: Macaws are highly intelligent, learn tricks easily—including how to escape their cages—and require lots of person-time. Although nothing seems as tropical as a macaw, these birds are difficult to care for properly because of the amount of exercise and mental stimulation they need. In addition, most macaws are simply too loud for the circumstances that most of us live in. People who have worked with many species of macaws suggest that if you are determined to look for a pet macaw, consider Hahn's, noble, or red-fronted macaws (*Ara rubrogenys)*. Likewise, experienced macaw parents suggest providing lots of thick, hard wood for chewing satisfaction.

Parakeets/Budgerigars

Scientific Name: *Melopsittacus undulatus*

Size: 7 in (18 cm)

Average Life Span: 6 years; reported maximum is 18 years.

Recommended Cage Size: Minimum, 18 × 18 × 24 in; preferred is an aviary or suspended cage, minimum length 4 ft (1.2 m). Although much smaller cages are used for parakeets, their health and temperament benefit from having more space.

Recommended Perch Size: ⅛–¾ in (31 mm–2 cm)

Talking Ability: Very good; large vocabularies are possible, but lack perfect clarity of speech.

Noise Level: Low

Pet Potential: Excellent; the best bird for beginners

Introduction: The best known of all parrots (properly called budgerigars; also called parakeets or budgies), this bird has been kept as a pet worldwide for many years. With many color varieties available, companions can have their choice of color. Highly adaptable and charming, these generally quiet birds have a pleasing chatter and can be taught to talk and perform simple tricks. Of any bird available, I would choose budgies, and I would choose to keep several. Uncomplicated,

The ever-popular budgie is bred in a wide range of delightful colors.

easy to keep, and easy for children and elders to handle, budgies are the perfect small parrot companion.

Origin and Habitat: Australia, generally the interior. They tend to favor open habitats over dense forests. Budgies have also become naturalized in Florida due to accidental (and purposeful, but illegal) releases.

Physical Characteristics: A small parrot with a long gradated tail. They have rounded heads and relatively small beaks. The sexes are alike, except that mature males have a blue cere and female and immature birds have a beige, brown, or tan cere. Adults and immature birds of both sexes have a white wing stripe except in some color mutations.

Mature male budgies have a blue cere (area above the beak where the nostrils are located).

Temperament and Personality: Friendly, these trainable birds are easy to care for and are not very demanding.

Most Popular Species: Although there is only one species, two types or styles of budgies exist in aviculture: the slimmer "American-style" budgie and the longer, large-chested "English" budgie.

Other Information: Although budgies' diet in the wild is principally seed, those birds fly tens of miles each day to gather their tasty morsels. For companion budgies, it is important to provide a wide variety of types of foods in addition to their favorite seed. Converting budgies to a healthy diet (many are feed only on seed) is a slow, painstaking process. However, your effort will be rewarded with a longer lived and healthier companion.

Budgies are genetically predisposed to many diseases, especially tumors. Consider the source to get the healthiest budgie possible and develop a relationship with a good avian vet.

Scientific Name: *Forpus*; there are seven species

Size: 4.5–5.5 in (12–14 cm)

Average Life Span: 4–9 years, depending on the species; reported maximums are 7–30 years.

Recommended Cage Size: Minimum, 18 × 18 × 24 in (46 × 46 × 60 cm); preferred is an aviary or suspended cage, minimum length 4 ft (1.2 m) so your parrotlet gets enough exercise

Recommended Perch Size: ⅛–¾ in (31 mm–2 cm)

Talking Ability: Questionable

Noise Level: Their twittering noise, made while feeding, is described as *tseet...tseet.*

Pet Potential: Good for small apartments and very fine first-time birds.

Introduction: These are adorable small birds; active, but not particularly affectionate. They can be fearless in spite of their size. These are the smallest parrots in aviculture; the pygmy parrots of New Guinea are smaller but are not kept as pets.

Origin and Habitat: Mexico, and Central and South America; introduced and naturalized in Jamaica. Most of the species are found in open and scrubby forest, but some are found in true rainforest, including the Amazon Basin.

Blue mutation of the Pacific parrotlet in flight.

Physical Characteristics: Very small, stocky parrots with short, wedge-shaped tails. The bill is large in proportion to the body size and has a notch in the upper mandible. Males and females have slightly different feather patterns, varying according to the species. In general, species appear green overall with blue or purple rumps and wing coverts. They have white eye rings and dark irises. Mutation colors range from white to yellow, to various shades of blue and violet.

Temperament and Personality: Feisty and playful; without proper training and socialization, parrotlets often become biters. Males may become possessive or aggressive. If kept with a mate, ensure the cage is large enough because males will become aggressive to females if kept in a small cage.

The blue-winged parrotlet is rarely seen in aviculture.

Most Popular Species: The green-rumped (*F. passerinus*), Pacific (*F. coelestis*), and spectacled (*F. conspicillatus*) are the most popular species, with the Pacific being by far the most common in aviculture.

Other Information: In the wild, these birds flock in small parties or groups of 5 to 50. Their principal diet includes seeds, berries, fruits, leaf buds, and blossoms. Parrotlets have a tendency to become obese if kept in small cages and not given enough exercise. They are active and vocal, twittering to attract attention in their feeding areas because they blend in with their surroundings.

Parrotlets enjoy swings and ropes, puzzle and foraging toys, and bird-safe wooden chew toys and branches (fir, pine, heat-sterilized pine cones, etc.). For their size, they are prodigious chewers. They also like to bathe.

Pionus

Scientific Name: *Pionus*

Size: 9.5–12 in (24–30 cm)

Average Life Span: 5–15 years, depending on the species; reported maximum is up to 24 years, although anecdotally these birds can live much longer.

Recommended Cage Size: 24 × 24 × 36 in (60 × 60 × 91 cm)

Recommended Perch Size: ¾–1 ¼ in (2–3.2 cm)

Talking Ability: Limited, but learns sounds and whistles

Noise Level: Relatively quiet; noise level comparable to cockatiels

Pet Potential: Excellent

Introduction: These medium-sized parrots are often overlooked because of their muted colors and quiet demeanor. These parrots offer everything you want in a large bird and less: less noise, less drama, and fewer demands. Every person who has a pionus parrot would not think of being parted from their companion. In fact, I would recommend that anyone looking for a gentle, quiet bird consider these species.

Origin and Habitat: Central and South America, from Mexico to northern Argentina; they live in forests, ranging from dry open forests to rainforests. The bronze-winged (*P. chalcopterus*) and the red-billed (*P. sordidus*) range up into the Andes Mountains.

White-capped pionus are common in both nature and in aviculture.

Physical Characteristics:
Medium-sized birds with short, square tails. The bill is stout and notched. Males and females are feathered alike, principally green or dark blue, with variations on head, neck, and under the tail, which make these parrots very attractive although somewhat muted in color when compared with macaws, for example. Like

Maximillian's pionus.

an opal, in the right light, you can see the many shadings of the pionus' feathers.

Temperament and Personality: Known to be quiet and steady birds, although individuals may vary. Usually gentle, smaller, and quieter than the related and superficially similar Amazons.

Most Popular Species: The species in aviculture are the blue-headed (*P. menstruus*), scaly-headed or Maximilian's (*P. maximiliani*), white-capped (*P. seniloides*), dusky (*P. fuscus*), and bronze-winged. The blue-headed is generally regarded as the best talker of the group.

Other Information: Like Amazons, pionus are prone to obesity. A pionus companion should keep a careful eye on the bird's weight. Pionus sometimes produce a sniffing or wheezing sound when frightened, which can be mistaken for respiratory distress. These birds emit a musky sweet odor that a few people find objectionable, although the scent isn't emitted constantly nor is it very strong.

Scientific Name: *Psittacula*; there are at least a dozen species.

Size: 15–23 in (38–58 cm)

Average Life Span: 6–10 years, depending on species; reported maximums are 12–33 years, depending on species.

Recommended Cage Size: Minimum, 24 × 24 × 36 in (60 × 60 × 91 cm); larger recommended

Recommended Perch Size: ¾–1 ¼ in (2–3.2 cm)

Talking Ability: Large vocabularies enunciated without perfect clarity

Noise Level: Moderate

Pet Potential: Good, but require careful training and socialization

Introduction: Also called ring-necked parakeets, these highly prized pets have a long history as companion birds, especially in Asia. Although these birds do not always talk as clearly as other parrots, they do amass large vocabularies. Ring-necks can be loud, and they require frequent handling to remain tame.

Origin and Habitat: The most widely distributed parrot clan, the psittaculas are prevalent throughout Asia, including India, Afghanistan, Pakistan, Thailand, southwestern China, and the Indochinese Peninsula, as well as in some parts of Africa. They are found in a wide range of habitats and are agricultural pests in some areas.

Physical Characteristics: One of the noticeable features of the ring-necks is the long tail in which the central pair of feathers are narrow. Psittaculas have heavy bills with a distinct notch in upper mandible. The bird's structure is elongated, with a distinctive ring around the neck in many species. Almost all are green with different colors in the head, neck, and beak. Some species have colorful breasts. Males tend to have more color in head and neck areas,

A male ring-necked parakeet is shown here; females have faint neck rings or lack them entirely.

and, in ring-necked species, the males have darker or more prominent rings.

Temperament and Personality: Intelligent birds, ring-necks can learn to talk and perform tricks. Ring-necks are said to be hardy and independent, and most do not seem to relish petting.

Some ring-necks talk well. Generally quiet, they can be tame and personable.

Most Popular Species: The most commonly kept psittaculas include the Alexandrine parakeet (*P. eupartria*), Indian ring-necked or rose-ringed parakeet (*P. krameri manillensis*), moustached

Moustached parakeet.

parakeet (*P. alexandri*), Derbiyan parakeet (*P. derbiana*), African ring-necked (*P. k. krameri*), and the smaller plum-headed parakeet (*P. chanocephala*).

Alexandrines make good pets; they appear to have an oversized red beak and are mostly green with a red wing patch. Mature males have a black and pink band surrounding the neck. This is the largest of the psittaculas.

Indian ring-necks can learn to talk and do tricks; they enjoy toys. Green, except for a red beak, males have a pink and black ring around the neck.

Moustaches sometimes learn to talk and do tricks. These birds are green except for a pink upper chest, a blue-gray head, and a band of black from lower beak to under the ear. They are very similar to the Derbyan at first glance. The Derbyan has a gray to purple breast rather than the rosy pink breast of the moustached parakeet.

Plum-headed parakeets need a lot of regular attention if they are to remain tame and not bite. However, they are gorgeous birds, with green bodies and blue tails. Males have vibrant purple and blue heads, while the females have gray heads.

Other Information: In the wild, these birds are known to feed on fruit, nuts, seeds, berries, blossoms, leaf buds, and nectar. They raid ripening crops, including corn, wheat, and rice. Most of the psittaculas are enthusiastic about destroying toys and should be given plenty of them to annihilate. Indian ring-necks have several color mutations, including blue, albino, and lutino. Some new color mutations may be predisposed to genetic problems that result in shorter life spans and increased sensitivity to bacteria and viruses.

Scientific Name: *Myiopsitta monachus*

Size: 11 in (29 cm)

Average Life Span: 6–7 years; reported maximum is around 30 years.

Recommended Cage Size: 24 × 24 × 24 in (60 × 60 × 60 cm)

Recommended Perch Size: ½–1.0 in (1.3–2.5 cm)

Talking Ability: Some; imitates sounds well

Noise Level: Moderate

Pet Potential: Moderate

Introduction: Commonly kept as a pet in many parts of the world, Quaker parakeets are hearty, if somewhat loud, companions. Able to talk and to imitate sounds, these little birds have a big personality and acrobatic tendencies. Legislation in various states has forbidden the sale of these birds because of their ability to naturalize and the size of their colonial nests, which are frequently constructed on top of power poles. The weight of the nests causes power outages, which make these little fellows very unpopular with most citizens. Agricultural communities are concerned that

Quaker parakeets pack a lot of personality into their tiny bodies.

these parakeets will breed and ravage crops. Prior to considering this species, check your local and state laws regarding the Quaker. Quakers are also called monk parakeets.

Origin and Habitat: Central Bolivia, southern Brazil, and Argentina. Introduced and naturalized in Puerto Rico, the United States, and a few places in Europe, their natural habitat is temperate to subtropical open forests, and they often adapt well to disturbed habitat, including paper plantations.

Physical Characteristics: Medium-sized parrot with a long, gradated tail. The heavy bill is notched in the upper mandible. Males and females are similarly feathered, predominantly green overall with a gray chest and forehead.

Temperament and Personality: Gregarious, they are playful and intelligent. However, they can also be very territorial, protecting their cage or play stands vigorously.

The colonial nests of Quaker parakeets can become heavy enough to topple utility poles.

Other Information: In the wild, their activities center on their huge colonial nests—they are the only parrot species known to build stick nests. Foods include seeds, fruits, berries, nuts, leaf buds, blossoms, and insects. Quakers also feed on crops including cereals and citrus orchards.

To cope with possible territorial behavior, be sure to stick train your Quaker so that you can remove and return him to his cage or play stand without being bitten during one of his territorial moments. Although this is a good practice with any species, this is a particularly important point with bird species known to be territorial.

Scientific Name: *Poicephalus senegalus*; there are at least eight other species in the genus.

Size: 8–11 in (21–28 cm)

Average Life Span: 6–10 years, depending on species; reported maximums are 16–36 years, depending on species.

Recommended Cage Size: 24 × 24 × 24 in (60 × 60 × 60 cm)

Recommended Perch Size: ½ –1 in (1.2–2.5 cm)

Talking Ability: They can talk but not as clearly as some other birds can.

Noise Level: Low to moderate

Pet Potential: Good, especially for smaller spaces

Introduction: These African parrots are excellent birds for small spaces and for people for whom interaction is important and talking less so. These are trainable birds and have good dispositions, especially if handled frequently from a young age.

Senegals are excellent parrots for people with small spaces.

Origin and Habitat: Sub-Saharan Africa; the various species range from savanna to tropical rainforest, with the Cape parrot (*P. robustus*) and the yellow-fronted parrot (*P. flavifrons*) occurring in mountainous habitats.

Physical Characteristics: Small to medium-sized stocky birds with short, square tails, and robust beaks. Their heads appear slightly too big for their

Meyer's parrot.

bodies. They are green or dark olive on the back, lighter green or brown on the neck, and have either an orange or a green belly.

Temperament and Personality: Playful, active, and usually gentle yet hardy, these little parrots can become territorial with sexual maturity. These birds can learn tricks and can talk, but are not usually noisy.

Most Popular Species: The Senegal is the most popular of this group. Other relatively common species include the Cape parrot (*P. robustus*), Jardine's or red-fronted parrot (*P. gulielmi*), the red-bellied parrot (*P. rufiventris*), Meyer's parrot (*P. meyeri*), and the brown-headed parrot (*P. cyptoxanthus*). The Cape parrot, largest of the *Poicephalus*, is often called the "gentle giant." With excellent talking abilities, this affectionate bird is mostly green with dark orange feathering on the head and bend of the wings. The Senegal has a gray-brown head and green starting at the throat and extending down to the chest. Below this is an orange-yellow patch, with green wings and back. Jardine's parrot is primarily green with black-edged feathers. There is patch on the forehead that ranges from orange to red, depending on the subspecies. The Meyer's is a brownish gray bird with blue-green chest and yellow at the wing bend and top of the head. The brown-headed parrot has a brown head and green body. The red-bellied male has a red-orange chest and an orange forehead band, green thighs, and a brown back. The female has a green chest. In other species, the sexes are difficult to impossible to distinguish visually.

Other Information: In the wild, foods include seed, fruits, shoots, and corn. Be sure to create a training program that anticipates territoriality, including stick training.

Resources

Chapter 1

10 Facts About Living With Parrots
www.birdchannel.com/bird-species/
find-the-right-bird/facts-about-parrots.aspx

American Federation of Aviculture
PO Box 91717
Austin, TX 78709
Telephone: 512-585-9800
Fax 512-858-7029
Email: afaoffice@afabirds.org
www.afabirds.org/

Avicultural Society of America
P.O. Box 3161
San Dimas, CA, 91773
Email: info@asabirds.org
www.asabirds.org

The Gabriel Foundation
1025 Acoma St.
Denver, CO 80204
Telephone: 303-629-5900
Fax: 303-629-5901
www.thegabrielfoundation.org

The Parrot Pages
www.parrotpages.com

Chapter 2

Avian Welfare Coalition
P.O. Box 40212
St. Paul, MN 55104
Email: info@avianwelfare.org
www.avianwelfare.org

Bird Placement Program
P.O. Box 347392
Parma, Ohio 44134
Telephone: 330-722-1627
Email: birdrescue5@hotmail.com
www.birdrescue.com/

Parrot Outreach Society
1205 Elizabeth St., Unit 1
Punta Gorda, Fl 33950
Telephone: 941-347-8876
Email: parrotoutreach@comcast.net
PaulParrotRescue@aol.com
www.parrotoutreachsociety.org

Parrot Rehabilitation Society
www.facebook.com/ParrotRehabilitationSociety

Petfinder
www.petfinder.com

Chapter 3

ASPCA's Toxic Plant List
www.aspca.org/pet-care/animal-poison-control/toxic-
and-non-toxic-plants

Disaster Preparedness
www.Ready.gov

Do It Yourself Ideas
www.aparrotsperch.org/DIY_ideas.php

Housing Your Bird and Setting up Your Bird Cage
www.beautyofbirds.com/housingbirds.html

Parrot Play Gym on a Budget
www.instructables.com/id/Parrot-Play-Gym-on-a-
budget/

Red Cross
www.RedCross.org

The Toymaker
www.birdsnways.com/birds/ideas.htm

Chapter 4
ASPCA Poison Control Center
Hotline: 888-426-4435
www.aspca.org/pet-care/animal-poison-control

Environmental Working Group's Guide
to Pesticides in Produce
www.ewg.org/foodnews/summary.php

Foraging
www.parrotenrichment.com/foraging.html

Foraging for Parrots
www.foragingforparrots.com

Growing Edible Sprouts at Home
www.learningstore.uwex.edu/
assets/pdfs/A3385.pdf

Chapter 5
The Alex Studies, Irene Maxine Pepperburg,
Harvard University Press, 2002

BehaviorWorks.org
www.behaviorworks.org/

Bird Hotline
Email: emailus@birdhotline.com
www.birdhotline.com

BirdChannel.com Travel Tips
www.birdchannel.com/bird-travel/

Good Bird, Inc.
www.goodbirdinc.com
www.youtube.com/user/GoodBirdInc

International Association of Avian Trainers
www.iaate.org

Karen Pryor Academy
www.karenpryoracademy.com

National Association of Professional Pet Sitters
1120 Route 73, Suite 200
Mt. Laurel, New Jersey 08054
Telephone: 856-439-0324
Fax: 856-439-0525
Email: napps@petsitters.org
www.petsitters.org

Natural Encounters
www.naturalencounters.com/

Pamela Clark, CVT
www.pamelaclarkonline.com

Parrot Behavior Analysis Solutions
www.tech.groups.yahoo.com/group/ParrotBAS/

Pet Sitters International
201 E King Street
King, NC 27021
Telephone: 336-983-9222
www.petsit.com

Chapter 6
Bird Grooming
www.birdchannel.com/bird-diet-and-health/bird-grooming/topiclist.aspx

Plucking vs. Preening vs. Molting
www.jamiesparrothelp.wordpress.com/2008/08/27/plucking-vs-preening-vs-molting

Chapter 7

Association of Avian Veterinarians
PO Box 9
Teaneck, NJ 07666
Telephone: 720-458-4111
720-398-3496
Email: office@aav.org
www.aav.org

Exotic Pet Vet.Net
www.exoticpetvet.net

HolisticBird.org
www.holisticbird.org

Chapter 8

African Grey Parrot
www.african-grey-parrot.com

African Grey Parrots
www.african-grey.com/home

Blue Front Amazon Parrots
www.bluefrontparrot.com

Budgerigar
www.budgerigar.com

The Budgie and Parakeet Place
www.budgieplace.com

Caique Parrots
www.caiqueparrots.com

Cockatiel.com
www.cockatiel.com

Cockatiel Cottage
www.cockatielcottage.net

Eclectus Parrots
www.eclectusparrots.net

Lineolated Parakeet Society
www.linniesociety.org

LinniesWorld.com
www.linniesworld.com

Lorikeets.com
www.lorikeets.com

MyToos.com
www.mytoos.com

National Cockatiel Society
www.cockatiels.org

Pionus Parrot's Website
www.pionusparrot.com

Poicephalus Parrots
www.poicephalus.org

QuakerParrots.com
www.quakerparrots.com

Talk Budgies
www.talkbudgies.com

Index

Note: Page numbers in **bold** indicate a photograph.

Photo Credits

Front Cover: PCHT/**Shutterstock**

Back Cover: Mila Atkovska/**Shutterstock**

Shutterstock Elena Abduramanova: 128; Naaman Abreu: 139; Sharon Alexander: 26, 188; Andy Dean Photography: 97; Apiguide: 221; Art man: 145; Mila Atkovska: 4; AZP Worldwide: 9; Geanina Bechea: 189; Mircea Bezergheanu: 218; Bigfish: 23; Sylvie Bouchard: 206; Bogdan Bulat: 71; Butterfly Hunter: 53, 213; Bryoni Castelijn: 129; Perry Correll: 202 (top); Neale Cousland: 208 (top); Judy Crawford: 138, 154; Cuson: 89; Cynoclub: 67; Henner Damke: 204; Pauline de Hoog: 171; Defpicture: 208 (bottom); Destinyweddingstudio: 143; Det-anan: 108; Dobermaraner: 112, 122; dragi52: 78; Linda Eastman: 34; Lindsey Eltinge: 118, 193; Dima Fadeev: 127; Fivespots: 190 (bottom); FrameAngel: 166; Irina Fuks: 179; Allen G.: 147; Gajus: 64; Sergei Gorin: 80; Reiulf Gronnevik: 215; Rob Hainer: 14; R.L. Hambley: 17, 162, 205, 224; Susan Harris: 157; Jennay Hitesman: 195; Drew Horne: 223; Chris Humphries: 152, 208 (center); Iordani: 125; Krotova Iryna: 168; Eric Isselee: 27, 111, 123, 197, 212 (bottom), 216; Istidesign: 100; Anton Ivanov: 181 ; Jackiso: 38; Nicky Jacobs: 57; Marina Jay: 88, 113, 190 (top); Kellis: 72; Keng88: 16; Kimmik: 19; Julia Kuznetsova: 174, 202 (bottom); Brian L. Lambert: 219; Jill Lang: 41, 55, 59, 61, 120, 124, 130, 158, ; Lana Langlois: 10; Lanych: 75; Lee319: 28, 191, 194; Rich Lindie: 217; Loraart8: 8; Lorcel: 144; Lsantilli: 40; Joyce Mar: 142; Lori Martin: 222; Michelle D.Milliman: 141, 183; Roger Costa Morera: 170; Multiart: 60; Murengstockphoto: 140; Christian Musat: 149; Napat: 84; Narongsak: 116; Neirfy: 99; olmarmar: 105; Jon E Oringer: 92; Alena Ozerova: 12; Kimberly Palmer: 58; PHB.cz (Richard Semik): 73; Photovova: 209; Lauren Pretorius: 32; RamonaS: 21; Redchanka: 6, 203; ReflectivePhotos: 82; RHIMAGE: 20; Nicky Rhodes: 42, 136, 198; Robert Gebbie Photography: 2212 (top); Robynrg: 56; Panu Ruangjan: 126, 210; Laurent Ruelle: 220; David Ryo: 110 ; Guy J. Sagi: 36; Shkvarko: 134 ; Juerg Shreiter: 86; Sim Kay Seng: 207; Thomas Skjaeveland: 48; Gina Smith: 214; Tracy Starr: 25, 45, 49, 50, 66, 155, 164, 173, 200, 201; Villiers Steyn: 225 ; Alexander Sviridenkov: 121; Tobkatrina: 199; toktak kondesign: 103; Virginija Valatkiene: 33; Kirill Volkov: 196; Waldru: 46; Wannachat: 187; WilleeCole Photography: 127; Worldswildlifewonders: 101, 184; Worraket: 176; Zurijeta: 114

i5 Studio: 192

About the Author

Carol Frischmann is an educator and writer who earned her B.S. in Science Education from Duke University. She is a pet columnist for television, the Internet, and for her own website, ThisWildLife.com. She is the author of *Conures*, *Cockatoos*, *Attracting and Feeding Backyard Birds*, and *Pets and the Planet*. Carol lives and works near the Grand Canyon, closely supervised by two African grey parrots.